Architecture in the Family Way
Doctors, Houses, and Women, 1870–1900

Architecture in the Family Way explores the relationship of domestic architecture, health reform, and feminism in late-nineteenth-century England. Annmarie Adams examines the changing perceptions of the English middle-class house from 1870 to 1900, highlighting the ways in which attitudes toward health, gender roles, and the home were played out in architecture.

Adams argues that the many significant changes seen in this period were not due to architects' efforts but to the work of feminists and health reformers. She reveals that, contrary to the widely held belief that the home symbolized a refuge and safe haven to Victorians, middle-class houses were actually considered poisonous and dangerous. Adams explores the involvement of physicians in exposing "unhealthy" architecture and designing improved domestic environments. She examines the contradictory roles of middle-class women as both regulators of healthy houses and sources of disease and danger within their own homes, particularly during childbirth.

Architecture in the Family Way sheds light on an ambiguous period in the histories of architecture, medicine, and women, revealing it to be a time of turmoil, not of progress and reform as is often assumed.

ANNMARIE ADAMS is associate professor of architecture, McGill University.

MCGILL-QUEEN'S ASSOCIATED MEDICAL SERVICES
(HANNAH INSTITUTE)
Studies in the History of Medicine, Health, and Society
Series Editors: S.O. Freedman and J.T.H. Connor

Volumes in this series have financial support from Associated Medical Services, Inc., through the Hannah Institute for the History of Medicine Program.

Architecture in the Family Way

Doctors, Houses, and Women,
1870–1900

ANNMARIE ADAMS

McGill-Queen's University Press
Montreal & Kingston · London · Ithaca

© McGill-Queen's University Press 1996
ISBN 0-7735-1386-8 (cloth)
ISBN 0-7735-2239-5 (paper)

Legal deposit third quarter 1996
Bibliothèque nationale du Québec

Printed in Canada on acid-free paper
First paperback edition 2001

This book was first published with the help of a grant
from the Canadian Federation for the Humanities, using
funds provided by the Social Sciences and Humanities
Research Council of Canada.

McGill-Queen's University Press acknowledges the financial support of the Government of Canada through the
Book Publishing industry Development Program (BPIDP)
for its activities. It also acknowledges the support of the
Canada Council for the Arts for its publishing program.

Canadian Cataloguing in Publication Data

Adams, Annmarie
    Architecture in the family way: doctors, houses, and
    women, 1870–1900
    (McGill-Queen's/Hannah Institute studies in the history
    of medicine, health and society: 4)
    Includes bibliographical references and index.
    ISBN 0-7735-1386-8
    1. Housing and health – England – History –
    19th century. 2. Architecture, Domestic – Health aspects
    – England – History – 19th century. 3. Architecture,
    Domestic – Social aspects – England – History –
    19th century. 4. Architecture, Victorian – Health aspects
    – England. 5. Architecture, Victorian – Social aspects –
    England. 6. Architecture and women – England –
    History – 19th century. I. Title. II. Series.
    NA7125.A33 1996   728'.01'03   C96-900010-3

This book was typeset by Typo Litho Composition Inc.
in 10.5/13 Caslon.

For Peter

Contents

Figures

Acknowledgments

This book concerns, among other things, the notion of "expertise" in the nineteenth century; it relies, nonetheless, on many twentieth-century experts. My dissertation advisers at the University of California at Berkeley were astute critics and gifted teachers: Dell Upton, Paul Groth, and Mary Ryan. Their broad interests in architecture and history were the inspiration for this project from the beginning. My fellow graduate students in architecture at UC Berkeley – Mark Brack, Kate Bristol, Greg Hise, Gulsum Nalbantoglu, Daves Rossell, Eric Sandweiss, David Vanderburgh, and Abby Van Slyck – contributed tremendously to this enterprise through the standards of excellence set by their own work.

In England I received generous assistance from many individuals and institutions. The staff of the British Architectural Library, the British Library, the National Art Library, the Archive of Art and Design, the Fawcett Library, the Wellcome Institute for the History of Medicine, the Royal Commission on the Historical Monuments of England, the Greater London Record Office and Library, English Heritage, the Institute of Historical Research, the Bethnal Green Museum of Childhood, Leeds University Library, and the Royal College of Midwives were all helpful in locating material that was often hard to find.

In Montreal, the opportunity to show most of the primary-source material in the exhibition "Corpus Sanum in Domo Sano: The Architecture of the Domestic Sanitation Movement, 1870–1914," at the Canadian Centre for Architecture in 1991–92, encouraged me to consider the material in completely new ways, inspired by the experience and insight of the staff, particularly Jennifer Couelle and Rosemary Haddad. I am grateful to the Canadian Centre for Architecture for permission to include material first shown in this exhibition and its accompanying brochure. During the final revisions to the dissertation, the staff of the Blackader-Lauterman Library of Art and Architecture and the Osler Library at McGill University were extremely helpful. For special assistance with the illustrations, I would like to acknowledge Catherine Draycott, Susan Hengel, Gary Kulik, Wayne Lebel, Leathea Lee, and Celine Mayrande.

The original research was generously supported by the University of California at Berkeley through a Humanities Research Fellowship and through the Ira Abraham Sr and Georgina Koenig Abraham Scholarship. The Social Sciences and Humanities Research Council of Canada funded the project with a doctoral fellowship. Further research support was given through an E. McClung Fleming Fellowship in American Cultural, Social, and Intellectual History at the Henry Francis du Pont Winterthur Museum in 1991–92. For this opportunity to compare the same ideas in American architecture I am sincerely grateful.

Many other individuals contributed to this project by commenting on this text, through the examples set by their own work, and in countless informal ways. Deserving special mention are Maureen Anderson, Vikram Bhatt, David Brady, Ricardo Castro, Zeynep Çelik, David Covo, Elizabeth Cromley, Derek Drummond, Rhona Kenneally, the late Spiro Kostof, Karen Hudson, Margaretta Lovell, Sally McMurry, Judy Metro, Eric Ormsby, Norbert Schoenauer, Pieter Sijpkes, Peta Tancred, and Neville Thompson. I have been fortunate in having the skilled research assistance of David Theodore, who improved the manuscript tremendously through his perceptive editing and persistent questioning. Many other students of McGill's School of Architecture, particularly those in the graduate program "Domestic Environments," have inspired this project through their own thesis research.

Much of the first chapter originally appeared as "The Healthy Victorian City: The Old London Street at the International Health Exhibition of 1884," chapter 15 of *Streets: Critical Perspectives on Public Space* (1994), edited by Zeynep Çelik, Diane Favro, and Richard Ingersoll, and I am grateful to the editors and to the University of California Press for permission to reproduce it here.

I am honoured to be part of the series of books edited by S.O Freedman and J.T.H. Connor, and am thankful for their suggestions and for the generous support of the Hannah Institute for the History of Medicine. I am grateful for the superb editing of Carlotta Lemieux and to the staff of McGill-Queen's University Press.

Finally, this publication is dedicated to Peter Gossage, who always believed it would be a book.

Architecture in the Family Way

Introduction

"Narrow indeed is the path in which a mother must walk ... Through her a blessing or a curse has been cast upon the world," noted Eliza Warren, the author of many popular advice books to women in the late nineteenth century.[1] Mrs Warren spoke perceptively of both the power and the complexity of Victorian motherhood. As a mother of eight children, she was an authority on the subject. Certainly the position was one of great influence in 1865. "All her past is summed up in it, the strength of her body, the attributes of her mind, her moral and spiritual individuality, are brought to a focus here," remarked one of the writers of a flourishing body of women's advice manuals, "and the whole of the future of her country and of the world depends on this work of hers."[2]

Perhaps Mrs Warren's personal experiences made it obvious to her that maternal power passed *through* her, as she remarked, affecting at once her immediate surroundings. Beginning about 1870, the power of middle-class women was associated in the minds of experts as well as ordinary people with the architecture of the house. "I am convinced a house is a sentient thing," Jane Ellen Panton instructed her women readers in 1888, "and becomes part and parcel of those who live in it in a most mysterious way."[3] This relationship – widely understood though seldom directly explicated at the time – is evident today in the ease with which Victorians spoke of the house as an extension of the body, and the body as a reduction of the house. In her capacity as the recipient and also the agent of such power, the Victorian woman – mother or not – occupied a shifting relationship to the built environment.

In this respect Mrs Warren was extremely perceptive in her description of women's power as both a blessing and a curse. Indeed, Victorian women's relationships to their homes vacillated between these extremes in the literature of health reform and feminism. As the regulators of systems devised to ward off disease (the blessing) and as the source of illness and danger (the curse), women simultaneously played both active and passive roles within their homes. Their bodies, like their houses, were the site of fierce social battles; health reform and feminism are only the most obvious of these campaigns.

Mrs Warren's statement also raises the question of a "path" for women – the physical space women occupied in the nineteenth-century city – and its degree of enclosure. Did Mrs Warren and other Victorian women simply follow paths already hewn for them by architects, doctors, and household advisers? Or did they deviate from these ideal courses or even cut new routes on their own to form the free-ranging world of female spaces in the nineteenth-century city? How did the architecture of the home affect the arrangements of new building types for women? How did the private lives of women at home modify the public realm?

Aspects of this project are an attempt to answer these questions and to assess the place of home in the social path of late-Victorian motherhood. In broader terms, this study explores the changing perceptions of the English middle-class house in the final three decades of the nineteenth century, with particular focus on the place of domestic architecture in the literature of health reform and feminism. The triad on which the study is based – house-body-woman – identifies domestic architecture and health reform as instruments of feminism, houses and bodies as targets of health reform, and doctors and women as agents of architectural reform. The close association of houses, bodies, and women around 1870 was activated through a coincidence of social factors at the time: the formulation of the germ theory, the availability of contraception, advances in women's political status and education, changing attitudes towards motherhood, the rationalization of housework, and the feminization of interior design. In addition to its direct impact on the middle-class conception of home, this house-body-woman triad also affected the practice of medicine and architecture. The seemingly divergent paths of nineteenth-century architects, doctors, and women converged in the middle-class home. Like Mrs Warren, doctors and architects defended their precarious places – their "narrow paths" in the nineteenth-century city – through the architecture of the middle-class house.

Most historians of architecture, medicine, and women have established the late-Victorian middle-class home as a relatively fixed institution in urban life – a "separate sphere," a product of a so-called "cult of domesticity" or "cult of true womanhood," and a refuge from a dynamic and unpredictable city.[4] These analyses presume the house to be a place that was both antithetical to and spatially separated from the world of science, politics, and men – a snug and comfortable refuge from a world that was not. "The conception of home," explained historian Walter Houghton, was "a source of virtues and emotions which were nowhere else to be found, least of all in business and society. And that in turn made it a place radically different from the surrounding world." Like John Ruskin, from whom his view of the middle-class home was largely drawn, Houghton described this difference in spatial terms: "It was a place apart, a walled garden, in which certain virtues too easily crushed by modern life could be preserved, and certain desires of the heart too much thwarted be fulfilled."[5]

Ruskin, too, had emphasized the differences between the home and the city. His ideal home was a sacred refuge from "terror, doubt, and division," assuming physical and emotional protection from the world outside as its primary objective. "So far as the anxieties of the outer life penetrate into it, and the inconsistently-minded, unknown, unloved, or hostile society of the outer world is allowed by either husband or wife to cross the threshold, it ceases to be home," he claimed, "it is then only a part of that outer world which you have roofed over, and lighted fire in."[6]

In this study, I purposely made use of alternative sources in order to construct a view of the house from the inside, to illuminate the roles played by nonarchitects in the making of the Victorian built environment, and to relate that information to the world outside. Evidence from this "inner world" of the home demonstrates that many of Ruskin's "anxieties of outer life" – the spread of infection, the rationalization of knowledge, scientific theories of sexual difference, the emancipation of women – continually invaded the late-Victorian middle-class home and were managed there by Victorian women; in this respect both the house and the housewife were vital "part[s] of that outer world," as Ruskin feared. While planners, architects, builders, decorators, and others involved directly in the physical arrangement of urban spaces obviously contributed enormously to the urban landscape of the nineteenth century, other people – including doctors and women – also played active roles in the development of domestic spaces a century ago. It is the house at the intersection of these public and private social issues that this book has attempted to explore.

The project, therefore, differs substantially from traditional architectural histories in its sources. Women's magazines, family advice books, Victorian advertisements, furniture store catalogues, medical texts and illustrations, plumbing manuals, and trade catalogues have been used in lieu of more commonly cited sources such as architectural drawings, architects' writings, and real buildings. As a result, the project is much more concerned with how people thought about houses than with how buildings looked or functioned. In the language of architectural representation, it deals more with changes in section and perspective than in plan.

This story is not to be found in the traditional sources of architectural history. For example, the authority physicians gained during the final decades of the nineteenth century as designers of an improved domestic environment is imperceptible from a reading of architectural journals during that time. Doctors attempted to analyse the house in section – as they saw the body – separating and categorizing the various systems as a way of understanding the whole. At the same time, descriptions and illustrations of the house in the women's popular press reveal the widespread association of female political power and control of domestic space. The decoration and management of the middle-class house expressed time liberated from reproduction and child care. Victorian feminists held political rallies in their drawing rooms, proffering their interest in decoration as qualifications for their right to vote. The rise of the perspective drawing as a "feminine point of view" was an attempt to reconstitute the house following the scientific analysis of doctors. For both Victorian men and women – despite these differences in perception – houses were an opportunity to learn about architecture and an instrument with which to express that awareness. Beyond the style of a building's elevation, the source of its historical references, and the reputation of its architect, nineteenth-century houses were a means by which people expressed their private lives in public.

By necessity, then, this study explores a period, 1870–1900, in which British architects were sharply criticized by the "users" of their buildings; middle-class householders blamed buildings and architects for many of the misfortunes brought about by urbanization, including poor health and the subjugation of women. In this respect, the Victorian middle-class home was a very public place. Its limits were challenged by various professional groups, the rights to its authority were debated by men and women, and its reform was devised differently by decorators, architects, doctors, engineers, and householders. This notion of the house as an overlapping or shared sphere between men and women has dictated the research methods of the study; I have attempted as much as possible to approach the house from the exterior and interior simultaneously, to understand its role in the supposedly public world of professional men, while at the same time uncovering the Victorian perspective of domestic architecture as women's space.

The book consists of five broad essays on Victorian bodies and space. Each section was conceived as an independent essay and makes use of a relatively autonomous set of sources. The healthy city, the rise of the "building-doctor," female regulation of the house, reproduction, and feminism were arenas that linked domestic life and architecture in the nineteenth century. Together these five chapters show that domestic architecture during the period 1870 to 1900 was not an orderly succession of steps towards a reformed, healthy house; rather, it was a profoundly paradoxical time in the history of health, women, and houses. Changing attitudes towards domestic architecture show how the lapse between the formulation of knowledge and its impact on domestic space could be appropriated by various groups for assorted political purposes. Scepticism in one field was seized upon to further causes in a seemingly unrelated field, as is often the case today; architecture is a way to measure this process.

Chapter 1 provides a general introduction to the nineteenth-century health movement through a visit to the International Health Exhibition, held in London in 1884. The architecture and literature of the exhibition reveal basic assumptions made by Victorians about health and urbanism. The fair's layout shows the different ways in which Victorians thought about healthy public and private space in 1884. While the fair promoted an image of public spaces as clean and pure, domestic space at the exhibition was seen as poisonous, dangerous, and in need of medical attention. Middle-class control of the healthy house promised control of the body.

The second chapter focuses on the middle-class house as the centre of professional squabbling between doctors and architects within the Domestic Sanitation Movement in Britain. Sanitary science devastated public confidence in the specialized training of architects, making middle-class householders wary of many building professionals. Physicians active in the movement undermined the authority of Victorian architects through their seemingly "scientific" approach to design. The doctors' systematic view of the house, drawing from the burgeoning field of physiology, exposed the shoddy workmanship and lack of principles they perceived in the practice of architecture at the time. Long-neglected design projects by Victorian medical experts reveal the impact of the movement on the ways people envisioned the relationship of the house and the city.

As doctors convinced the public that houses and architects were to blame for the spread of disease, middle-class women became the physicians' most trusted allies in the domestic health movement as the chief "inspectors" of domestic architecture. This responsibility also meant that women were often blamed when sickness struck a family member. Chapter 3 examines the active "control" of healthy domestic architecture that was gained by middle-class women after 1870 as the house was increasingly seen as an extension of their bodies.

Chapter 4 explores the effects of "house-body" thinking on women in the nineteenth century from another point of view, through the spatial implications of conception in the Victorian cultural landscape. Pregnancy, more than any other factor, marked a fundamental change in the relationship of Victorian women's bodies to their surroundings. Just as the city actively shaped and affected the lives of those who resided within its bounds, so did pregnant women affect the life developing inside their bodies. They were told to regulate their participation in the urban social realm, both for their own protection and, in a sense, for the protection of those around them. The evidence of this change is in the "architecture of confinement": the lying-in room of the middle-class house.

The final section, chapter 5, explores the place of the middle-class house in the "woman question," the Victorian feminist movement. While the home is often seen as the place from which feminists tried to escape, their public image as domestic beings actually played a positive role in the emancipation process. A survey of articles in the women's press illuminates the practice of a form of "spatial feminism," advocated by authors such as Jane Ellen Panton, who did not necessarily favour female suffrage per se but who suggested that women's control of their houses and bodies would grant them more power. The place of domestic ideology in the design and construction of public architecture for women is also explored in this section.

The forces that compelled the close association of houses, bodies, and women between 1870 and 1900 arose concurrently, gently reinforcing one another as they gained momentum; these chapters, considered together, are an attempt to explore simultaneous concepts of domestic life and architecture during three tumultuous decades. In Victorian times, as well as today, perceptions of the body illuminate significant notions about architecture. By reconstructing the shifting boundaries between the body, the room, the house, and the city, it is hoped that this book will serve to document, illuminate, and widen Mrs Warren's "narrow path."

1 The International Health Exhibition of 1884

The main entrance to the Old London Street was through Bishopsgate, an imposing Norman arch sliced through the Roman city wall.[1] The wide opening, above which towered a statue of William the Conqueror, was framed by two monumental towers. Narrow slits of windows hinted at the dark, confined prison cells within their massive and weather-worn masonry walls. Through the gateway, the picturesque sweep of the archaic street was breathtaking (fig. 1.1). Buildings of four or five storeys cast their darkening shadows across the narrow passageway to Elbow Lane. Crowds jostled their way in and out of such popular commercial establishments as the Rose Inn and the Cock Tavern, passing beneath half-timbered façades whose heaviness was relieved only by bands of tiny discoloured window-panes. "By hammer and hand all arts must stand," warned a sign over the iron workers' shop. A sudden widening of the street just past Isaac Walton's house afforded a generous view of the old wooden church tower. A small staircase on the south side of the street ascended to the second-floor level of the buildings, where "darksome little upper rooms" were filled with a mismatched array of tapestries, furniture, and utensils.[2] The windows would not open; the thick panes of glass distorted the view of the crowd below slowly making its way towards Elbow Lane. Most of the visitors wore fashionable dresses or suits; others wore the working attire of three centuries earlier.

The Old London Street was a brilliant ploy on the part of the executive council of the 1884 International Health Exhibition. Billed as a means of illustrating the overcrowded spaces, dark interiors, and inflam-

Figure 1.1
The Old London Street at the International Health Exhibition (*Illustrated London News*, 2 Aug. 1884, supplement) Collection Canadian Centre for Architecture, Montreal

mable building materials that were common in London before the plague and devastating fire of 1666, this reproduction of a medieval street – composed, as the fairgoers were told, of "honest structures" rather than "pasteboard and painted canvas delusions" – was the most popular attraction of the exhibition, appealing in its picturesqueness to "lovers of Art."[3] "The mind and the eye of the average sightseer do not derive any very ecstatic pleasure from the contemplation of models of drain-pipes, sewer-traps, cisterns, pumps, roof-slates, joists, filters and ventilators," a visitor remarked. "Life is not made sweeter to him by the inspection of samples of disinfecting fluids or 'Illustrations of the Chemistry and Physiology of Food and Nutrition.'"[4]

The Old London Street was part of a group of special displays – consisting of fireworks, flower shows, illuminated fountains, and other attractions – that were intended to lure crowds to the exhibition in the hope that they would go on from there to explore the vast displays of drainpipes and ventilators or to attend one of the lectures on "sanitation,"

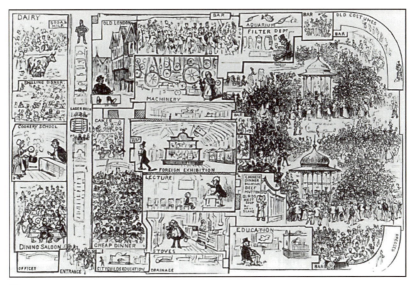

Figure 1.2
An "Insane-itary Guide to the Health Exhibition" (*Punch*, 30 Aug. 1884, 98) Courtesy of McGill University Libraries, Montreal

which formed the truly instructive element of the fair. The cartoonists at *Punch* were evidently aware of the twofold agenda of the fair. They published a humorous "insane-itary guide to the health exhibition," which offered their readers one itinerary for instruction and another for pleasure (fig. 1.2).

The International Health Exhibition (IHE), or "The Healtheries" as it was called at the time, was intended by its promoters to celebrate international progress in the scientific study of health.[5] "Sanitary science" was a relatively new field in the late nineteenth century, but by the 1880s it had become a fairly autonomous discipline, as illustrated by events such as the IHE.[6] By then, courses in sanitation were taught in most schools; hygiene was the subject of royal commissions and government boards; and sanitary institutes were common in many English cities. Divided into two main sections, "health" and "education," the IHE focused on recent reform in food, dress, the dwelling, the school, and the workshop. Although no earth-shattering technological innovations resulted from the exhibition, it served to raise both the consciousness and the fears of the middle-class population on matters of sanitation.[7]

Implicit in the IHE's program was the relatively new but already firmly planted belief that the environment had a direct impact on public health.

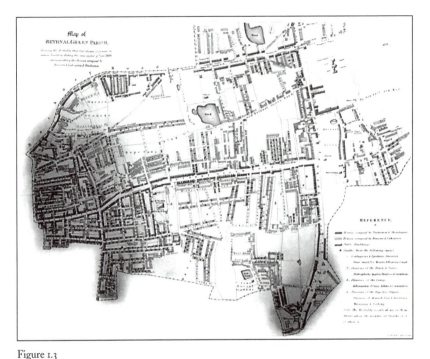

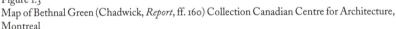

Figure 1.3
Map of Bethnal Green (Chadwick, *Report*, ff. 160) Collection Canadian Centre for Architecture, Montreal

Edwin Chadwick's *Report on the Sanitary Condition of the Labouring Population of Great Britain* (1842) had given credence to the argument that the "environment," which included housing, was a major factor in the spread of illness.[8] According to this national survey of health, disease nearly always occurred in "connexion with the physical circumstances" of the patient. Chadwick's mapping of the incidence of disease demonstrated a direct link between environment, particularly housing, and health.[9] For example, he indicated the location of four common illnesses in the east London neighborhood of Bethnal Green by placing a brown "mist" of ink on an ordinary map (fig. 1.3). As a result of his findings, Parliament passed the first Public Health Act in 1848.[10] The pivotal effect of Chadwick's report on the Victorian perception of the city has been noted by historian James Walvin, who pointed out that "to believe that poverty and disease were functions of personal failings was to argue that little could be done about them. To locate their causes (largely if not completely) in the environment was to claim that they could be improved by changing that environment."[11] Historian Jean-Pierre Goubert credits

Chadwick's report with the full recognition of the problems associated with supplying water to areas of the city.[12]

The spirit of optimism and impetus for improvement inspired by Chadwick's popular book focused new attention on the reform of domestic architecture and constituted a basic tenet of the rising Domestic Sanitation Movement, which is explored further in chapter 2. The subject of this chapter, London's International Health Exhibition of 1884, represents a distillation of the major issues addressed by the movement as well as the meeting place of its most important figures. From the exhibition's architecture, as well as from the vast literature produced for it, we can extract a representative sketch of the relationship of health to public and private space in 1884.[13]

The International Health Exhibition followed the Fisheries Exhibition of 1883 in a series of thematic fairs sponsored by Queen Victoria and the Prince of Wales. It was largely accommodated within the buildings and courts constructed for its predecessor, though its organizers pointed with pride to "the intricacy of the ground plan," which was made possible by the "large number of new annexes, courts, corridors, and detached buildings" constructed for the IHE.[14] The health exhibition took place in South Kensington, on the grounds of the Royal Horticultural Society, between the Royal Albert Hall and the Natural History Museum (fig. 1.4).[15] Parts of the Royal Albert Hall and the City and Guilds of London Technical Institution, on Exhibition Road to the east, were also appropriated for the IHE. Most of the displays were housed in long, narrow galleries at the south end of the grounds, adjacent to the Natural History Museum on Cromwell Road (fig. 1.5). The north end consisted of a grand terraced court and garden, which contained a memorial to the Great Exhibition of 1851 – a forceful reminder of the history of the area as the setting of other successful public exhibitions – and magnificent fountains. A grand axis, Central Avenue, bisected the site from north to south. The main entrance was in the southeast corner, off Exhibition Road.

The flurry of activity resulting from the fair extended well beyond the boundaries of the exhibition site. Anticipating the four million visitors who attended the event, vendors filled the streets of South Kensington leading to the grounds with stands and displays of "useless productions."[16] These stalls of cork mice, china dolls, and tin mechanical alligators supposedly prepared the visitor for the plethora of hygienic devices exhibited within the boundaries of the IHE.[17] Meanwhile, railway companies offered discounts to all districts within sixty miles of the metropolis,

Figure 1.4
Site plan of the International Health Exhibition, London, 1884 (*International Health Exhibition Official Guide*, title page) Collection Canadian Centre for Architecture, Montreal

allowing "country cousins to 'do' the exhibition in a day."[18] Fair attendance exceeded all recorded estimates, presumably drawing crowds away from many other cultural events. A satirical cartoon in *Punch* featured a huge "Miss South Kensington" luring people from the city's theatres with a gigantic magnet called "The Healtheries" (fig. 1.6).

The crowds attending the health exhibition were a testament to the widespread interest in the new field of sanitary science, as well as to the Victorian faith in the power of spaces and things – supposedly "useful productions" – to improve public health. Heating and cooking apparatus, clothing, shoes, machinery, food, ambulances, lighting, furniture, and baths, among other objects, were displayed by individual manufacturers and grouped according to subject. The illustrations of the fair reveal that most of the displays were arranged in large shop windows or in small shoplike stalls constructed inside the open exhibition halls (fig. 1.7). Belgium, China, India, and Japan were represented by separate national pavilions, in and around which were exhibited objects that were more or less related to health in these countries.[19] The focus of the IHE, however, was on health reform in England.

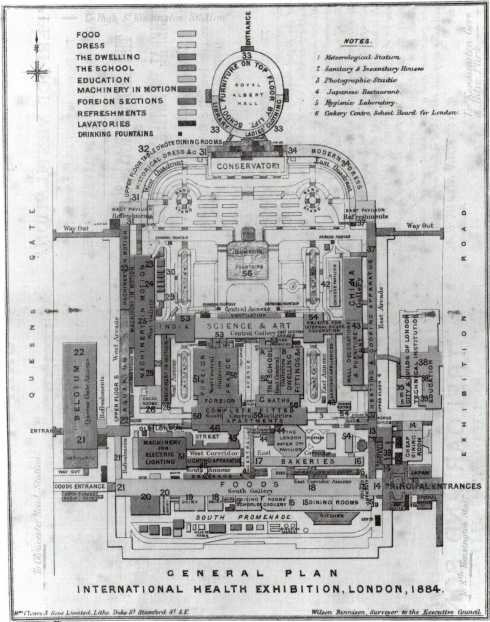

Figure 1.5
General plan, International Health Exhibition, London, 1884 (*International Health Exhibition Official Guide*, between 32 and 33) Collection Canadian Centre for Architecture, Montreal

Figure 1.6
Miss South Kensington attracting theatre crowds (*Punch*, 26 July 1884, 39) Courtesy of the
Winterthur Library, Printed Book and Periodical Collection

Food, dress, furniture, and houses of the past were juxtaposed with
contemporary productions of the same items in order to illustrate and
celebrate Victorian progress in the field of sanitation. This pointed juxta-
position of historical and contemporary artifacts communicated a clear
message to the fairgoers: living conditions in 1884 were much healthier
than they had been in the past. This message was expressed not only by

Figure 1.7
Displays at the International Health Exhibition (*Illustrated London News*, 2 Aug. 1884, 117)
Collection Canadian Centre for Architecture, Montreal

the architecture of individual buildings and the displays of objects within them, but by the visitors' "experience" of moving through the entire grounds, inside and outside buildings, in the dynamic interplay of changing sights, smells, and sounds through which the fluid ground plan naturally led them. The Old London Street, the fountains, the architecture, and the display of the individual ventilating tube could be read – at one level – as a lesson in the progress of sanitary science. At the same time, the design of the IHE glorified the productive organizational capacities of the municipal government and manufacturers; it was the streamlined, rationalized structure of the industrial corporation and the city bureaucracy that seemed to offer hope in the present against what Victorians were warned to fear about the past.

In this sense, the display of water at the fair assumed special importance as a self-congratulatory promotional gesture by municipal water companies touting their role in the recent "cleansing" of London, as well as being a direct reference to the importance of clean water in the Victorian conception of disease control.[20] Decorative pools and drinking fountains could be found throughout the grounds of the IHE. This "conspicuous consumption" of water for apparently purely recreational use in the main court of the IHE was much more than an aesthetic choice; it was a public celebration of the city's good health in 1884.[21]

In both its sheer quantity and its illumination, the water displayed at the exhibition was, at the very least, "novel as well as ingenious" to the Londoner of the 1880s.[22] The magnificent "illuminated fountains" – the "greatest attraction" of the IHE – in the main courtyard were visible from a great distance, for a single jet of water 120 feet high rose from an island in the centre of the "water garden." Some 250 smaller jets and sprays of water "in the most fantastic designs" surrounded the island, changing constantly in their form and lighting (fig. 1.8).[23] The prime location of the fountains, on the axis between the central gallery and the memorial to the exhibition of 1851, was a further indication of the importance of water in the larger political agenda of the plan.

The sophisticated technology behind the elaborate water displays at the IHE was invisible, intriguing the crowds with its seemingly magical qualities (fig. 1.9). Giant arc lights cast a range of colours on the fountains, producing "the most varied effects to be attained, the water sometimes appearing red, at others purple, and again, when the white beam falls on it, the falling spray against the dark background of the sky resembles showers of diamonds."[24] One visitor described the lighting effects as a "stream of fire"; electric lights were shot through the jet of water inter-

Figure 1.8
The fountains illuminated (*Illustrated London News*, 2 Aug. 1884, 112) Collection Canadian
Centre for Architecture, Montreal

nally, so that it seemed as if the water itself was the source of illumination, rather than the reflecting surface.[25] Advertisements of the health
exhibition claimed that it was the "largest display of electric lighting in
the world" (fig. 1.10). Colonel Francis Bolton, examiner of the Metropolitan Board of Works, personally worked the display from the clock tower
in the courtyard, sending signals to five men who controlled the lights
from a cramped machine room under the island. Meters on the western
side of the centre basin recorded the quantity of water for the enthusiastic crowd.

In this magnificent display of electricity and waterworks, the Metropolitan Board of Works had succeeded in turning its mundane operations
into the stuff of fantasy and drama in the name of public health. "Londoners can no longer complain that they are deprived of all means of out-
of-door enjoyment at night," boasted the author of the official guidebook
to the exhibition.[26] Ernest Hart, an organizer of the IHE, pointed to the
fountains as the exhibition's most important contribution. "The metropolitan water companies appeared in a new light at this Exhibition, and
entered the arena as caterers for pleasure, amusement, and instruction of
the public, Hart explained when assessing the fair's overall influence." "It

Figure 1.9
Behind the scenes at the fountains (*Illustrated London News*, 2 Aug. 1884, 93) Collection
Canadian Centre for Architecture, Montreal

is no small thing to have acquired the conviction that our open spaces
may be, and should be, much more largely devoted to the open-air recreation of the people than they are at the present moment." Hart observed
that London's parks were nothing more than "dreary desolate areas of

Figure 1.10
Advertisement for the International Health Exhibition (*Illustrated London News*, 2 Aug. 1884, 115) Collection Canadian Centre for Architecture, Montreal

darkness ... unused in the evenings for any wholesome or moral purpose." He saw the IHE as both a physical and a moral model for the city: "Why should we not learn from the success of the music and the lighting of the gardens of the Health Exhibition, that our great parks should all be lighted by the electric light at night ... and should make those places, which are now not only useless but scandals to the metropolis, the sites of healthful and innocent recreation?"[27] In this way, the popularity of the illuminated fountains linked issues of urban safety and health, projecting an atmosphere of optimism for the use of public spaces at night in the city.

Although its value as a spectacle and as a model for the real city was undeniable, the health exhibition was condemned by many critics, who held that the connection to health had been interpreted by the commissioners and exhibitors far too broadly: "'This is the Health Exhibition – Where is the health?' and the popular answer was, 'Outside in the gardens.'"[28] As many of the visitors noted, the music, lighting, and water drew the crowds out of the exhibition halls to fill the exterior spaces.[29] But beyond the water gardens' obvious role as an attraction to the overall event, they were the vehicle of one of the IHE's most potent lessons.

In 1854, John Snow had proved that cholera, which had raged through London killing thousands in 1832 and 1848, was transmitted primarily through infected water; he had shown that each victim in Westminster

Figure 1.11
Section of the Thames Embankment (*Illustrated London News*, 22 June 1867, 632) Collection
Canadian Centre for Architecture, Montreal

had consumed water from an infected pump in Broad Street.[30] This revelation was followed by desperate calls for cleaning the River Thames, from which the water supply of London, the world's largest city, was drawn. Hot weather during the summers of 1858 and 1859 attracted further attention to the condition of the Thames, and "the Great Stink," as it was known, forced politicians into action.[31] Through massive urban restructuring – a new sewer system, the embankment of the river, and widespread slum clearance – London attempted to "cleanse" itself (fig. 1.11).[32] The Metropolitan Board of Works, created in 1855, was charged with constructing a new system to dump sewage into the river at a significant distance from the city.[33] Joseph Bazalgette's solution, an 82-mile-long drainage system, was one "of the greatest engineering feats in a great age of engineering."[34] Clean water, as a result of largely invisible technology, became clearly associated in the minds of the citizenry with victory over disease.

The basic ideas behind Bazalgette's sewer system were the interception and separation of sewage from the river. Until the 1850s, refuse had been stored in cesspools or cesspits in yards or streets. These were often connected to street drains, discharging untreated sewage directly into the

Thames, from which the city's drinking water was drawn.[35] Bazalgette's ingenious sewers, designed in 1854, discharged their deadly contents twelve or fourteen miles below the metropolis, at which point the sewage was diluted and transported an additional twelve miles by the ebbing tide.[36] His entire system was based on separation, whereas Paris installed a "combined system."[37] The embankment of the Thames – a new river's edge – was part of the larger project undertaken by the Metropolitan Board of Works. The embankment was to serve two purposes: to remove the deposits of foul matter that often collected on the mud banks at the river's side and to increase the velocity of the water, preventing the collection of solid waste in the city's centre.[38] These massive public works were a major political accomplishment, following years of heated public debate. "The spade, the shovel, and the pick," reported the *Illustrated London News* in 1859 with great relief, have finally "taken the place of pens, ink, and debate."[39]

Water was also employed to clean the streets of London following the construction of the sewer system and embankment. The watering carts used before this time had simply dampened the dust and dirt on the streets, but more sophisticated machines were now developed to carry garbage and dirt to the gutter, thereby removing refuse completely from the street by disposing of it in the sewer system. The "Hercules Street-Cleansing Machine," for example, was used in the Strand in 1890; a threewheeled vehicle pulled by one or two horses, it consisted of a cylindrical 300-gallon water tank over a screw-shaped, india-rubber revolving roller (fig. 1.12). Operated by a single driver, the "Hercules" could clean an astonishing 7,250 square yards per hour.[40]

As a subtle reference to this idea of sanitary progress, the clean water theme continued throughout the site plan of the International Health Exhibition in pools, fountains, and even in architecture. The Water Pavilion, for example, an octagonal building constructed especially for the fair, was jointly sponsored by the eight water companies that supplied London at the time.[41] In the centre of the building was a cast-iron fountain; a single jet of water rose from the mouth of a swan, whose neck was clasped by a young boy. An observer remarked that the statue was "an emblematic figure, no doubt, signifying the cupidity of the water companies."[42] A journalist in *Punch* was even less sympathetic, clearly disappointed with the building following a rumour that "these monopolists were about to atone for a past of mismanagement and extortion, by affording a display that would soften the heart of the most indignant economist."[43]

Figure 1.12
"Hercules Street-Cleansing Machine" (*Sanitary Record*, 15 Feb. 1890, 402) Collection Canadian Centre for Architecture, Montreal

The water theme was carried outward from this central motif throughout the rest of the building, recalling "the venerable squirts of Trafalgar Square."[44] The basin surrounding the fountain was decorated with water lilies and other aquatic plants. From its edges, eight streams of water representing each of the city's water companies were directed towards the middle of the fountain. Scenes of the River Thames decorated the walls of the pavilion. Each company displayed, "behind a glass screen, an actual section of the materials of its filter bed," as one journalist described: In each angle is a tap and a drinking-cup, so that persons who feel that they 'may well abide it' can drink the water of all the different companies and compare them."[45] It is hard to imagine Londoners of the 1850s drinking water that appeared to have come from the River Thames!

The elaborate use of water at the IHE, even in this artistic guise, was a direct reference to the significance of clean water in the Victorian conception of disease control. But on another level it operated as a subtle counterpoint to the quaint but lamentable picture painted by the architecture of the Old London Street. The Water Pavilion, in its location and architecture, and in the sensual experience that it offered visitors, was the antithesis of the old street.[46] In this way the water companies portrayed themselves as a relief, or even protection, from a horrific past.

As an amalgam of buildings from different eras and different parts of London, the Old London Street was less an accurate representation of an actual street than a creative recombination of "typical buildings, of which

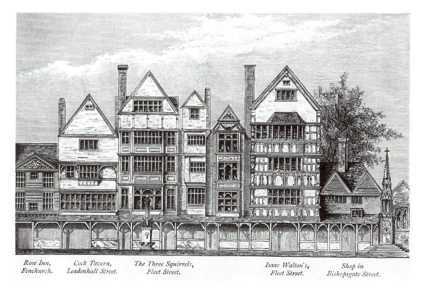

Rose Inn,   *Cock Tavern,*   *The Three Squirrels,*   *Isaac Walton's,*   *Shop in*
Fenchurch. *Leadenhall Street.*   *Fleet Street.*   *Fleet Street.*   *Bishopsgate Street.*

Figure 1.13
Elevation of the Old London Street (*Art Journal* 4 [1884]: 162) Collection Canadian Centre for
Architecture

authentic drawings have come down to us."[47] The scale of the exhibit was
equally misleading; the reproductions of medieval buildings that lined
the street were much smaller than the actual structures they represented
(fig. 1.13).[48] Furthermore, any realism on the part of the Old London
Street was invalidated by signs, advertisements, and evidence of modern
technology.[49] Old London, presented in this fictional, miniaturized
model, clearly communicated to visitors that the mistakes of the past,
which had resulted in horrifying plague and fire, were now understood
and would therefore never be repeated. As one observer perceptively remarked, "As it stands, the sole relation of the old street to Health is a
negative one."[50]

"New London," the healthy city, was represented by more "positive"
displays: the Water Pavilion and the other displays of water in the site
plan. In every way, the architecture of the new building was a subtle response to the conditions simulated in the Old London Street. Its decorative motifs, drawn from water and plant life, provided an obvious
counterpoint to the austere simplicity of medieval buildings, which recalled death and destruction from plague and fire. While the Old London Street was essentially an enclosed space, with its buildings intended
to form a backdrop like a stage set, the Water Pavilion was only one part

of a complex series of relatively open spaces, linked by water, leading to the illuminated fountains and eventually to the memorial to the exhibition of 1851.

The Old London Street and the Water Pavilion offered an illustrative lesson in the value of municipal control over the public landscape. London's open spaces – the street, the court, even the river – were described as unquestionably clean and healthy by the promoters of the health exhibition in 1884. More dangerous and in need of closer inspection, according to the architecture of the IHE, were the private spaces of contemporary London. It was within the parlours, nurseries, and particularly the walls of the typical middle-class home that many experts believed diseases were accommodated and spread. And it was at home, the health exhibition tried to convince its middle-class audience, that one's personal health was really controlled.

Not surprisingly, then, domestic architecture was the subject of a major display at the exhibition – the Sanitary and Insanitary Dwellings. These two sectional models, representing an "improved" and an "ordinary" house, formed the exhibit on the architecture of the home and its relationship to health. The purpose of the models was to demonstrate common errors in building construction (in the Insanitary Dwelling), compared with the apparently "correct" way to build (in the Sanitary Dwelling). Unlike the other displays at the fair, the message was not based on a comparison of objects that dated from before and after the rise of the health movement. Rather, it represented real and ideal contemporary middle-class housing. Again, its value as a social lesson overlapped with its significance as commercial advertising.

Like all architectural models, the Sanitary and Insanitary Dwellings were intended as abstractions of a situation in the real world; they were full-sized sectional models of two houses.[51] Constructed in a conspicuous location in the open space adjacent to the central gallery, the model houses were extremely popular, probably because their scale was large enough to allow visitors to move through the spaces.[52] By this careful manipulation of the visitors' movements, the Sanitary and Insanitary Dwellings expressed a very different message from the overall plan of the exhibition. While the architecture of the fair declared the unhealthy living conditions of the past to have been "healed" by the productive organizational capacities of the municipal government and London's water companies, these models expressed the direct conviction that London's houses were still very sick and were in need of medical attention and constant regulation. This message was stated explicitly by the models' architectural forms.[53] Visitors entered the basement of the unhealthy house, ascended through three levels representing the various rooms in a typical house, and then crossed a passage to the top floor of the second model, the healthy house. The four levels of this second building were then seen in descending order. The tour finished in the basement.

The Insanitary Dwelling was intended to incite fear by its resemblance to one's own house. "*How* can that be unhealthy?" asked a visitor. "We have exactly the same kind of thing in *our* house, and that is not unhealthy!"[54] The exhibit warned by implication that the architect or plumber might have hidden such dangerous details in the walls, transforming ordinary houses into "death traps." The visitor's fear was heightened by the fact that the sanitary flaws illustrated in the Insanitary Dwelling were not immediately apparent. A journalist in *Punch* described a typical visit:

You are requested to enter by the basement. You obey, and discover first a dear old dust-bin – just like the one you left at home. Capital! You inspect the kitchens and scullery, and find them all that can be desired. A house-agent entering this house on his books would certainly write down, "Excellent domestic offices" … You are very pleased … Undoubtedly a very desirable residence, and yet (and you congratulate yourself upon the fact) only a counterpart of the mansion you have left at home. Just like your own, in fact. You are in raptures upon making this discovery. You have been so pleased and excited that you have not examined everything in detail. You have got a general impression, and now you consider the time has arrived for a closer inspection. The room you are standing in is remarkable for a bright, cheerful wall-paper. You think how well it would show up pictures, when a placard hanging from a nail catches your eye. You draw near. Surely some mistake here! … Horrible! The cause of your admiration is the Handmaid (or rather the Machine-made) of Death![55]

The subtlety of the sanitary flaws thus augmented the insecurity of visitors, convincing them that their own homes might contain such dangerous materials and construction details, which they might have overlooked.

The major problems illustrated by the house concerned drainage and ventilation. According to the guidebook, construction errors were apparent as soon as one entered: the dustbin was placed improperly against the wall; the basement floor had dangerous direct communication with the damp ground; and the soil pipe was located inside the house. The ground floor contained, among other frightening errors, an unlit and unventilated water-closet, with a dreaded "pan closet" and "D-trap." In addition, the walls were decorated with arsenical wallpaper. The next floor saw the direct connection of the rainwater and soil pipes. The attic level illustrated the dangers of an inaccessible water cistern; from this floor, visitors also witnessed the soil pipe releasing sewer gas just outside the bedroom windows.

From this level the visitors, who by now were concerned about the resemblance of this architecture to that of their own homes – and who were often "deeply depressed," according to one account – would pass over what presumably was some form of bridge to the uppermost floor of the second model, the Sanitary Dwelling.[56] In this way, the designers of the exhibit ensured that visitors saw the second house as an alternative to the situation in their homes. The unidirectional movement through the unhealthy house and the forced exit through the healthy world supplied by manufacturers meant that visitors were obliged to see the models in this "before and after" sequence. The Sanitary Dwelling was thus offered as a corrective to the unhealthy house, just as the Water Pavilion had seemingly corrected the architectural mistakes of the Old London Street. The difference, of course, was that the old street represented a situation more than two hundred years earlier than the fair, while the Insanitary Dwelling was intended to represent contemporary domestic architecture. The significance of this spatial sequence did not pass unnoticed in the *Architect*, though it was not stated explicitly. "We cannot by any possibility miss any of the lessons intended for our learning," noted the journal.[57]

The Sanitary Dwelling, as one might expect, was antithetical in every way to the unhealthy house, including the way in which it was experienced. Visitors descended through its spaces, whereas they had ascended through the first house. Also, the second model was as instructive by what was missing as by the features that were present. For instance, the second floor, the visitors' entry level, had a noticeable absence of arsenical wallpaper. This might have gone unremarked if the visitors had not just seen poisonous wall-coverings in the Insanitary Dwelling. As a sort of rebuttal to the first house, the second model also boasted an easily inspected cistern room. Stopcocks were visible on all pipes; the water could be turned off at any time.

The first floor of the healthier house had separate water supplies. Floors were parquet, a dust-free, easy-to-clean surface. The water-closet and sink were in the correct position, on the outer wall of the house with windows for light and ventilation. Electricity was provided throughout the Sanitary Dwelling, consuming no oxygen and producing no emissions, visitors were assured. On the ground floor, paint had been substituted for arsenical papers, and the walls and ceiling in the basement were covered in "Duresco," a surface easily cleaned with cold water. Outside the Sanitary Dwelling, visitors entered the yard, the site of a separate servants' water-closet. A six-inch concrete foundation was visible beneath the entire building, and the escape pipe for sewer gas was well above the living spaces of the house. The names of manufacturers whose appliances were shown in this healthier house were listed in the guide.

The Insanitary and Sanitary Dwellings are revealing of the ways people thought about health and houses in the mid-1880s. After about 1870 there was a widespread belief that a house could cause sickness or that domestic architecture itself was sick because it was connected to other houses and to the city. It is this presumption – the close association of the body and the house – that enabled doctors and women to appropriate domestic architecture as a tool of empowerment in the late nineteenth century, as we shall see in subsequent chapters.

Although the germ theory had been postulated in the 1860s by Louis Pasteur and had been further developed in the following decades by Joseph Lister and Robert Koch, the houses at the IHE expose the existing uncertainty – as late as 1884 – regarding the ways diseases spread.[58] The fair organizers' subtle insistence on the culpability of architecture – on the arrangement and materials of the house itself – reveals their fundamental faith in visible, even spatial, explanations for internal states, despite evidence to the contrary. The model houses, for example, illustrate fears stemming from several prebacteriological explanations of disease transmission, such as the miasma theory, whose followers believed that infection generated spontaneously in sewage, filth, or earth and was then transported by foul air.[59] Contagionists, on the other hand, believed that infection was spread by "animate contagia" through direct contact.[60] The focus of the sanitarians on ventilation and drainage in the model houses at the IHE – on the danger of breathing and drinking contaminated material – is an illuminating index of the state of the debate over the spread of infection at that time.

Concentration on the middle-class house was a relatively late development in the Victorian health movement.[61] Sanitarians at mid-century had focused their reform efforts on large-scale municipal improvements such as the sewers and the Thames embankment, and on working-class housing.[62] Appalled by the overcrowded slums, the open gutters of raw sewage, and the inadequate water supply, they had conducted exhaustive surveys of sanitary conditions in working-class neighbourhoods. It was

not until about 1870 that British sanitarians turned their attention to the
health of the urban middle class.[63] At the same time, they altered their
approach to health reform. Rather than imposing urban improvements
from above through municipal controls, they tried to convince educated
middle-class householders to regulate their own physical health through
the sanitary regulation of their houses.

This program of enlightened self-improvement was a basic tenet of the
new field of "sanitary science."[64] As several social and medical historians
have noted, it also reflected fundamental changes in the ways people
thought about disease. Before the Victorian era, disease and death had
typically been associated with unseemly or inappropriate behaviour. But
sickness and death could be prevented, the large-scale municipal reforms
at mid-century had proven, if people followed the scientific laws of
health. For members of the middle class, the house thus became the instrument through which they could demonstrate their awareness of scientific knowledge as well as their desire to self-regulate health.

After 1870, then, the spread of infection reflected the ignorance of the
middle-class householder rather than any incompetence on the part of
the physician. Although public health improved in the second half of the
century, cholera, typhus, typhoid, and a host of other debilitating illnesses continued to travel mysteriously through urban centres, seemingly
defying the salubrious effects of isolation and separation.[65] The obvious
failure of proposed explanations for disease transmission left physicians
"conceptually helpless" for most of the century.[66] The inability of Victorian physicians to arrest the spread of infection which they presumed
they understood was translated by the medical profession into an apparent failure of Victorian architecture and architects.[67]

The houses at the IHE illustrate this frustration in the blame that physicians directed at architects, plumbers, and builders, and in the continued precautions taken against miasmatic and contagionist explanations
for the spread of infection. The primary concern of the miasmatists was
ventilation. Both Chadwick and Florence Nightingale were confirmed
miasmatists. Nightingale pioneered the "pavilion" system of hospital design, based on her belief that surrounding each patient with copious
amounts of fresh air would inhibit the spread of disease between patients.[68] In the design of houses, however, there were fewer formulae for
ventilation, though reformers were no less passionate about the need for
plenty of fresh air in the home.

Most sanitarians recommended the absolute avoidance in the home of
all vapours emitted from sewers and sewage – "sewer gas," as it was

called.[69] The correct place for water-closets, householders were told, was on the exterior walls, with complete disconnection between the drains and the interior of the house through the use of traps and other fittings.[70] Pipes should ventilate into the open air, well above the level of any windows, according to the example set in the Sanitary Dwelling.

The dangers posed by sewer gas were as hotly debated as the broader theories of disease transmission. Sanitarians argued about whether sewer air was actually poisonous or simply promoted other diseases.[71] While some doctors attributed the spread of diphtheria, typhoid fever, and pleuro-pneumonia to breathing sewer gas, others insisted that sewer air was actually healthier than most other environments. Experts on this side of the debate even went so far as to recommend the location of hospitals *near* sewers. "As the sewer air is so much purer than the general atmosphere," said one doctor, "we shall probably have sanitaria established at the sewer outfalls, where there must be an abundance of sewer air."[72] Benjamin Ward Richardson, who was among the most vocal medical doctors involved in the health movement, argued for the complete avoidance of sewer air in the home. He believed sewer gas caused "sewer-air fever," or "continued fever," a disease that typically attacked the inhabitants of a single contaminated house and rarely spread between houses.[73] The evidence on both sides of the sewer-air debate was based on the health of sewer workers. Everyone agreed, however, that sewer air was extremely unpleasant. It was for this reason that the "pan closet" and "D-trap" shown in the insanitary house at the IHE were considered extremely dangerous by sanitarians. These devices held sewage, rather than flushing clean, and therefore seemingly poisoned the occupants of a house.

Tuberculosis, or consumption, was also thought to be encouraged by bad air, more from lack of ventilation and dampness than from noxious poisons.[74] The high rate of TB in the British army of the 1850s was linked to the "foetid and unwholesome atmosphere" of barracks.[75] As a result, sanitarians prescribed well-ventilated rooms and corridors, insisting that both water-closets and bedrooms have windows. Experts claimed that even the process of breathing contaminated rooms: "The water given out in respiration is loaded with animal impurities; it condenses on the inner walls of buildings, and trickles down in foetid streams, and evaporates or sinks into the walls, leaving the impurities on the surface. On this account, a peculiar disagreeable smell may often be perceived in rooms which have long been inhabited, especially rooms which have been inhabited by large numbers of persons, and the wall-surfaces of which have not been often renewed."[76]

Novels of the period document the change in middle-class habits from the earlier aversion to drafts to the acceptance of bracing fresh air in interior spaces as the century closed: "Some one – a young person – opens a window, and some one – an old person, Lady Lancaster, I think it is – shuts it again. Lady Lancaster has that rooted aversion to fresh air which characterized the last generation."[77] Similarly, the *Sick Chamber* by Robert W. Weir is typical of the way patients, especially those suffering from tuberculosis, were shown in the Victorian period; they were almost always close to large open windows. In Weir's picture, an open window in the room in which a young woman has just died not only indicates the way to heaven but also illustrates contemporary uncertainty regarding the cause of her death (fig. 1.14).

In advising householders to open their windows, experts also warned their readers of the dangers of drafty rooms. The architectural solution to this dilemma was the ventilating tube, often referred to as "Tobin's tube" after a popular version. Hospitals and schools adapted the system first. A tube or pipe inserted directly into the exterior wall of a building provided fresh air to interiors without the discomfort of drafts; the supply was usually regulated by a lid at the mouth of the pipe. Dr Edward Blake illustrated a ventilation system based on the same system in 1880 (fig. 1.15). He recommended heating the fresh air at the point of entry and ventilating the room from behind a continuous wainscoting.

Victorian building materials were also believed to be dangerous. Wallpapers were commonly manufactured with arsenic in order to achieve bright colours, particularly shades of green. As illustrated in the Insanitary Dwelling at the IHE, experts believed that these papers emitted toxic fumes that were responsible for various illnesses, including enteritis (bowel inflammation), diarrhoea, nausea, depression, asthma, headache, and skin irritations.[78] Like other aspects of the reformers' agenda, not everyone agreed on the dangers of arsenic in the home.[79] The evidence cited for the risks associated with wallpaper was usually an improvement in the patient's condition after removal of the material made of "devil's dust."[80]

The Victorian obsession with drainage was fuelled by enthusiasm for all three theories of the spread of infection; experts feared not only the gases escaping from sewers and sewage but also the accumulation of sewage in the dwelling. Drains and cesspools, said the sanitarians, often leaked into wells and ground water, and they gave examples of these leakages in their publications. For instance, Dr T. Pridgin Teale claimed that an outbreak of typhoid at a boys' school was caused by the connection

Figure 1.14
Sick Chamber (steel engraving after Robert Walter Weir, unknown source,
c. 1860) Courtesy of McGill University Libraries, Montreal

between the water-closet and the supply of drinking water at the institution. Thirty boys fell ill two weeks after one of their colleagues had contracted the disease at home.[81]

By 1884, as is evident by the architecture of the International Health Exhibition, the revolutionary germ theory had clearly not resolved the problematic relationship between bodies, illness, and domestic space. The major display on the home did not, like the exhibitions on public life and spaces, celebrate victory over disease. Rather, the Insanitary Dwell-

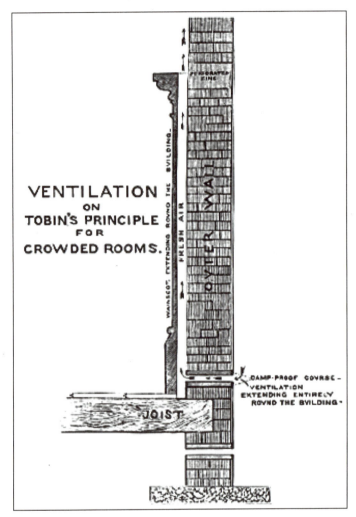

Figure 1.15
Ventilation through tube or pipe in exterior wall (Blake, *Sewage Poisoning*, 51)
Courtesy, Hagley Museum and Library

ing underlined the notion of the middle-class house as a poisonous, dangerous place, where illness passed through walls, water, people, and things, seemingly defying the system of physical barriers prescribed by contemporary science.[82]

The reform of domestic architecture was a fundamental aspect of what Oswei Temkin has described as a "willingness to rationalize the conduct of life in accordance with medical rules," which he claimed smoothed the emergence of hygiene, bacteriology, and asepsis in the late nineteenth century.[83] Indeed, in their attempt to understand and explain the relationship between houses and health, medical experts fragmented the house into its constituent parts. They broke down the walls of the building, exposing the drainage systems that were supposedly poisoning middle-class families, in an attempt to explain the relationship of the parts to the whole in the maintenance of healthy bodies. This program of rationalization can be read at every level of the reformers' agenda, from the systematic and diagrammatic ways they explained healthy architecture, to the literal, sectional character of the models at the IHE. The professional implications of the program were enormous: an expansion of the practice of medicine and a concurrent contraction of both the public's faith in architecture and its confidence in Victorian architects.

2 Doctors as Architects

The audience gasped as the lecturer described in detail the horror he had felt as a young boy when his father lifted the dilapidated floorboards of their family home; below, in the pungent earth, was a foul drain. This was the reason, the father had explained to his son, that their beloved home was overrun with rats. On further investigation, the father and son had discovered that the scullery sink, at some distance from the house, ran directly into a drain, emitting an extremely foul smell. "Disconnection between the house and the drainage system," Dr T. Pridgin Teale explained, "is the basis of domestic sanitation." He pointed to two diagrams posted on the wall of the makeshift lecture room to illustrate this. Large, simple, line drawings showed two houses in section; they looked like the Sanitary and Insanitary Dwellings that stood just outside the door of the IHE's central gallery, where the lecture was being held. Brightly coloured arrows showed poisonous gases penetrating the floors and walls of the house. The audience was mesmerized and strained to catch every word of architectural advice offered by the celebrated physician.

Mr F.S. Powell thanked Teale at the end of his lecture. "Tonight's guest is held in high regard not only by his own colleagues in the medical profession," explained Powell, "but well beyond that field. Dr Teale has added substantially to our understanding of the application of science to the domestic arrangements of a home." The crowd applauded enthusiastically, and many of those present approached the podium with questions for Teale concerning the situation in their own houses. Then, anxious to check their homes according to the "scientific principles" of which Teale had spoken, they left the central gallery and headed towards the main gate of the International Health Exhibition.[1]

T. Pridgin Teale's authority in architectural matters was typical of the "building-doctors" of the Domestic Sanitation Movement. As a surgeon in Leeds he had expanded his medical practice to include the assessment of his patients' houses, having first attempted to check the "health" of his own house. These investigations of unhealthy architecture were illustrated in his book *Dangers to Health* (1878); plate 1 showed what he believed to be the typical sanitary flaws in the construction of ordinary English houses (fig. 2.1).[2] "Many of the medical men of this town," Teale wrote in the introduction, "have recently gone into the question of the sanitation of their own houses ... [becoming] more keenly alive to possible sources of illness among their patients."[3] Teale's conviction that more than one-third of all illness could be traced to defective house drainage convinced him of the merits of publishing a book "on a subject which at first sight may appear to be outside the lines of my strictly professional work."[4]

This chapter examines the professional implications of the Domestic Sanitation Movement as various doctors, with a range of positions and backgrounds, expanded the "lines" of their work to encompass the middle-class house. The consequences for the architectural profession in England were devastating.[5] A "systematic" view of the house professed by the medical doctors was embraced by the middle class, with the result that there was a widespread wariness of building professionals. Design based on scientific principles boosted the confidence of physicians, and it also informed much material culture of the period. From the tiniest pipe fitting to master plans for entire cities, good design was described in terms of its adherence to "principles" and "systems."

Medical doctors shaped the perspective of the public health movement in the years following Chadwick's report. Edmund Alexander Parkes is often considered the founder of the "science of modern hygiene."[6] The Parkes Museum of Hygiene in London was established in his memory in 1877.[7] Chadwick had been assisted by several doctors in his exhaustive survey of the nation's health; physician Thomas Southwood Smith, whose supplementary study to the Poor Law commissioners' report of 1838 paved the way for Chadwick's work four years later, has also been called "the intellectual father of the public health movement."[8] "It is from the ranks of the medical profession that our modern prophets have mostly risen," proclaimed engineer W.P. Buchan in reviewing progress in drainage in 1888.[9] While architects, engineers, plumbers, city officials,

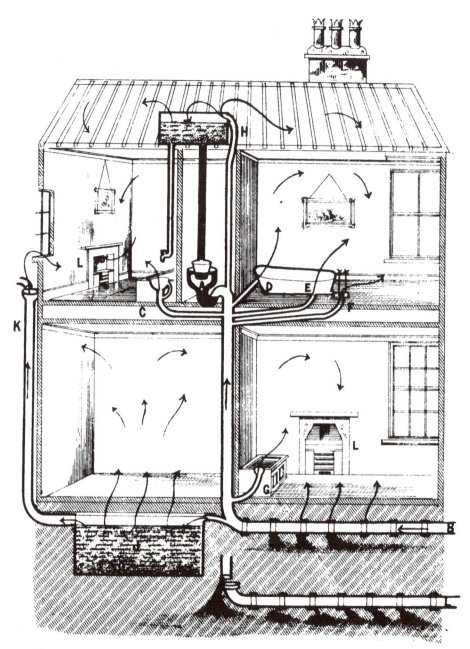

Figure 2.1
House with every sanitary arrangement faulty (Teale, *Dangers to Health*, 1881 edn., plate 1)
Courtesy of McGill University Libraries, Montreal

and lay people contributed to the movement, the domestic sanitarians were, by the 1870s, a coherent and highly visible group whose common goals were defined in terms of a primarily medical discourse.

This was largely because of the prominent position of the doctors in defining the group's perspective on the environment. Since sanitation was based on the notion of health as a public concern, nineteenth-century sanitary reform demanded the expansion of traditional conceptions of disease from the scale of the individual to that of the community. Lord Stanley explained this change of scale. Whereas sanitary science, he said, meant "that science which deals with the preservation of health and prevention of disease in reference to the entire community," by contrast, "medical science in the ordinary acceptation of the term … deals with the case of each individual separately."[10]

Thus, as sanitarians, physicians were concerned with how the spaces between bodies accommodated illness, rather than simply how the body acted as a setting for disease. They extended the scope of their investigation from the body to the room, the house, the street, and the city – visible and observable spaces in which they could attempt to control the seemingly invisible paths of diseases through air, streets, walls, water, people, and things.[11]

In applying their command of physiology to urban and domestic spaces, physicians defined a new form of expertise in building construction and architecture. Like Teale, many of those associated with the Domestic Sanitation Movement became, in a sense, "building-doctors," called on to diagnose, treat, and heal architecture, much as they might treat a patient. Many doctors even designed buildings. The homoeopathic physician John James Drysdale designed a suburban house in Liverpool in 1861; his medical colleague John Williams Hayward adapted Drysdale's unique system of ventilation to an urban site in 1867.[12] It was not unusual, in the 1870s and 1880s, for doctors to design model houses for the public to visit, or to prescribe the use of materials and the proper orientation for new buildings. Like Teale, many Victorian doctors lectured on the design of healthy houses. The physicians' apparent expertise in assessing the delicate relationship of health to the environment, in the guise of a more "scientific approach" to architecture, appealed to a middle-class population that was desperate for new solutions to seemingly insoluble health problems.

The doctors' "colonization" of the middle-class house depended on a widespread acceptance of the notion that houses were sick. The models at the health exhibition, as we have seen, showed how diseases were believed to have entered middle-class houses, even as late as 1884. The germ theory, of course, had postulated that spatial separation would prevent the spread of disease.[13] The host of diseases still plaguing the late-Victorian city had therefore transgressed the boundaries that had been carefully constructed between spaces; according to the theory, these boundaries should have arrested the spread of contagious diseases.

Victorian middle-class suburbs, for example, were enormous gestures of withdrawal from cities that were perceived as unhealthy, dangerous, and crowded. Real and imagined lines were constructed around suburbs such as Bedford Park (built outside London in the 1870s) through the distances travelled to reach them, the size and cost of the houses, the consistency of the architectural imagery, and the resulting homogeneity of the residents. These social and architectural distances were intended to shield middle-class families from the perceived threat of working-class people, immigrants, and others who did not fit an increasingly narrow definition of acceptable neighbours.

Similar boundaries were constructed around and within typical middle-class houses, acting as a form of spatial health insurance. Hedges and fences, front gardens, and elaborate entry halls constituted impenetrable systems of filters and barriers between the interior of the house and the unpredictable nature of the street. An advertisement for Bedford Park from 1881, hailing the west London suburb as the healthiest place in the world, showed a woman and child in a spacious garden, sheltered from other gardens and from the street by a tall wooden fence and a row of plants.[14]

The building-doctors demonstrated convincingly how these boundaries were nonetheless penetrated by invisible substances carrying deadly diseases. Many of them noted how infection refused to respect class lines. The American sanitarian Harriette Plunkett explained: "A man may live on the splendid 'avenue,' in a mansion plumbed in the latest and costliest style, but if, half a mile away, in range with his open window, there is a 'slum,' or even a neglected tenement-house, the zephyr will come along and pick up the disease-germs and bear them onward, distributing them to whomsoever it meets, whether he be a millionaire or shillingaire, with a perfectly leveling and democratic impartiality."[15]

Teale's picture-book, like the Insanitary Dwelling at the IHE, illustrated these processes most powerfully. In the book, as in his lectures, he showed how poisonous substances penetrated the walls of a newly built row of terrace houses that had been erected on a former dump site (fig. 2.2). Even the drawing Teale used revealed his reservations about the ca-

Figure 2.2
New terrace built on former dump (Teale, *Dangers to Health*, plate 50) Collection Canadian
Centre for Architecture, Montreal

pability of real architecture to protect its inhabitants. The building was
represented in an extremely light outline in order to emphasize how the
deadly gases rising from the former rubbish heap could easily penetrate
the nearly transparent structure. Similarly, Teale's "House with every
sanitary arrangement faulty" (see fig. 2.1) illustrated the potential of poisonous substances (germs) to penetrate the foundations and roof of a
house. The drains of the house overflowed into a rainwater tank under
the floor, while the soil pipe of the toilet on the upper floor ventilated
into the water-closet cistern, which supplied the drinking water for the
family. The drawing implied that the ample base and roof structures of
the house did nothing to protect the spaces inside.

Boundaries drawn between individual family members within a house
were similarly violated by disease, explained the doctor. The Victorian
house contained numerous specialized rooms, allowing family members
to spend a considerable amount of time in isolation. A standard plan for
houses of all classes had rooms leading off a single corridor and stairway,
and consequently encounters with other family members were both predictable and controllable. This facilitated seclusion of the sick without
any disruption of the family's normal use of the house. But Teale and
other doctors showed how a house's drainage system effectively demolished the physical separation of rooms; corroded pipes inside the walls
rendered the walls completely useless in fighting illness. Teale's illustra-

tion showed how the circulation system in a house did not enable the bedrooms and other separate spaces to be protected when they were in fact connected through the drainage system.[16]

Adding to the fear aroused by the doctors' warnings was the horrifying reality of the death rate. Despite the precautionary measures "built in" to the middle-class urban landscape by 1870, many diseases were obviously still not under control. As the doctors showed, tuberculosis, typhoid, and a host of other chronic or fatal illnesses were transported on the cool, fresh breezes of suburbia, where they ignored the fences and hedges, and permeated the thick brick walls of middle-class villas. Without considering possible shortcomings in their own treatment of disease, many doctors blamed buildings and architects for Victorian medicine's failure to cure.

The doctors' destruction of middle-class faith in domestic architecture as preventive medicine was a complex process consisting of three main strategies. First, the physicians active in the health movement discredited the authority of building professionals and workmen – namely, architects and plumbers – by exposing their supposedly substandard work to the public. The Insanitary Dwelling at the International Health Exhibition was a perfect example of these techniques. Secondly, they openly criticized the general practice of architecture, blaming its lack of "scientific principles" for the spread of disease in cities. As part of this step, the doctors themselves attempted to rationalize architecture, to systematize the house the way modern physiology had systematized the body, through their illustrations and descriptions of architecture as well as through demonstrations of their own ability in design. Finally, the physicians cemented their monopoly on the middle-class house by "negotiating cognitive exclusiveness."[17] This last stage of their program involved convincing the public of the exclusive ability of medical experts to perform sanitary house inspection. The immediate effect of these efforts was a significant shift in the ways ordinary people thought about architecture; the house became a form of preventive medicine only when regulated by its occupants under the watchful eye of medical experts. This careful regulation is the subject of chapter 3.

"The question that underlies the whole contention," stated an author in the *Sanitary Record*, "is whether gentlemen accredited in physic or surgery, who cannot be supposed to know the difficulties and constant outcomes of engineering science, can compete with engineers and architects."[18] The physicians active in the movement were explicit in their criticism of building professionals. According to Benjamin Ward Richardson, a major spokesman for the medical profession on the subject of domestic sanitation, most of the major diseases of the nineteenth century had been introduced and promoted by "errors of construction."[19] The exposure of substandard work by architects and plumbers thus formed the doctors' primary agenda. "When we have discovered what is wrong," said Teale, "we are more than half way to what is right." Teale referred to such house defects as "the rascalities of dishonest builders."[20]

The reported number of insanitary houses in the final decades of the nineteenth century is astounding. Teale, as previously mentioned, attributed faulty drainage to one-third of all illnesses in Great Britain. William Maguire, a Dublin engineer, checked three thousand houses between 1860 and 1890; of these, he believed that only one per cent (thirty houses) were healthy.[21] Richardson's assessment was equally bleak. "It has been declared upon examination," he stated, "that not above one out of three first-class houses have been found to be safely drained."[22]

Nearly all the books written by doctors for householders included instructions such as Teale's on the "self-diagnosis" of houses using common household objects. Doctors explained the widespread "poor health" of houses by stating that architectural practice (presumably, unlike their own field of medicine) lacked rational principles. "As a rule, in second-class, and, indeed, in many first-class houses," observed physician George Vivian Poore in 1887, "the ventilation and illumination of the staircase never trouble the mind of the builder or his architect."[23] Poore included in his book the plan of a house that featured what he considered to be healthy ventilation and lighting. "It is the principle only which I wish to illustrate. If the principle be sound, the method of carrying it out will certainly be improved by the experience and cunning of the trained architect."[24]

While doctors saw medicine as a model for architecture and engineering, practitioners of those professions tended to see the fields as complementary. "The professions of medicine and architecture are in no way rivals," asserted engineer William Eassie, "both sciences are necessary to the realisation of a perfect piece of architecture, be it cottage, mansion, school house, theatre or hospital." "It is due to the medical profession," he added, "to state that its members have ever been foremost in pointing out the danger of mass practices that were unwittingly [produced] by their architectural brethren."[25]

The physicians' demand for "principles" in architecture was typical of the general formation of Victorian professionalism, as historian Burton Bledstein has noted. "Principles" reinforced the need for specialized professions, serving as well to distinguish professionals from tradesmen or craftsmen, who supposedly worked more by methods of trial and error.

"The professional excavated nature for its principles, its theoretical rules, thus transcending mechanical procedures, individual cases, miscellaneous facts, technical information, and instrumental applications," explained Bledstein.[26]

This establishment of "principles" in nineteenth-century fields expressed a familiarity with contemporary "science."[27] Systematic or scientific thinking at this time meant the mastery of a body of knowledge that appeared to follow precise rules. The distinguished thinkers of Victorian science, such as Charles Darwin, explained the great mysteries of the age through the postulation of understandable rules. Following the rules or steps – emulating the scientific model – would guarantee predictable results. Thus it promised a certain degree of control over a given situation.

From this perspective, the sanitarians were extremely "modern." They claimed that systematic or scientific design would guarantee good health. Indeed, Richardson declared that the "scientific" view of the house was the major objective of the Domestic Sanitation Movement. In the introduction to one of the most important texts produced by the group, *Our Homes, and How to Make Them Healthy*, he explained his motives: "In the dialogue between Socrates and Critobulus, which Xenophon invents, he makes Socrates declare that the ordination of the house is the name of a science, and that the science means the order and increase of the household. It is in the spirit thus expressed that the writers of this work enter on their task. They aim to make the ordination of the house the name of a science, – the science of domestic sanitation."[28]

According to the doctors, the main problem was that most architecture of the 1870s and 1880s failed to reflect contemporary "scientific" research, particularly the new understanding of the effects of the environment on the health of the body. Recent public buildings constructed in London were held up as evidence. "That our architects have by no means grasped these facts," one observer noted, "is amply demonstrated by the style of some recent public buildings."[29] The newly completed Law Courts were particularly poor in this respect, he said, as were numerous schools in England.

Not only did architects fail to understand environmental health, implied the doctors, but the field of architecture itself was becoming far too diversified: "Perhaps there is no profession that calls for such varied qualifications as that of the architect – qualities that are not very commonly found in combination, the qualities of the artist, the scholar, and the engineer. An architect should have considerable scientific knowledge, be sympathetic, that he may readily assimilate the ideas of his clients, and have plenty of administrative capacity."[30] Architects, of course, were not the only specialists blamed by the physicians; plumbers, too, were held responsible for the spread of "house diseases." "Next to the mother-in-law," noted Mrs Plunkett, "the plumber is the best-abused character of the period."[31] According to the doctors, plumbers often misfitted pipes and joints, allowing dreaded sewer gas to leak into both soil and houses. They also allegedly substituted inferior materials in an effort to save money, knowingly "poisoning" the inhabitants of houses.

Plumbers and plumbing became the subjects of intense public scrutiny when the Prince of Wales almost died of typhoid in 1871.[32] He is said to have remarked, "If I were not a Prince, I would be a plumber."[33] The medical journal the *Lancet* conducted a thorough investigation of the prince's lodgings, paying particular attention to Londesborough Lodge in Scarborough, presuming a connection between its sanitary arrangements and the prince's illness. Although the lodge had been inspected by a contractor before the prince's visit, the Lancet Sanitary Commission uncovered several defects.[34] Ten years earlier, Albert, the prince's father and Queen Victoria's husband, had succumbed to the same disease, as had his cousin the king of Portugal. Supposedly passed through the atmosphere rather than through direct communication, typhoid was described by physicians as being "far more fatal to sufferers of the upper class and of the middle period of life than to patients of the poorer kind." Albert's death, like the near-death of his son a decade later, had prompted a "medical" investigation of his royal residence, Windsor Castle.[35]

In 1896 the *Lancet* published a "Special Commission on Plumbers' Work," in which it examined the drainage system of two typical London houses and specified what it considered to be the appropriate costs of plumbers' labour for various alterations or details. The commission noted that plumbers received relatively low pay because their work was "less observable" than that of others, such as decorators.[36] "There are few professions or trades," commented a journalist, "in which more reliance must be placed on the honour of those who are engaged in them; for, from the very nature of the case, the plumber's work is for the most part entirely unseen, and it might easily be scaped without anybody being a bit the wises – at least, for an indefinite time."[37]

In their defence, the plumbers, like the architects, blamed the absence of professional standards:

Before an English ship can sail out of any port on our British coast, it must be pronounced sea-worthy by a fully qualified and experienced surveyor under the

Government, and the captain who is to steer the vessel, as well as the officers and engineers, must each and all hold certificates as to their fitness for their respective positions. But *any* place enclosed within four walls, and roofed, or even semi-roofed over, may be inhabited, however dangerous to the health of the occupants it may be, and *anybody*, whether qualified or not, may plan the sanitary arrangements of a house, and *anybody* may do the plumber's work and drainage.[38]

The physicians demanded the registration of plumbers in order to guarantee a certain standard of "scientific" competence. Plumbers should not learn their trade by rule of thumb, "but in accordance with the scientific knowledge of it that has been acquired in recent years," said the physicians, referring to their own progress in the field.[39] Plumbers must be taught "principles," they insisted, just as they had stressed the need for principles in the profession of architecture.[40] "The modern plumber must face modern work," said Peter Fyfe, chief sanitary inspector of Glasgow, "or stand aside and make way for a new class of municipal tradesmen in departments only divided by a very thin partition wall from that in which he was reared."[41]

The *Lancet* commission on the work of plumbers suggested that the only hope for the future lay with the medical profession; the commissioners encouraged doctors to enlarge the boundaries of their professional terrain to include the houses of their patients, though they acknowledged the delicacy of the situation: "The power of the profession for good would be increased if a larger number of its members would follow the example of many and use their influence, so far as their opportunities will allow, to suggest that the sanitary condition of the patient's home should be ascertained in an obstetric or serious surgical case; but this is a matter of great delicacy."[42] Teale dedicated his popular book to his colleagues who had "studied, investigated, and corrected the sanitary arrangements" of houses, "in the hope that what [was] perhaps a small minority, [would] before many years [were] over, become a large majority of the medical men of the United Kingdom."[43]

The physicians' relegation of architects and plumbers to a subsidiary status in the reform of middle-class houses depended heavily on the creation of what Bledstein has called an "atmosphere of constant crisis."[44] The vast literature on architecture produced by the doctors and such highly publicized exhibitions as the Insanitary Dwelling at the IHE, as well as the doctors' seeming willingness to inspect buildings and cities, served to convince the public of the need for immediate action. In this way, as historian Patricia Branca has explained, "many of the health guides increased anxieties more than they allayed them."[45] Widespread familiarity with such concepts as "house disease" and "sewer gas" – and their attendant consequences – created work for the doctors and underlined their authority through fear and intimidation.[46]

So desperate did the situation appear that by the 1880s a new profession had been sanctioned to police the work of builders and architects. "Sanitary inspectors" were expected "to keep the country clean" by checking the drainage systems and materials of all new buildings.[47] The training of these inspectors varied, but admission to the profession was granted only to those who had passed a test and gained a diploma of merit granted by the Sanitary Institute. "This functionary must have science behind his back," stated a journalist in the *Sanitary Record*. "It has been too much the fashion, especially in smaller places, to take for granted that any quondam policeman, or active man of good character and fair business habits, was sufficiently qualified to enter on the duties of sanitary inspector."[48]

Building professionals were not unaware of the power their medical colleagues had gained in architectural matters. Architects remarked, for example, that while the Prince of Wales had appointed four medical men as commissioners to the International Health Exhibition, the committee included no architects or engineers.[49] In drawing attention to this situation, the architects openly acknowledged the unique qualifications of medical doctors in assessing the influence of buildings on health:

It is a matter of regret that while there are no fewer than four medical men, there is no architect and no engineer on the Commission; but this omission may perhaps not prove so detrimental to the object we believe to be one of the most important of those which the exhibition contemplates – the demonstration of the influences which the architectural design of buildings exerts on those who occupy them, and the way in which every part of a building, and the structure as a whole, should be so framed as to promote their health. Physicians are quite as much alive to this as any other class of observers, perhaps more so, and they know better than many other people that such influences as these, though they have been too often overlooked or ignored, are of primary importance to individual and public health.[50]

At the same time, the architects defended their professional territory by insisting that too much "science" was harmful to architecture. A journalist in the *Architect* explained:

It is very much to be suspected, when we ask the apparently simple question – what a London house is, that some of those eminent scientists who are now so devoted to the study of its organisation may be fast approaching a condition of mind which must cause them before long to abjure the shelter of a roof altogether for fear of being poisoned underneath ... Even our respect for science has its limits, and in all cases of philosophic enthusiasm we are bound to remember that the history of such endeavour is full of examples of the failure of the most excellent motives because of the most guileless mistakes.[51]

The reaction of the two professions to the effectiveness of the Insanitary and Sanitary Dwellings at the International Health Exhibition is equally illuminating. The medical profession, represented by opinions voiced in the *Lancet,* found the model houses to be an "important addition" to the fair and considered the insanitary house a fair representative of London's dwellings. "This 'shocking example' is not overdone," the doctors claimed. "The defects shown come daily under the eye of medical men, and as we walked through this dwelling, visions of sore-throat, headache, malaise, typhoid, diarrhoea, and puerperal fever filled the mind." The physicians hoped that "every plumber in Great Britain" might "find an opportunity to [inspect the houses]."[52]

The architects, on the other hand, although impressed by the model houses, insisted that the lessons offered by the display were intended not for them but for "the large number ... who go to the great show-grounds determined to see everything." The reviewer for the *Architect* found the construction flaws greatly exaggerated: "It need scarcely be said that those to whom the idea was entrusted to carry out have in the one case selected the worst systems and appliances, and almost gone out of their way to make every arrangement as bad as it could well be." The journalist defiantly concluded: "There are no new ideas that we can see enunciated in the arrangements of these two houses."[53]

The architects blamed general living conditions in London for the insanitary state of most houses. Bad weather was the most common reason given for the peculiarly English indoor lifestyle. "Even in transacting their business, men hasten from shelter to shelter, instead of assembling in the *piazza* or sauntering along the *boulevard*," the architects maintained. Moreover, the burning of pit-coal for heat and gas for lighting inside tightly concealed "boxes" rendered the interiors of houses highly artificial.

The architects also pointed to the increased demand for interior sanitary facilities as the reason for unhealthy houses. When water-closets and pumps were located outside the house, they said, domestic architecture was much healthier. The demand made by "fine" people for more sophisticated plumbing had given rise to the "science of the plumber." The present unhealthy lifestyle of London's middle class, they believed, resulted more from an unnecessary demand for luxury and comfort than from a lack of scientific understanding on the part of architects: "A London house has become simply a highly artificial cage for a group of highly artificialised animals; and the worst of the matter is that, the more the inmates demand in the way of advanced artificiality, the more they themselves become artificialised. In plainer language, the more they 'cosset' themselves, the more cosseting they must have; the more comfortable they are, the more delicate they grow."[54] The solution, according to the architects, was a return to a more natural, less scientific house. Houses would be healthier as a result of open windows, outdoor exercise, and the prompt removal of "at least half of all that the plumber has brought into it."[55] The architects were also quick to underline the limits of the doctors' authority in building: "In arrogating to themselves any exclusive capacity to remedy the faults in dwellings, the medical officers of health are unwise, and the most strenuous opposition would come from some of their own body. If an engineer were to profess to treat disease, the absurdity would at once be seen, but it appears to be overlooked when a medical officer of health professes to deal with engineering and construction."[56]

Nevertheless, the overall impact of the Domestic Sanitation Movement on the prestige of the architectural profession in England was devastating. Robert Edis was the architect most closely associated with the movement, and his name continues to be invoked in the discussion of the architectural aspects of domestic sanitation.[57] Best known as the designer of the British pavilion at the World's Columbian Exposition in Chicago in 1893, Edis had a substantial practice in domestic architecture in England.[58] Although he was both an architect and a sanitation "expert," his role in the movement (and at the IHE) was limited to that of an adviser on decoration and furniture. Architect E.W. Godwin was cast in an equally minor role; he contributed a history of costume to the International Health Exhibition in which he claimed that the history of dress and of architecture had run parallel courses.[59]

The fact that these carefully circumscribed roles were given to such prominent architects as Edis and Godwin at an international health exhibition is telling. The Domestic Sanitation Movement directed the attention of architects away from drainage, ventilation, and other systems that connected domestic space with urban space, causing them to focus on the planning, decoration, and furnishing of houses.[60] While doctors and manufacturers argued over the hazards of untrapped drains and ventilating tubes, architects were left to debate the "healthiness" of undecorated surfaces, curtainless windows, built-in furniture, nonpoisonous wallpapers, and (in Godwin's case) the benefits of loose clothing. Since they were not to be trusted with the plumbing and ventilation of buildings – the real matters of sanitation – architects marketed themselves in a new light, as the exclusive arbiters of "beauty."

Edis lectured and published widely on the subject of healthy furniture and decoration.[61] In many ways, he acted as the most important link between the architectural profession and the sanitarians, belonging as he did to both groups. His allegiance in the professional debate, however, lay with the architects.[62] Indeed, he deflected the blame cast by doctors on architects onto builders and landlords. In a lecture on "The Building of London Houses," Edis pointed out "the hopelessness of any real improvement in the building of London houses until effective legislation brought the 'speculative builder' under such control and supervision that he should be obliged to give up the scamping work, the defective materials, and the utter disregard of all sanitary requirements which now characterise 99 per cent of new construction. The problem, he insisted, was that 'competent' architects only erected one per cent of London houses."[63]

Edis's lecture at the IHE was a recapitulation of the major ideas in his best-known book, *Decoration and Furniture of Town Houses* (1881), which, as members of the press frequently noted, was based more on what not to do to ensure a healthy house than on specific recommendations. Edis warned "those about to furnish" to avoid anything in houses that was likely to hold dust, to avoid arsenical wallpapers and thick carpets, and to furnish and clean the nursery with great care.[64] As an architect sympathetic to the health movement, it is telling that Edis felt his place was to explain to the general public the relationship between art and health, rather than construction or architecture and health.

According to Edis's doctrine, "beauty" determined the healthiness of a house. While he admitted that many people considered clean water and pure air to be the major determinants of a healthy building, he insisted that the design of furniture and wallpaper had an equally significant impact on personal health. He detested ready-made furniture, advocating instead the use of custom-made pieces. This attitude did little to endear Edis to furniture manufacturers, who were extremely concerned after his

Figure 2.3
Messrs Jackson and Graham's "fitments" as applied to a bedroom (*Cabinet Maker and Art Furnisher*, 1 July 1884, 3) British Architectural Library, RIBA, London

lecture at the IHE that the audience had been left with the impression that "every ordinary and portable bedroom suite is a disseminator of disease and death." One reviewer of the lecture recommended Edis's pamphlet, "for it will do much to reform, if it does not remove, many old friends."[65]

Edis presented his architectural ideas in an exhibition for Messrs Jackson and Graham at the IHE (fig. 2.3). Described as a scheme of "fitments," the display exemplified Edis's method of treating the room "as a complete and indivisible thing" rather than as a collection of "isolated articles." The mantelpiece extended up to the electric light on the ceiling; cupboards continued along the top of the walls, creating recesses that contained a writing table and a toilet table. As one visitor noted, at first glance this philosophy of decoration and furnishing appeared to be the work of a builder rather than a furniture maker, but Jackson and Graham's exhibit was meant to demonstrate that such work could be successfully carried out by a furniture-making company.[66] Just as doctors had infringed on the traditional territory of architects, architects were now blurring the boundary between their responsibilities and those of decorators and furniture makers.

The influence of the physicians involved in the Domestic Sanitation Movement extended far beyond their scathing criticism of current architectural practice; these building-doctors also designed houses and cities, illustrating that they could do what architects did, only better. Although it was never constructed, Richardson's "Hygeia" was the most ambitious "design project" by a medical professional.[67] A utopian city for a population of 100,000, it was never even illustrated; it existed only in the description Richardson read at the 1875 annual meeting of the Social Science Association in Brighton. He dedicated the city to Edwin Chadwick.

The "plan" of Hygeia involved 20,000 houses on 4,000 acres of land. Richardson suggested that each of the buildings should be constructed on brick arches because of the water retention problems of a clay substratum. Whereas in most English cities, he explained, kitchens and servants' quarters were located below grade, only subways carrying currents of fresh air and other services would be built beneath Hygeia. He hoped this would not "shock" housewives.[68]

The city was ordered by three wide east-west boulevards, beneath which special railways would be constructed to carry the "heavy traffic" of the city.[69] The generous width of the streets was intended to encourage both the thorough ventilation and the natural illumination of the houses, which were to be surrounded by green spaces, planted with trees and shrubs. Richardson imagined the streets of Hygeia paved with "wood pavement set in asphalte," because he believed the material to be quiet, easy to clean, and durable.[70] His system of subways to facilitate street cleaning would significantly reduce the number of "gutter children," he insisted. "Instead of the gutter," claimed the optimistic doctor, "the poorest child has the garden."[71]

The houses of Richardson's Hygeia were to be constructed of brick cavity walls, allowing thorough ventilation and heating; the interior walls were to be of a washable glazed brick. "The after adornment of the walls is considered unnecessary, and, indeed, objectionable," stated Richardson.[72] The kitchens were sited on the uppermost levels of the houses. The sewers ran along the floors of the subways; this underground system also functioned as a way of distributing water and gas directly to each house. Such a system, the doctor insisted, would diminish the diseases that were prevalent in most English cities and would decrease the death rate to eight per thousand; a cartoonist in *Punch* illustrated the ironies of the design project by showing the physicians of Hygeia out of work (fig. 2.4).[73] Since Richardson was an avid supporter of temperance, no alcohol was permitted in Hygeia. Also forbidden in the homes of his utopian city was any industrial work, such as tailoring or dressmaking. "That this is a common cause of disease," said Richardson, "is well understood."[74]

Figure 2.4
Doctors in Hygeia. (*Punch's Almanack for 1876*) Courtesy of McGill University Libraries, Montreal

Richardson's grasp of planning principles was obviously extraordinary. However, the significance of Hygeia was not in its architecture but in the fact that the doctor had clearly abandoned all hope of "curing" the existing built environment and saw starting over on a new site as the only way to achieve good health. In this respect it was prophetic of Ebenezer Howard's scheme for a garden city more than two decades later, as well as foreshadowing many of the urban planning schemes of the twentieth century.

Other physicians were less ambitious in the scale of their design ideas but were more specific in their prescription of architectural details. Dr George Vivian Poore illustrated his capabilities as a designer in the plan of an individual house with the help, as he acknowledged, of his friend the architect Thomas W. Cutler.[75] Poore's triangular "bungalow facing south" (fig. 2.5) allowed "those who lived in it [to] enjoy a maximum amount of sunshine and fresh air without exposure to cold winds."[76] The plan had apparently been adapted by Cutler for a real convalescent home in Epping Forest.[77]

Like Richardson, Poore had far-reaching ideas about the complete re-design of cities. What differentiated his work from that of the other building-doctors was that he dared to criticize London's new sewer

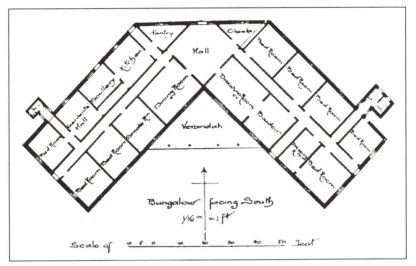

Figure 2.5
Bungalow facing south (Poore, *The Dwelling House*, 14) Collection Canadian Centre for Architecture, Montreal

system. Poore claimed that the system just adopted by the metropolis was "based on an utterly wrong principle," for the soil rather than the river should be the repository for sewage.[78] Modern sewerage, he said, led to overcrowding by allowing houses to be built higher than previously. Indeed, the real danger came from the fact that modern houses were built without any curtilage. Water and fuel were no longer delivered by hand to the upper floors of houses, and therefore taller buildings caused no great inconvenience to the occupants. Poore pointed to American hotels as models of unhealthy buildings:

"Five hundred rooms, passenger and luggage lifts to every floors, 1,000 electric lights, hot and cold water laid on to every room, bath-rooms on every floor," is the kind of advertisement put forward by an eight-storeyed hotel without an inch of curtilage. Without steam power, without water under pressure, and without water-carried sewage, such Yankee monstrosities were not possible, whereas nowadays the loftier the hotel so much the greater is the profit, because extra storeys do not increase the ground-rent.[79]

Furthermore, said Poore, the dangerous overcrowding in London after the construction of the sewer system was completely invisible in the official documents, and people were therefore misled into thinking that

London had become a safer place to live. The recent tendency to live in suburbs and commute to work in the city meant that the statistical death rate had only appeared to improve. Anticipating our interest, Poore warned: "Some historian of the future may draw the conclusion that the decay of London set in acutely about the year 1871, unless he should perchance discover that ... this population is one mainly of adult males, and since, if they get ill in the City they don't die in it, the death-rate keeps down, and we like to think it is a wholesome place for a young man to work in."[80] Building regulation, Poore believed, was the only hope. He called for a standardized relationship between the volume of a building and the area it was to occupy. Under the system currently in practice, he noted, "the volume of sewage to be dealt with may be doubled or trebled without any increase of the area drained by the sewers."[81]

Poore's vision of an ideal city, like Richardson's, existed only in the realm of the written word and was based more on political reform than on revolutionary physical change:

If every house were compelled in the future to have a curtilage bearing a definite proportion to the cubic contents, there would be an end of these towers of Babel, which shut out from us the light and air of heaven; the price of building land would fall; it would be possible to make some calculations as to sewage; and the excessive overcrowding of a city would be prevented. Without such a regulation great sewage schemes must in the end make the sanitary condition of a city worse rather than better.[82]

Regulation, decentralization, and cremation, Poore believed, were the real solutions to the poor health of the city.

Poore's work resembled Teale's more than Richardson's in that Poore supported his proposals for new design by a thorough inspection and analysis of existing houses in London. He explained his findings by using a house featured in the *Lancet* in 1896 (fig. 2.6). But like Richardson (and unlike Teale), Poore believed the faulty construction of London houses to be irreparable. He outlined four major problems in his sample house: the volume of the building was inappropriate for its area; the depth of the house was too great; the largest level was below the street; and there was no back door.[83] Poore suggested extensive and expensive renovations to the house, based on the report on plumbing in the *Lancet*. "It is said that eels get used to skinning," explained the doctor-architect, "and so the Londoner becomes very blind to the failings of the house which he inhabits."[84]

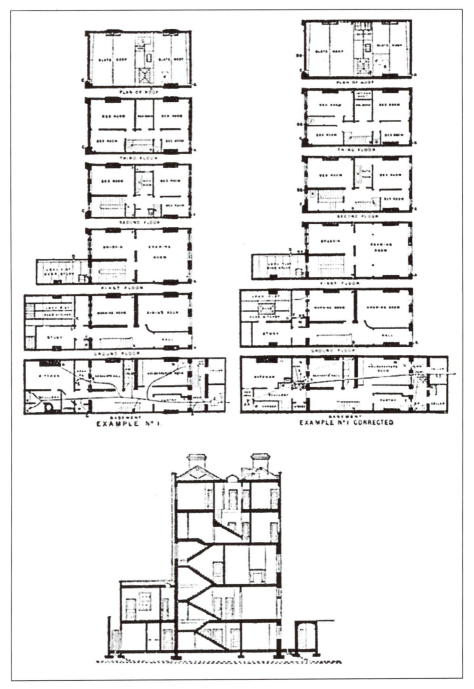

Figure 2.6
Typical London house analysed by Poore (Poore, *The Dwelling House*, 4–5) Collection Canadian Centre for Architecture, Montreal

Poore's emphasis on the geometry of the house and his reliance on an architect in drawing and realizing his design ideas recalled the influential work of the American phrenologist Orson Squire Fowler. In 1849 Fowler had published *A Home for All; or, the Gravel Wall, and Octagon Mode of Building*, which advocated walls constructed of concrete and described what he believed to be the best shape for a house: the octagon.[85] Although the volume included some references to health, particularly with regard to ventilation, Fowler's overall intention was to make houses more affordable and to use space more efficiently, rather than to improve the health of the inhabitants. His preference for concrete, in fact, came from his belief that the earth's supply of wood was finite.[86]

Certainly, at mid-century it was more typical of authors of architectural texts to link the character of inhabitants to the forms of their houses rather than to suggest a relationship between their bodies and domestic space. "Indeed, other things being equal," stated Fowler, "the better a man's mentality, the better mansion will he construct, and the characteristics of the house will be as those of its builder or occupant."[87] Fowler went beyond this simple link between architecture and human character, suggesting that people possessed a "building faculty," presumably drawn from "inhabitiveness," a phrenological faculty.[88] Phrenology postulated that the disposition and character of a person might be ascertained through the shape of his or her head. Like other phrenologists, Fowler saw housing as a way in which Americans could improve their lives.

Fowler's ideas were certainly known in England. His younger brother Lorenzo Niles Fowler – with whom he published such works as *Phrenology Proved, Illustrated, and Applied*, and with whom he founded a publishing firm – moved to London in 1863. Lorenzo Fowler lectured extensively throughout Great Britain, and several of his lectures were published in London. Interestingly, Lorenzo's wife Lydia Folger Fowler was a graduate of Syracuse medical college and lectured on the diseases of women and children. However, Orson Fowler had no special training in science or medicine.[89] Perhaps his interest in the connection between geometry and character (the book includes lengthy calculations of the superior efficiency of the eight-sided form) stemmed from his lifelong interest in phrenology. Fowler's houses were extremely modern, particularly in the way the major rooms opened into one another rather than connecting through a corridor (fig. 2.7). His time-and-motion analyses of the way housework might be performed in the home (illustrated by the dotted lines through the plan, for example)

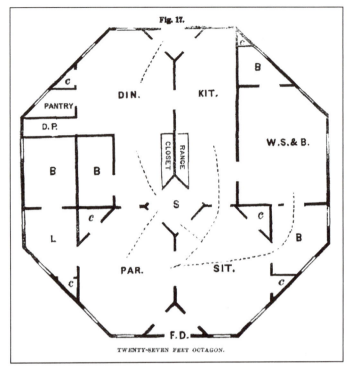

Figure 2.7
Octagon house, designed by Fowler (Fowler, *A Home for All*, 97)
Collection Canadian Centre for Architecture, Montreal

foreshadowed by nearly seven decades the well-known movement diagrams of Christine Frederick, pioneer of the home economics movement in America.[90]

Many other British medical experts supervised the sanitary "renovation" of their houses and opened them to the public, like Teale, rather than designing ideal houses, as Poore and Fowler did, or prescribing sanitary renovations. Thomas Wakley, editor of the *Lancet*, "determined that his house should have every improvement known to science, and also serve as a model and means of instruction." In 1889 he invited "sanitary experts" to examine the changes carried out by Rowland Plumbe, architect, in the "healing" of his house: covers were fixed in the traps; sinks and basins were provided with outlet pipes; and the ventilating pipe was continued up to the roof. "Until householders consider these matters as of vital importance, architects and builders will continue to treat them as

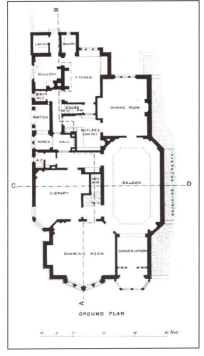

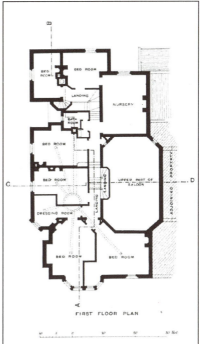

Figure 2.8
Ground plan of House no. 1. (Drysdale and
Hayward, *Health and Comfort in House Building*) Collection Canadian Centre for Architecture, Montreal

Figure 2.9
First floor plan of House no. 1 (Drysdale and
Hayward, *Health and Comfort in House Building*) Collection Canadian Centre for Architecture, Montreal

subordinate features of design," commented a visitor in a review of
Wakley's house in a popular women's magazine.[91] Like the books doctors
wrote on architecture, Wakley's house had, by implication, reflected neg-
atively on the architectural profession.

Homoeopaths John Drysdale and John Williams Hayward went even
further in their critique of architects' work. These Liverpool physicians
designed and built two houses in the 1860s in order to illustrate a unique
system of ventilation. Following the medical model, they then observed
and recorded the occupants' health for ten years.[92] "House no. 1," designed by Drysdale, was constructed in a Liverpool suburb in 1861 (figs.
2.8–2.11). Rather than ventilating rooms individually, the design called for
a single system of air flow.[93] The entire house was ventilated with heated
fresh air through a chamber located under the central staircase; used air

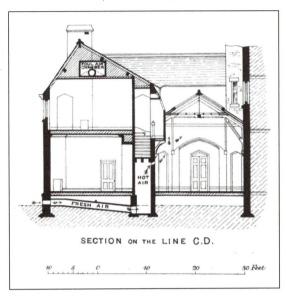

Figure 2.10
Section of House no. 1 (Drysdale and Hayward, *Health and Comfort in House Building*) Collection Canadian Centre for Architecture, Montreal

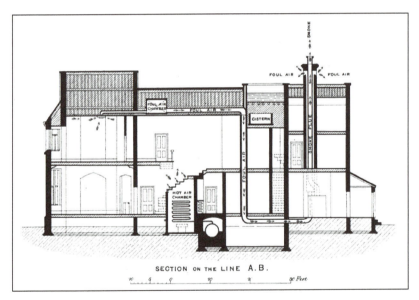

Figure 2.11
Section of House no. 1 (Drysdale and Hayward, *Health and Comfort in House Building*) Collection Canadian Centre for Architecture, Montreal

was removed from each room through a perforated ornament in the ceiling, then carried along a zinc tube into a foul-air chamber below the roof. The vitiated air in this chamber was then vented above the house through the exhaust shaft in the kitchen chimney.

After ten years, "House no. 1" was considered by its owner to be "pleasant," "warm," "airy," and "comfortable." "So completely unobtrusive and self-acting" was the system that tenants were apparently unaware of its existence. One resident was so impressed after having spent the winter in the house that he had another one constructed using its principles.[94] Dr Inman, author of *On the Preservation of Health*, described his visit to the model building: "I never once during my prolonged visit felt either too hot or too cold. Neither before nor since have I been in a residence which seemed to be so thoroughly comfortable, and the doctor and myself were soon at work over the plan of another."[95]

Six years later Hayward built "House no. 2," attempting to improve on Drysdale's ventilation system and at the same time to adapt the design to an urban site (figs. 2.12 and 2.13).[96] In 1868 he presented his ideas to the Architectural Society of Liverpool, where the house was "received with approbation" and was described in the society's proceedings.[97] One physician actually lived in this house for four years, during which time he apparently experienced a dramatic improvement in his health: "Whereas previously, when living in ordinary houses, he frequently suffered from bronchitis and quinsy, he has never had either disease since living in his present house: and a member of his family who had previously to spend several winters in a warm climate, is now able to remain at home and go about in the open air all the year round. For the prevention of disease we hold such a house to be a most important auxiliary."[98]

Drysdale and Hayward justified their authority in designing this "auxiliary" to good health by stating in the beginning of their book that physicians had more opportunity than other members of the community to see the interior arrangements of houses. "And no one realises as he does," they continued, "the true nature of any defects of construction, warming, or ventilation which bear upon the health and comfort of the inhabitants."[99] The two doctors claimed that they experienced no "difficulties or unpleasantness" with the architects on the project. They had little confidence, however, in the initiative of architects to reform houses, for it seemed to them that the interests of architects were exclusively aesthetic. Like other physicians active in the Domestic Sanitation Movement,

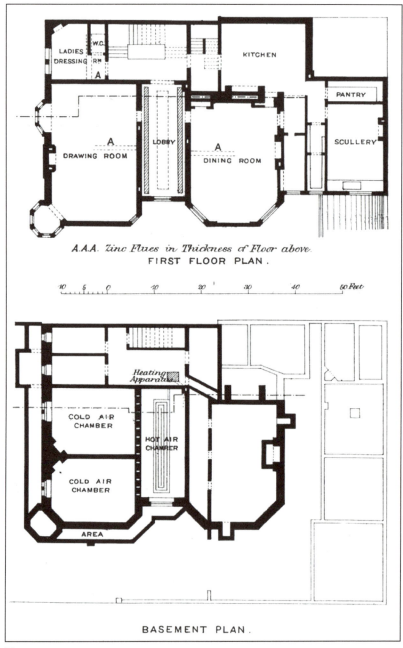

FIRST FLOOR PLAN.

A.A.A. *Zinc Flues in Thickness of Floor above.*

10 5 0   10   20   30   40   50 *Feet*

BASEMENT PLAN.

Figure 2.12
Plans of House no. 2 (Drysdale and Hayward, *Health and Comfort in House Building*) Collection
Canadian Centre for Architecture, Montreal

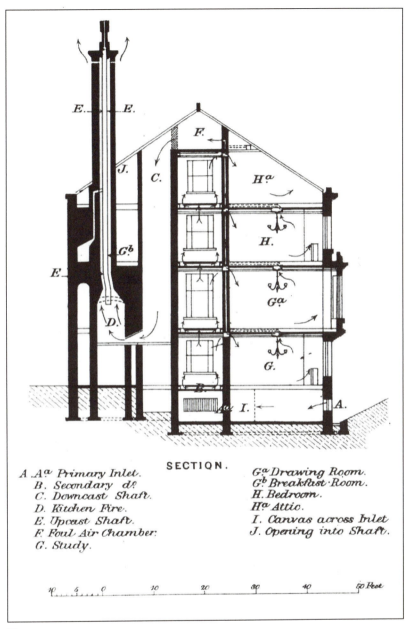

E. E.

F.

J.

C.

Hᵃ

Gᵇ

H.

E.

Gᵃ

D.

G.

B.

Aᵃ I. A.

SECTION.

A Aᵃ Primary Inlet.
  B. Secondary dᵒ.
  C. Downcast Shaft.
  D. Kitchen Fire.
  E. Upcast Shaft.
  F. Foul Air Chamber.
  G. Study.

Gᵃ Drawing Room.
Gᵇ Breakfast Room.
H. Bedroom.
Hᵃ Attic.
I. Canvas across Inlet
J. Opening into Shaft.

10 5 0   10   20   30   40   50 Feet

Figure 2.13
Section of House no. 2 (Drysdale and Hayward, *Health and Comfort in House Building*) Collection Canadian Centre for Architecture, Montreal

Drysdale and Hayward regarded members of the medical profession as the primary agents of change:

Architects would, indeed, have some difficulty in initiating any change involving extra expense, because the public naturally object to increase of cost, of the benefits of which they are not convinced; nor are architects specially likely of themselves to introduce changes that involve expense without display, as their sphere lies more with beauty and elegance of the exterior than with the sanitary conveniences of the interior. Consequently we must not look for much improvement in house building until the public themselves are convinced of the advantage, to comfort as well as health, of having warmed and ventilated houses; it is therefore hoped that medical men especially, who are the best able to appreciate these benefits, will embrace every opportunity of pressing these matters on the attention of the public.[100]

Drysdale's and Hayward's architectural efforts are compelling evidence of the variety of medical specialists who were drawn to spatial solutions for illness. As noted above, both Drysdale and Hayward practised homoeopathic medicine, a popular system of therapeutics based on the principle that "like cures like." Homoeopaths prescribed treatments or drugs for their patients that were intended to produce symptoms similar to those of the disease being treated, and they favoured extremely small doses.[101] Homoeopaths were widely ostracized in the nineteenth century. Medical schools expelled faculty members who practised homoeopathic principles, and mainstream medical journals avoided the subject for fear of jeopardizing sales.[102] Yet both Drysdale and Hayward were outspoken proponents of homoeopathy. Each served as president of the Liverpool Homoeopathic Medico-Chirurgical Society.[103] Drysdale was co-editor of the *British Journal of Homoeopathy* and was influential in reforming homoeopathy itself, which became less distinguishable from regular medicine in the final decades of the nineteenth century.[104]

The physicians' "negotiation of cognitive exclusiveness" – their attempt to monopolize domestic sanitation by convincing the public of their exclusive ability to check sanitary architecture – was strengthened by their suggestion that the diagnosis of houses was precisely the same enterprise for which their authority was already well established in all branches of medicine; houses, they implied, were like bodies. To this end, doctors explained domestic architecture using the language and illustrative techniques of contemporary physiology. Houses and bodies were represented in the Victorian popular press in cross section to show the complex networks of overlapping "systems." This type of drawing emphasized the flow and interplay of air, water, waste, and other substances through the structure. As the physiological systems of respiration, circulation, and digestion were inextricably linked in the human body, so too, implied the doctors, must ventilation, drainage, and the supply of fresh water work together in a house.

A typical physiological drawing of the period illustrating this approach is George Lewes's digestive tract of a dog, which appeared in the *Physiology of Common Life* in 1858 (fig. 2.14). As historian Bruce Haley has explained, physiology "came to occupy a central position in scientific thought" in the nineteenth century. The "vital activities of human beings" emphasized the "wholeness of the body."[105] To a lay audience, illustrations of buildings based on this physiological model appeared much more scientific than traditional architectural drawings, for they revealed the disease-ridden drains and pipes which, as Teale pointed out, often passed unnoticed in the real world because they were out of sight.

Journals of the time featured parallel series on houses and bodies, referring to the illustrations of the body in explaining the house, and vice versa. In the popular family magazine *Baby*, for instance, a series in twelve parts called "Outlines of Physiology and Hygiene" ran consecutively with a twelve-part series entitled "Health in Our Homes."[106] On the subject of ventilation, the author referred readers to the illustration of the lungs in a previous volume (fig. 2.15).[107] The implication was that houses and bodies operated by the same principles.

The medical profession's "colonization" of the middle-class house was seen by the urban middle class as a heroic effort to predict, and hence to control, this seemingly uncontrollable movement of illness from house to house. It was also seen as an attempt to protect the public from the unacceptable standards set by the building professions. By assuming professional responsibility for the sanitary condition of houses – particularly for drainage, ventilation, and illumination – doctors presumed that such external conditions would necessarily determine the health, or the "sanitary condition," of the bodies that inhabited the space. This conceptual convergence of the body and the house was embraced by an anxious urban population as a conscious attempt to control disease.

The distinctions between body and house became sufficiently blurred in the 1870s and 1880s that doctors also employed the reverse metaphor, explaining the body in terms of the house. The notion that the body was actually occupied or inhabited, like a building, was carried to an extreme by the American author-doctor Mary Wood-Allen. In her book *The*

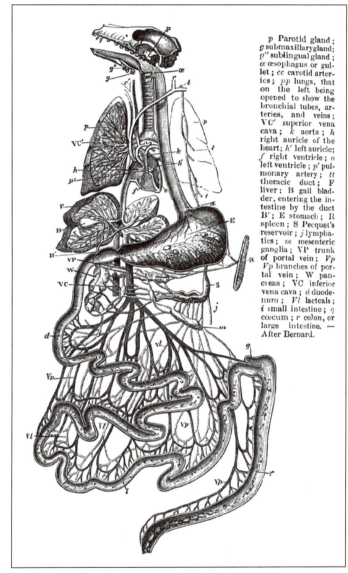

p Parotid gland ;
g submaxillary gland;
g'' sublingual gland ;
œ œsophagus or gullet ; *cc* carotid arteries ; *pp* lungs, that on the left being opened to show the bronchial tubes, arteries, and veins ; V C' superior vena cava ; *k* aorta ; *h* right auricle of the heart; *h'* left auricle; *f* right ventricle ; *o* left ventricle ; *p'* pulmonary artery ; *tt* thoracic duct ; F liver ; B gall bladder, entering the intestine by the duct B'; E stomach ; R spleen ; S Pecquet's reservoir ; *j* lymphatics ; *m* mesenteric ganglia ; VP trunk of portal vein ; *Vp Vp* branches of portal vein ; W pancreas ; VC inferior vena cava ; *d* duodenum ; *Vl* lacteals ; *i* small intestine ; *q* cœcum ; *r* colon, or large intestine. — After Bernard.

Figure 2.14
Digestive tract of a dog (Lewes, *The Physiology of Common Life*, 1: 230). Courtesy of McGill University Libraries, Montreal

Man Wonderful in the House Beautiful, she used the metaphor of the house-body to warn of the dangers of "guests," such as alcoholic stimulants.[108] And she began her popular textbook of physiology, *The Marvels of Our Bodily Dwelling*, by stating: "Let us study the body as a house in

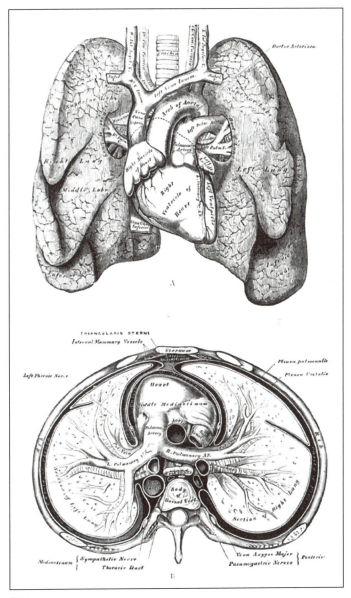

Figure 2.15
Illustration of a lung (*Baby*, July 1890, 175) Courtesy of the British Library, London

which we dwell here on earth, a house created by a divine Architect, fitted up with every comfort, divided into many rooms, each with its own appropriate furniture and adapted to its own especial use. It is a beautiful building, more exquisitely adorned than any structure of man's creation."[109] Wood-Allen pushed the body-house analogy to an extreme, describing, for instance, the stomach as a kitchen, the skin as sheathing, and the brain as electrical equipment. She admitted that the analogy was not original; it was "as old as literature." Her personal contribution to the idea, she said, was that she had "united metaphor with scientific facts."[110]

Just as the traditional boundaries between the body and the house were demolished by the domestic sanitarians, so were the conceptual boundaries destroyed between the house and the city. The sanitarians saw the body, the house, and the city as part of a single system, which was dependent on "scientific" principles for its healthy regulation. At the scale of the city, Chadwick himself had argued that reform could be achieved only through drainage, cleanliness, and improved ventilation, as if the city were a gigantic house. As Graeme Davison has noted, Chadwick also delighted in urban schemes in which "the supply of gas and the supply of water may be carried on together."[111]

In their view of the body, the house, and the city, the sanitarians were obsessed with drainage; the removal of human waste from all three "structures" was at the heart of the Victorian battle against infection. In treating most illness in the late nineteenth century, physicians prescribed a generous dose of laxatives or purgatives. They believed that the body was at its strongest and was best able to ward off disease when it was empty of fecal matter. This assumption, underlined by the fear of noxious odours, which had been reinforced by the miasmatists, was extended to the house and the city. Richardson proclaimed: "A basic principle in domestic sanitation is to take care that everything that is generated in the house and that is of an excretive, offensive, and injurious form, shall be prevented accumulating in the dwelling. Whether it be dust or refuse, or remnants of food, or sewage, it is necessary that it be removed as it is produced."[112]

Similarly, Bazalgette's sewers were the great intestines of the city, removing human waste to a location outside the metropolis. Before the sewers were built, refuse had been stored in cesspools or cesspits, which were contained within the yards of middle-class houses and were shared between houses in poorer neighborhoods.[113] While the earlier system was obviously less healthy, it meant that middle-class city dwellers were aware of the location of their own waste – supposing, mistakenly, that the waste of their neighbours or of the slum across town had little effect on their immediate surroundings.

This same attitude is reflected in the commercial products of the period. Based on the actions of human digestion and respiration, drainage and ventilation were "systematized" to protect the body from the city by means of the house. The Banner system of house drainage (fig. 2.16), for example, was an extremely popular tripartite trap system. According to its designer, E. Gregson Banner, it was superior because it was based on the human body. The trap, inlet pipe, and cowl had breathing power like the lungs, and the major benefit of the system was "continuous extraction."[114]

The Robert Boyle Company in London also marketed its ventilation fittings as "systems," implying that the ideas behind its products were based on scientific laws. Its catalogue featured sectional drawings of rooms, with the picture of a billiard room, for example, showing how the whole room worked as a single system, from the ventilator on the roof to the hidden fresh-air warmer under the billiard table (fig. 2.17). Other companies featured illustrations resembling the illustrations published by Teale. The Durham Company, for instance, showed a section of a "city house"; in this system, the thick walls of the building seemed to afford a layer of protection between the municipal sewer system and the interior of the house (fig. 2.18).

As we have seen, the doctors gained much of their confidence in architectural matters from what they believed to be their superior qualifications in assessing healthy bodies. While some physicians, such as Drysdale and Hayward, claimed that this came from having seen more house interiors than other professionals, Teale, Richardson, Poore, and most of the other building-doctors simply extended their established expertise in assessing bodies to the "diagnosis" of patients' houses.

Architects, however, were equally confident of their qualifications in domestic sanitation. At the beginning of a three-day conference of the Royal Institute of British Architects (RIBA) at the International Health Exhibition, architect Robert Kerr stated his hope that "this opportunity would be embraced by architects of London to expound more particularly those principles which they, having to do with those matters professionally, understood so much better than any other section of the community."[115] Indeed, the theme of the architects' meetings at the IHE was "The Sanitary Construction of Houses."[116] After introductory remarks by the president of the RIBA, eleven papers were read by prominent architects on subjects ranging from waterproofing roofs to the hygienic value of colour. Discussion followed, led by Kerr. A major concern of the participating architects was the sense of their powerlessness in

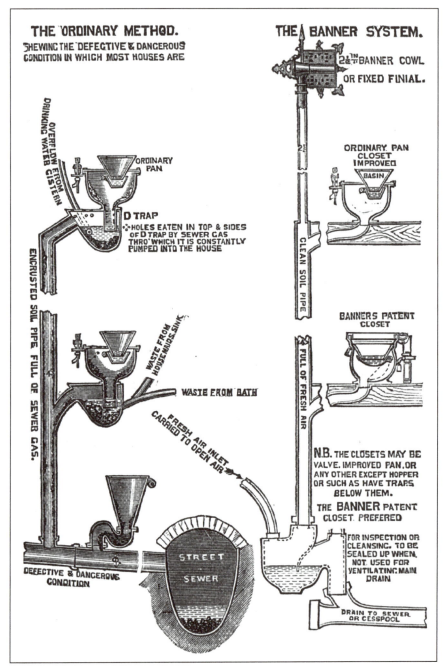

Figure 2.16
Diagram of the Banner system of house drainage (Banner, *Wholesome Houses*, 37) Collection Canadian Centre for Architecture, Montreal

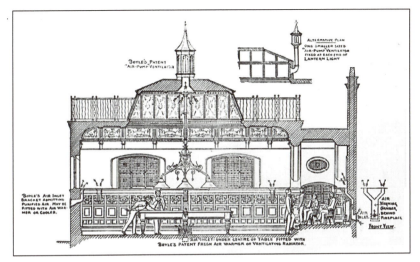

Figure 2.17
Diagram of the Boyle system of ventilation as used in a billiard room (Boyle, *The Boyle System of Ventilation*, 59) Collection Canadian Centre for Architecture, Montreal

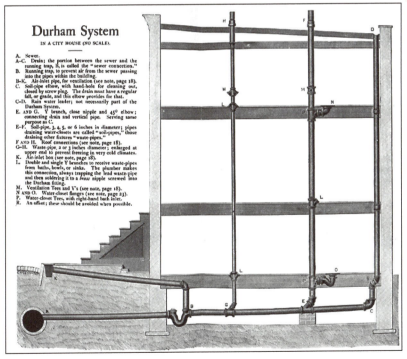

Figure 2.18
City house drainage system (*The Durham Patent System of Screw-joint Iron House Drainage*, 16–17) Collection Canadian Centre for Architecture, Montreal

the health reform of middle-class houses. If only the houses of the middle class were designed by architects, they stated over and over again, their profession would not be in its present hopeless situation. Architect T. Hayter Lewis concluded the meetings by acknowledging the work of "eminent men in other professions." He said, "we gladly accept their most valuable help, and we feel bound to keep well abreast with them in their scientific work, and to bring the results of their labours into a tangible form."[117] On this note, the meeting adjourned.

3 Female Regulation of the Healthy Home

"Woman's sphere," observed Harriette M. Plunkett, "has had a great many definitions." To illustrate her idea of women's place in sanitary reform, the author of *Women, Plumbers, and Doctors; or Household Sanitation* included in her book a sectional drawing of a standard middle-class house, labelled "A properly plumbed house – Woman's Sphere."[1] Drawn in the manner of Teale and the other house-doctors, it showed the exterior connections of a building to the municipal sewer system, as well as its ventilation and water supply (fig. 3.1). Woman's sphere "begins where the service-pipe for water and the house-drain enter the street-mains," explained the American author, "and, as far as sanitary plumbing goes, it ends at the top of the highest ventilating-pipe above the roof."[2]

Plunkett was not alone in designating domestic sanitary responsibilities to women. Ada Ballin, the editor of *Baby* magazine and the author of numerous books for women, also considered the examples set by women in the home to be significant contributions to public health:

It is a glorious thing for us to think that health-science is mainly to be taught and practised by women; that women are now going about among the people as apostles of health, teaching them how to be well and happy, and that this movement is gaining impetus every day. Oh, yes, my readers may say that is doubtless all very good and noble, but we cannot all frequent the shrines as missionaries of the goddess Hygeia. Certainly not; not every woman is suited, or can have the opportunity to do so; but yet, by attention to herself, her children and her home,

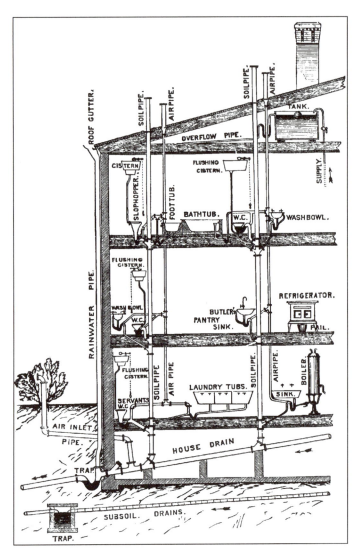

Figure 3.1
A properly plumbed house – Woman's Sphere (Plunkett, *Women, Plumbers and Doctors*, 112) Collection Canadian Centre for Architecture, Montreal

she can work in the good cause. Let her make her own home a temple of the goddess, and she will have done her duty.[3]

Sanitarians noted women's supposedly innate interest in health and also their familiarity with the construction and arrangement of the house. "The men of the house come and go; know little of the ins and outs of anything domestic; are guided by what they are told, and are practically of no assistance whatever," asserted the physician Benjamin Ward Richardson. "The women are conversant with every nook of the dwelling, from basement to roof, and on their knowledge, wisdom, and skill the physician rests his hopes."[4]

Plunkett and Richardson were also typical in their focus on the spatial limitations that defined women's place in late-nineteenth-century health reform; both sanitarians described women's sphere as being within the physical boundaries of the middle-class house. Throughout the literature of the period, the so-called separate sphere – or woman's sphere, as Plunkett called it – was synonymous with the female-led middle-class home.[5] While men toiled in the city, a public world, middle-class women were thought to live in an essentially private, domestic realm bounded by the exterior walls of the house.[6]

Few historians have challenged this notion of a spatial separation of men and women in English or North American urban life.[7] According to most accounts, the period since the Industrial Revolution has been marked by sharper distinctions between the experiences of men and women, reinforced by the breakdown of the extended family as a unit of production.[8] Since the mid-eighteenth century, the story goes, home and work have increasingly been differentiated by geographical location, architectural style, and gender associations. "As the workplace became separated from the home," observed Jane Lewis in a major social history of nineteenth-century English women, "so a private, domestic sphere was created for women, divorced from the public world of work, office and citizenship."[9]

As a result, the history of the nineteenth-century home, like the building that is its focus, has been gendered female. Concentrating on the differences between the middle-class house and the city, rather than on their similarities, historians have painted a picture of home that "assumed a universality of experience and meaning."[10] A "cult of domesticity" in the late nineteenth century supposedly made the house antithetical in every way to the city. The city was aggressive while the house was passive; the city was unpredictable while the house was stable; the city was corrupt while the house was virtuous. In terms of architectural style, public architecture relied on universally accepted principles for its meaning. The house was personalized, emotional, exclusive, and sheltered from the public gaze, like the Victorian woman.

"Control" of the separate sphere (the house), in terms of its health, was largely the responsibility of middle-class women. The medical discourse that emerged from the Domestic Sanitation Movement in the 1870s radically changed women's relationship to the home and to the city. The conceptual blurring of the body, the house, and the city exposed women's control of domestic space and their participation in the urban realm. This chapter explores the female regulation of domestic architecture during the period 1870–1900. It also examines the significance of a new field of endeavour for women, domestic science, which focused on the house as a subject of study, debate, and reform. As a feminized component of the medical profession, domestic science provided a significant public arena for feminist critiques of the middle-class house, while at the same time expressing time liberated from the constraints of reproduction and child care. The emergence of this new field at this particular time also illustrates how public debates over the virtues of art and science were simultaneously played out in both the woman and the house. Neither the woman nor the house, then, was as separate as most histories of the period would have us believe.

This idea of the middle-class house as a separate domestic sphere was not invented in the twentieth century. Like Plunkett, many Victorian women described the separateness of their lives from the public world of their fathers and husbands, adopting the metaphor of the sphere to emphasize their isolation. Jane Ellen Panton, the author of more than thirty popular advice books for women in the late nineteenth century, was typical in her description of Victorian women's lot in spatial terms: "A woman's sphere is domestic, more or less, she cannot alter it by stepping out of it."[11] Advisers earlier in the century had even noted the exclusion of men from the world of home. It was the right of every wife, said author Sarah Ellis, to have "a little sphere of domestic arrangements, with which the husband shall not feel that he has any business to interfere, except at her request, and into which a reasonable man would not wish to obtrude his authority, simply because the operations necessary to be carried on in that department of his household are alike foreign to his understanding and his tastes."[12]

There is no doubt that Victorian women's choices in life were extremely limited, as many excellent studies have shown.[13] Women had no access to property or wages, for example, during most of the nineteenth century. Nor did Victorian women exercise any real political power; they could not even vote in England until 1928.[14] Victorian women were not lawyers, and few were doctors. None were architects.[15] Some were teachers and nurses. Most were mothers and homemakers. In the realm of opportunities, the spheres of women and men were unquestionably distinct.

In most other respects, however, the social worlds of nineteenth-century middle-class women and men overlapped considerably. For example, although women undoubtedly spent more time than men in the home, they exercised enormous power in the so-called public sphere of economics. If a family rented out a room to a lodger, for instance, it was the woman who handled this arrangements, generating a sizable percentage of the family income within supposedly "separate" space. Middle-class women in the nineteenth century typically controlled the employment of servants; they hired, trained, paid, and fired the men and women who looked on their houses as workplaces as well as residences.[16] They also managed the elaborate round of social events that helped secure their husbands' place in the public world of finance and manufacturing.[17] In addition, most women managed the purchase of food and clothing for their families; they balanced the family books, exercising, in many cases, considerable economic expertise. The rise of the department store in the business districts of cities is testament to women's economic power in the consumption of ready-made goods.[18] The sphere of women encompassed, in a very real way, the public spaces, rural landscapes, commercial enterprises, and private rooms of nineteenth-century England. Gender distinctions depended on women's behaviour in public places.[19] If anything, the range of spaces accessible to Victorian women was far wider than that open to Victorian men.

Nor was the world of home shielded from the influence of men. The daily lives of middle-class husbands and fathers had an enormous impact on domestic life.[20] Although architectural historians have focused in their consideration of gender on rooms associated with women's experiences – the parlour, the kitchen, the nursery – as many rooms in the house were relegated to men's special use. The dining room, for example, was often occupied exclusively by men when women left the table after eating.[21] Victorian dining-room furniture was often dark and massive in appearance, supposedly satisfying masculine tastes (fig. 3.2). Decorators Rhoda and Agnes Garrett maintained that the gloomy atmosphere of most dining rooms in London was to "remind one of the British boast that every Englishman's house is his castle, and that he wishes neither to observe nor to be observed when he retires into the dignified seclusion of this, the especially masculine department of the household."[22] In larger houses, the library, study, smoking room, and billiards room were designed especially for the man of the house. The separation of these spaces from the family rooms was necessary for the proper transaction of business (and smoking), but their difference was

Figure 3.2
Man smoking in a dining room (Loftie, *The Dining-Room*, 6) Courtesy of McGill
University Libraries, Montreal

also marked in material terms by the presence of books, maps, scientific
equipment, and weapons.[23]

Indeed, the spatial separation of men and women was one of the most
prominent features of the typical Victorian house, and the degree of separation was a significant indication of class.[24] While the dining room,
study, and smoking room were associated with the husband, the drawing
room, boudoir, and morning room were the wife's realm. It was in these
rooms that the elaborate ritual of women's morning calls took place, as
well as other important occupations for middle-class women, such as
reading novels, writing letters, and doing handiwork.

Men's association with the dining room depended on the withdrawal
of women to the drawing room after dinner. In plan, the dining and
drawing rooms were often set off in direct opposition to express these
gendered associations. The "masculine departments" were commonly lo-

cated at the front of the house, the more "public" part of the plan, while women's rooms were in the back or were removed from the street level altogether, apparently protected by this distance from public space. The plan of a typical London house cited by Poore and published in the *Lancet* (fig. 3.3) shows this configuration of rooms. The dining room is adjacent to the main entrance of the house while the morning room is in the rear. The lady's drawing room and boudoir are on the first floor, above the unpredictable and presumably noisy activity of the street.

The prospect of rooms and their means of access in a typical Victorian house were also clearly gendered. Men's rooms, particularly the study or library, often included a separate entrance "to admit the tenants, tradesmen, and other persons on business, as directly as possible to the room in question, and no other part of the house," while women's rooms often looked out on flower gardens or even on a "lady's walk."[25] Men's rooms were thus open and accessible to the outside world, while women's spaces were most often intended to be closed and inaccessible. Most experts recommended the complete separation of men's and women's rooms. Robert Kerr, for instance, considered connection between the dining and drawing rooms "a clumsy contrivance."[26] The author of another popular advice book observed that the drawing room and dining room were the reverse of each other in every way.[27] The location of the rooms on different levels, of course, secured separation and guaranteed relatively predictable meetings between men and women in the house.

In terms of decoration, too, men's and women's rooms were directly opposed. "The relations of the Dining-room and Drawing-room," explained Kerr, "are in almost every way those of contrast."[28] He saw the ideal drawing room as being "entirely ladylike" in "cheerfulness, refinement of elegance, and what is called lightness as opposed to massiveness."[29] Hermann Muthesius, whose classic *English House* of 1904–05 is a perceptive analysis of the contemporary British house plan, said that the drawing room had a "light, pleasing impression and a general air of *joie-de-vivre*."[30] The Garretts described the decoration of the drawing room as "light and airy" compared with the "heavy and sombre" dining room, for in the former "the ladies of the family are told that it is now their turn to have their tastes consulted."[31] According to the Garretts, the drawing room was devoted "to the lighter occupations of life."[32]

The entire Victorian house – its location, arrangement, style, and size – also served to situate men (and women) in a culture ordered according to class.[33] Like clothing, language, behaviour, and even smell, the house expressed to the public world the aspirations and economic mobility of

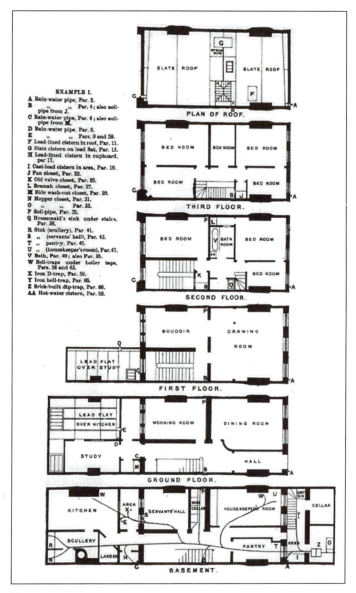

EXAMPLE I.
A Rain-water pipe, Par. 2.
B   "   " Par. 4; also soil-pipe from J.
C Rain-water pipe, Par. 6; also soil-pipe from M.
D Rain-water pipe, Par. 8.
E   "   " Pars. 9 and 59.
F Lead-lined cistern in roof, Par. 11.
G Slate cistern on lead flat, Par. 13.
H Lead-lined cistern in cupboard, par 17.
I Cast-lead cistern in area, Par. 19.
J Pan closet, Par. 22.
K Old valve closet, Par. 25.
L Bramah closet, Par. 27.
M Side wash-out closet, Par. 29.
N Hopper closet, Par. 31.
O   "   " Par. 33.
P Soil-pipe, Par. 35.
Q Housemaid's sink under stairs, Par. 38.
R Sink (scullery), Par. 41.
S   " (servants' hall), Par. 43.
T   " pantry, Par. 45.
U   " (housekeeper's room), Par. 47.
V Bath, Par. 49; also Par. 35.
W Bell-traps under boiler taps, Pars. 56 and 63.
X Iron D-trap, Par. 59.
Y Iron bell-trap, Par. 65.
Z Brick-built dip-trap, Par. 66.
AA Hot-water cistern, Par. 52.

Figure 3.3
Plan of a typical middle-class house (*Lancet*, 4 July 1896, supplement) Wellcome Institute Library, London

all its inhabitants. The healthy house, "from basement to roof," as Mrs Plunkett described it, was an equally important expression of women's participation in the public urban realm.

The association of middle-class women with health in general was not new in the Victorian period. As many historians have noted, before the rise of the modern profession of medicine, women of all classes had played significant roles as domestic healers in their homes. In the seventeenth century, Lady Anne Clifford described her mother as "a lover of the study of medicine and the practise of Alchemy." It was said that "she prepared excellent medicines that did good to many."[34] Cooking, brewing, and distilling – traditionally women's work – were closely associated with healing.[35] Sickness and dying were much more private conditions than today, and both were overseen by women within the home.

The expectations of the nineteenth-century sanitarians stemmed from this long-standing belief that domestic health was an innately female concern; women were considered "natural" healers and nurturers because they bore children. Victorian scientific theories of sexual difference also saw women as passive, intuitive, and tender – qualities that were considered appropriate to caring for the sick.[36] "Sick-nursing" was seen as a natural extension of domestic labour. As Lewis has noted, it was not until 1891 that the census in England differentiated hospital nurses from household servants.[37] The emergence of modern nursing in the nineteenth century as a profession particularly suited to women is testament to all these beliefs.

By then, too, it had often been stated that women were particularly adept at preventive rather than therapeutic or curative medicine. Their experience in raising a family supposedly endowed them with special abilities in maintaining good health in the household and preventing the spread of disease once it entered a home. Pioneering female physicians later in the century used the seemingly urgent need for preventive medicine to strengthen their campaign for more women doctors. "We should give to man cheerfully the curative department, and women the preventative," proclaimed Dr Harriot Hunt in 1852.[38] This perception that women's place in the profession of medicine was complementary to men's eased the way for women to enter the predominantly male field.

As in the profession of medicine, so it was in domestic sanitation. Women's role in the reform of domestic architecture focused on preventing the spread of infection within the house – by inspecting and maintaining the sanitary aspects of the house, by caring for the sick according to modern "scientific" principles, and by keeping the house clean, especially free of dust. As we saw in chapter 2, the responsibility for repairing or healing the already "sick" building – like the restoration of sick bodies – was the charge of male physicians.

Women's isolation in the home was used to advance their role in domestic sanitation, as Dr Richardson so clearly stated: "I press this office for the prevention of disease on womankind, not simply because they can carry it out ... but because it is an office which man never can carry out; and because the whole work of prevention waits and waits until the woman takes it up and makes it hers. The man is abroad, the disease threatens the home, and the woman is at the threatened spot. Who is to stop it at the door, the man or the woman?"[39] This parallels women's "progress" in other fields, where their supposed experience as mothers was used to strengthen their position outside the home as practitioners of "social" or "civic maternalism."[40]

But the reformers' enthusiasm and support for female collaboration worked in other ways as well. Teaching women the "laws" of sanitary science and expecting them to realize these laws in the home meant that any subsequent sickness or death was considered to be the result of women's failure to follow the rules.[41] "The gospel of sanitation must find its chief preachers and exponents in the women who make the house into the home, or by neglect turn it into a trap for the four deleterious D's, Darkness, Damp, Dirt, and Disease. Slovenly women ... are factors of disease, and cleanly housewives acting forces against the possibility, or for the suppression, of sickness," reported a reviewer of Dr Richardson's *Household Health*.[42] The next chapter focuses on one particular way in which Victorian women were "factors of disease." Here we will concentrate on their role in the prevention of sickness.

The domestic sanitarians expected middle-class women to be amateur inspectors of their houses, maintaining minimal standards of healthy architecture by detecting architectural defects. Typical house inspection covered a wide range of tasks, including checking the connection of the house to the municipal sewer system, the orientation of the building, and the materials used in the walls, as well as inspecting for water purity and measuring dampness and air movement in the interior of the house.[43] A proliferation of books and articles appeared in the 1880s and 1890s instructing women on how to inspect the work of the "ignorant or indolent plumber," builder, or architect.[44] The authors included tips on drainage, ventilation, lighting, furnishing, and the arrangement of rooms, covering the architecture of the house thoroughly for their female readership. Attention to these sanitary matters, claimed one sanitarian, could decrease the death rate by half.[45]

The inspection of the house was usually conducted in a series of tests, which were spelled out in detail and illustrated in the women's advice literature. The "peppermint test," to check the drainage system, consisted of running peppermint oil into a drain from the exterior of the building.

If a minty smell was detected inside, the house was considered insanitary. The oil could also be mixed with a can of boiling water, as recommended by William Maguire in his popular plumbing manual, then poured down the soil pipe from the roof. Maguire pointed out that this test was "troublesome" and required "delicate handling." The person pouring the peppermint oil into the pipes had to remain on the roof for a considerable time, otherwise one might bring the peppermint smell into the house and ruin the test.[46] Special machines, resembling modern vacuum cleaners, were commercially available to assist householders in the diagnosis of their houses (fig. 3.4).

Air quality in the house was also regulated by women. A simple test of holding a candle to the keyhole of an interior door would illustrate how the fire in a room could draw "drain-derived air" from other sources (fig. 3.5).[47] A candle test could also identify joints of soil pipes that had been soldered with "inferior material" (figs. 3.6 and 3.7).[48] Lead pipes often developed holes over time, explained Dr T. Pridgin Teale. His diagrams offered few clues of how householders could gain access to the drainage systems hidden within their floors and walls, but he nevertheless insisted that the candle test could give sure evidence that "sewer gas" was leaking from faulty pipes.

Other aspects of house inspection were far more sophisticated. Reinsch's test, for example, to detect arsenic in wallpapers was a complicated procedure involving hydrochloric acid and copper foil.[49] The experts suggested that women conduct the test only if a chemist or public analyst could not be employed to do so. In this procedure, pieces of the questionable wallpaper were placed in a test-tube of hydrochloric acid and water. If a piece of copper foil dipped in the boiling liquid turned black, the wallpaper was arsenical (fig. 3.8). Other tests described in the press required less equipment or scientific knowledge.[50]

The titles of articles in popular ladies' magazines in the final decades of the nineteenth century suggest that women may have participated in decisions regarding the health of houses long before problems were evident. The authors of "Where Shall My House Be?," "The Site of the House," "Walls," and "Drainage" provided middle-class women with comprehensive information on building design, including issues of health in the home.[51] The design of domestic architecture was thus a form of preventive medicine regulated entirely by women. "She may have something to do with the building of the house at some time," observed an expert in 1899.[52]

Again, this gendering of responsibility worked in two ways. If a wife and mother was solely responsible for major design decisions that were

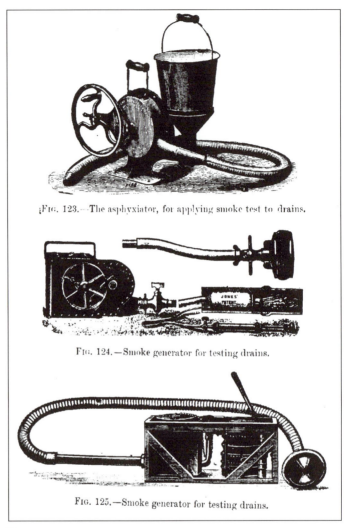

Fɪɢ. 123.—The asphyxiator, for applying smoke test to drains.

Fɪɢ. 124.—Smoke generator for testing drains.

Fɪɢ. 125.—Smoke generator for testing drains.

Figure 3.4
Machines for testing drains (Maguire, *Domestic Sanitary Drainage and Plumbing*, 194) Collection Canadian Centre for Architecture, Montreal

thought to affect the health of the family, it followed that any defects or illness that subsequently emerged were essentially her fault. In addition, it meant that a woman's poor health was regarded as a result of her own actions. By insisting that middle-class women's health had declined rather than improved as the reform of domestic architecture presumably progressed, doctors implied that women's faulty choice or

"A" window shut. Flame at the keyhole horizontal.

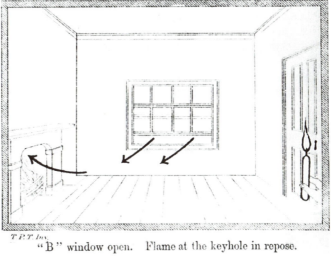

"B" window open. Flame at the keyhole in repose.

Figure 3.5
Teale's candle test (Teale, *Dangers to Health*, plate 3) Collection Canadian Centre
for Architecture, Montreal

regulation of sanitary systems were more to blame than their own inability to cure.[53]

"House-choosing," as Panton called it, was a standard chapter in late-
nineteenth-century domestic manuals for women. Selecting a family
residence was one of the many tasks that a young couple performed together

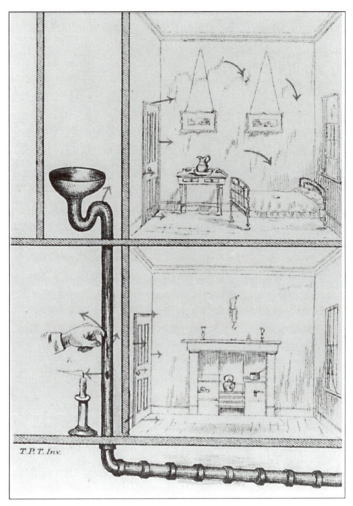

Figure 3.6
Test for faulty material (Teale, *Dangers to Health*, plate 19) Collection Canadian
Centre for Architecture, Montreal

before (or just after) marriage. According to most authors, women were
expected to make most of the decisions regarding the family's place of
residence, sometimes but not always with the advice of their husbands.[54]
They were always solely responsible for any aspect of the house affecting
the family's health. For example, although both husband and wife probably participated in the general inspection of a house before its lease or
purchase, the more detailed investigation of plumbing and drainage were

Figure 3.7
Test for putty joints (Teale, *Dangers to Health*, plate 18) Collection Canadian
Centre for Architecture

the responsibility of the wife. The previous generation of women, reported Plunkett in 1885, had left inspection of the "semi-telluric" region
of the house to their husbands, whereas modern women "rise above the
beaten paths of cookery and needlework to some purpose." "A new
sphere of usefulness and efficiency opens with the knowledge that in sanitary matters an ounce of prevention is worth a ton of cure," she asserted.
"There is nothing in hygiene that [a woman] can not comprehend."[55]

As well as becoming amateur inspectors of their houses, Victorian
women learned about science and medicine by nursing sick family members, just as their mothers and grandmothers had done. Indeed, the primary location for middle-class medical care at this time was the home. It
was even the site for major surgery. Hospitals, especially those in large

Figure 3.8
Test for arsenic (Murphy, *Our Homes*, 372) Collection Canadian Centre for Architecture, Montreal

urban centres, were seen as the causes of death rather than as places to heal, since their mortality rates were extremely high. It was not until the turn of the century that the hospital was considered preferable to the home as a site for middle-class medical treatment, for by then it was understood to be cleaner and more appropriate than the home. As a result of Joseph Lister's explanation in 1867 of the role of living organisms in the putrefaction of wounds, cleanliness and antisepsis were practised so that hospitals gradually became curative places.[56] Around the turn of the century, many operating theatres were redone with new easy-to-clean materials and were rearranged to include specialized sterilizing and recovery rooms, which obviously were not available in typical middle-class houses.[57]

Women's role in the home involved much more than the simple isolation of the patient in a bedroom. As sick-nurse, a woman's responsibility included monitoring the room temperature and humidity, overseeing the patient's meals, and ensuring the patient's isolation from other family members. The difference between the Victorian woman's care for the sick and her great-grandmother's was that the late-nineteenth-century sickroom was ordered with "hints" from a medical expert according to modern "scientific" principles.[58]

"However skilfully designed the arrangements of a house may appear to be," commented Mary Ann Barker, author of *The Bedroom and Boudoir*, "it is impossible to know whether a great law of common sense and practical usefulness has guided such arrangements, until there has been an illness in the house." Family sickness entailed considerable rearrangement of the spatial relationships between family members, as well as the ways spaces were perceived. "Many smart and pretty-looking bedrooms are discovered by their sick owner to be very different abodes to what they seemed to him in health," noted Lady Barker.[59]

Women's major responsibility in caring for the sick at home was ensuring the isolation of the family member in the sickroom. The sickroom was an ordinary bedroom that was often set aside and especially furnished in anticipation of illness in the house. Catherine Gladstone described the benefits of such planning in the book she authored for the International Health Exhibition:

As we must prepare, in every dwelling-house, for the contingency of illness, how desirable it would be for *all* houses, even of moderate size, to have some one corner suitable for a sick-room! If space admits of such a room being entirely isolated from the rest of the house, so much the better; but much may be done by at all events securing two rooms opening into each other, with windows, doors, and fireplaces where they should be, with hot and cold water supply within easy reach, and a closet properly placed.[60]

Many authors not only recommended the careful planning of special rooms for the sick but also advised that they be constructed differently from ordinary bedrooms, with "double sashes and double wall," for example, "to exclude the sound of the elements without."[61]

Mrs Gladstone did not explain why she recommended having two sickrooms, though she probably subscribed to the widespread belief that a "change of rooms" improved a patient's health. Children were often moved to a spare bedroom when they were ill, not only to prevent the infection spreading to other children but because it was feared the illness might infect the room itself. Maud Sambourne, daughter of the cartoonist Linley Sambourne, was temporarily accommodated in the spare room of the family home in Kensington. Her mother Marion Sambourne's diaries record the concern she experienced when 12-year-old Maud fell ill in 1887 and the frequency with which doctors visited the family's sickroom. On 10 February 1887, Marion wrote, "Maudie no better, v. feverish & in pain, Dr O came four times."[62]

The "construction" of a special room or suite of rooms for a family member within the home often involved considerable rearrangement of room uses, as previously mentioned. Mrs Panton suggested choosing a room at the top of the house. In the case of a house that was being built to a family's specifications, she advised that the sickroom be separate from the main building – an annex that could be reached by an interior passage and an exterior door. The door between the passage and the sickroom should be of plate glass so that a mother could observe her sick child without risk of infection. As additional protection, Panton suggested that a sheet soaked in carbolic acid should be hung on the door. The doctor would enter the sickroom from the exterior door. The decorations and furnishing should be extremely cheap, Panton advised, because they would be destroyed after every illness.[63]

Most sickrooms were less elaborate than Panton's version. Certainly, most families did not construct special annexes to their houses. They simply "emptied" ordinary rooms of furnishings, clothing, and any other contents as a way of securing separation of the sick from the healthy members of the family. The back of the house was better than the front, and upper levels were preferable to lower floors, experts said, because of the need for perfect quiet. Too much furniture was believed to "confuse" sick people. "As a rule, in a severe illness" warned Lady Barker, "sick people detest anything like a confusion or profusion of ornaments or furniture." Like others, she associated successful nursing with the removal of "things" from the room:

I have known the greatest relief expressed by a patient, who seemed too ill to notice any such change, at the substitution of one single, simple classical vase for a whole shelf-full of tawdry French china ornaments, and I date the recovery of another from the moment of the removal out of his sight of an exceedingly smart modern dressing-table, with many bows of ribbon and flounces of lace and muslin. I do not mean to say that the furniture of a sick-room need be ugly – only that it should be simple and not too much of it.[64]

The American author and social reformer Charlotte Perkins Gilman described the sense of confinement, even imprisonment, she had felt in a "big, airy room" because of its "smouldering unclean yellow" wallpaper.[65] Her well-known story, "The Yellow Wallpaper" (1892), recounted her quick mental disintegration while spending time in a former nursery at the top of a rented summer house. The tale has become a classic in women's history and is also significant for the clear links drawn by the author between architecture and women's power, a subject that intrigued Gilman throughout her prolific career.[66] Seldom mentioned, however, is that in "The Yellow Wallpaper" she blamed her husband John, a physician, for her inability to get better.

An emptier room was also easier to clean, protecting the next occupant from infection. Catherine J. Wood suggested that women should remove all carpets and curtains, retaining only a table and washstand in the sickroom.[67] While every family could not afford to destroy and replace the room's contents, care was certainly taken to clean the sickroom and its contents thoroughly after an illness. Like the regular cleaning of the house, this was entirely the woman's responsibility.

The above advice of Wood and others is evidence of the widespread debate at the time over the role played by household objects in the spread of infection. It also shows that medical experts as late as the turn of the century continued to create an "atmosphere of constant crisis" in the middle-class home. Articles with titles such as "Books Spread Contagion," "Contagion by Telephone," and "Infection and Postage Stamps," as well as many experts' insistence that diseases were continuing to spread because of women's negligence, must have boosted both the standards of cleanliness (and sales of sickroom furniture) and maternal guilt.[68]

The sanitarians also promoted cleanliness in the home by specifying the use of new materials inside the house. This advice, of course, assumed that there would be considerable renovation to house interiors. The sanitarians' "prohibition against dust," for example, discouraged the use of upholstered furniture and the elaborate decoration that was popular at mid-century. W.H. Corfield recommended the use of tiles throughout the house; Douglas Galton, an authority on hospital design, suggested that interior walls be made of metal or cement to avoid the accumulation of dust. Most experts' advice was less drastic, suggesting simply that one avoid heavy curtains and difficult-to-clean furniture.[69]

Commercial manufacturers took advantage of woman's role as sick-nurse in the home by promoting health-inducing products that were supposedly less disruptive to the household. The "Arema" vaporiser, for example, would prevent the spread of all infectious diseases while a woman slept, read, or worked (fig. 3.9). Not surprisingly, the International Health Exhibition of 1884 brought together hundreds of manufacturers selling devices specially for invalids and sickrooms. Many of these were marketed to women. Messrs Doulton and Company, the major manufacturer of domestic tiles at the time, set up a special pavilion at the IHE.[70]

In terms of material culture, however, health reform had its greatest impact on the design of beds. The most drastic change was the popularity of metal beds, which had formerly been used only in institutions. It was believed that metal, like tiles, harboured less dust and absorbed no

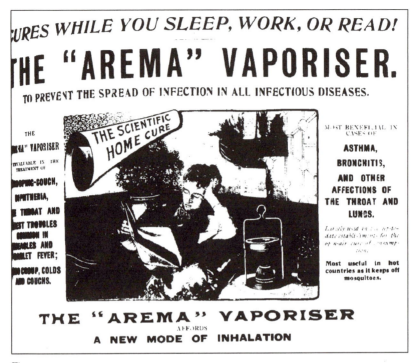

Figure 3.9
Advertisement for the "Arema" vaporiser (*Baby*, June 1905, xi) Courtesy of the British Library,
London

humidity; it was thus intrinsically cleaner than wood. The leading manufacturer and distributor of beds in London, Heal and Son, exhibited an
ideal small bedroom at the IHE (fig. 3.10). Although the other three
pieces of furniture in the room were wooden, the bed was metal.

Physicians also advised different "environmental" conditions for the
treatment of various illnesses in the home. After about 1870, the authors
of articles advising women how to nurse sick family members nearly always focused on the arrangement of the sickroom rather than on the
therapeutic treatment of illnesses.[71] Through the arrangement of the "architecture," women were expected to prevent the spread of infection in
the house. A fever, for example, required that the sickroom have either a
small fire or none at all, thorough ventilation, and minimal furniture. A
completely different "architecture" was recommended for the treatment
of measles: closed windows and an open door.[72] Victorian women thus
practised domesticity, as historian Regina Markell Morantz has noted,
"not as a cult, but as a science."[73]

Figure 3.10
Heal's model bedroom at the IHE (*Illustrated London News*, 2 Aug. 1884, 108) Collection Canadian Centre for Architecture, Montreal

Women learned about science in the public and commercial districts of cities. The Ladies' Sanitary Association (LSA) – which was originally called the Ladies' Association for the Diffusion of Sanitary Knowledge – was formed in 1857 by a group of women who believed that most of the "debility, disease, and premature mortality in this country arose from the ignorance of the masses respecting the commonest laws of health."[74] The LSA offered courses in sanitation, sponsored lectures on various aspects of hygiene, and distributed thousands of tracts aimed at instructing women on sanitary matters.[75]

Like the "healthy house" literature written for women, the LSA material emphasized that it was women who were responsible for health in the home, particularly with regard to the importance of the building in preventing disease:

The architect may allow for windows, but who is to open them at proper seasons? Or as regards medicine; the physician may prescribe and the apothecary may send in the dose, but who is to administer it at the stated hour and with the proper limitation of quantity? It is the house-mother who must do all these things, and we must teach her why and how to do them. We do not need only to persuade her to do this or that, we need to inspire her with a living horror of ill health, and to make her see that the bodily welfare of her husband and children chiefly depends on herself.[76]

The women attending the first annual meeting of the LSA were told by the Reverend Charles Kingsley that each of them was in a position to save three or four lives in the following six months. "It is in your power, ladies, and it is *so* easy," he said.[77]

The LSA was an active force in British health reform until its disbanding in 1900. The diffusion of sanitary knowledge to English women of all classes was its principal mandate, and it attempted to establish branches in towns throughout the country rather than concentrating its efforts in London. Not surprisingly, the initial supporters of the LSA were from the upper and middle classes. During the early years of the association, its principal organ was the *English Woman's Journal,* a magazine that published articles on many aspects of women's reform.[78] The LSA and the journal shared office space on Princes Street, Cavendish Square. The early membership counted among its executive several well-known male sanitarians such as physician Thomas Southwood Smith, as well as social reformers such as Charles Kingsley. The women present at the first annual meeting included a countess and a marchioness as well as several "ladies." By 1882, the LSA was patronized by the Princess of Wales, the Crown Princess of Germany, the Princess Christian, and Princess Mary of Teck.[79]

The association's major architectural consultant was Henry Roberts, best known as an author and as a reformer of working-class housing. As the honorary architect to the Society for Improving the Condition of the Labouring Classes, he had been an obvious choice as the designer of model dwellings for Prince Albert in the Great Exhibition of 1851.[80] Roberts's lecture to the LSA on the connection between housing design and health was the third of five lectures in a course for women given at the Kensington Museum in 1860.[81] Roberts was extremely precise in his description of women's role in sanitary reform. He divided the improvement of dwellings into three classes. The first class was government measures; the second included public bodies, voluntary associations, and employers; the third was personal influence, for which he believed women were primarily responsible. Like other sanitarians, he noted women's involvement with the building itself:

Ladies can exercise a personal influence by either teaching or causing to be taught, the benefits resulting from a free admission of pure air and from personal and household cleanliness. They can facilitate the attaining of such articles as whitewash brushes and ventilators, as well as the mending of broken windows. They may also enforce, more especially on wives and mothers, a careful attention to the many details which conduce so much to health and domestic comfort, and render home attractive rather than repulsive to husbands and sons.[82]

Besides the national scope of the LSA network, special conferences were organized to instruct women on health in the home. The first of these was held in Portsmouth in 1892. "The preservation of health is, after all, mainly a woman's question," reported a journalist covering the conference. "What the municipality may do in the way of providing drainage is no doubt important: but the custody of the health of the inmates is largely in the hands of the mistress of the house. We cannot expect, therefore, to see that degree of improvement in the public health that might be attained, until our mothers and sisters, our wives and daughters, have made much greater progress in a knowledge of the most elementary sanitary laws."[83]

The sanitarians acknowledged that previous sanitary knowledge had been passed down through generations of women, "from mouth to mouth," as they said. But now, they claimed, women's sanitary knowledge should be systematized and regularized, in keeping with the "scientific" times: "Our grandmothers were not complete ignoramuses, but their knowledge belonged to the pre-scientific period. They learned what they knew from the current proverbial philosophy of the home, which was without system, and often without rule. What we require now is a more carefully-ordered knowledge about common things, and their bearing upon bodily health."[84]

As if to compensate for the restrictions placed on women's role in health reform, doctors and building professionals described domestic sanitation as an expression of female power. "There is great talk in some quarters about 'Woman's Rights'; this is one of them, to see that the house is kept clean and wholesome," wrote S. Stevens Hellyer in his popular handbook on plumbing.[85] Richardson admitted that domestic sanitation might not fulfil some women's visions of equality but quickly pointed out that this new mission for women was nevertheless "greatly advanced and more nobly utilised than it is at this time." He added: "Nay, perchance, when she has heard me to the end and has well considered the tremendous power which the completed scheme would give to her sex, she might feel that her ambition would be more than satisfied by its accomplishment."[86]

Beginning in the 1870s, women's sanitary responsibilities in the home were professionalized under the name of domestic science or domestic economy. Like medicine and architecture, the new "field" was configured to follow precise and predictable rules, was subject to examination (not registration), and became the subject of formal programs of education. "Wifeliness, which for centuries has been attributed to natural charm, is demonstrably a science," proclaimed the pioneers of the new field.[87] As Barbara Ehrenreich and Deirdre English have noted, "scientific house-keeping" depended heavily on real connections to the male world of science.[88]

"[The home maker] must know a good deal about physics," stated an expert in 1899, "because that is basal to all the plumbing in her home, basal to the whole subject of ventilation, to the whole material side of the home."[89] Like Catharine Beecher in the United States, proponents of the new field argued that proper housework was based on scientific prin-ciples. "It is a Profession," claimed Phyllis Browne, the author of several housekeeping manuals, "and to qualify for it a girl needs systematic train-ing and methodical practice."[90] Beecher's ideas were promulgated in En-gland in the 1890s by her sister-in-law Eunice Beecher. "There is nothing that can lighten labour," she said, "like method and regularity in per-forming it."[91]

The first annual congress on domestic economy was held in Birming-ham in 1877 to discuss the teaching of domestic science as a part of the general education of girls.[92] Several sanitarians, including Edwin Chad-wick, read papers to the newly assembled organization. A journalist re-porting on the conference noted what he considered a peculiar omission:

We are not aware if domestic architecture has yet been taken up as a profession by women – but we feel convinced that when this is the case it will prove not only lucrative to themselves, but most valuable to the community. The dreary monotony of our street architecture would be done away with, and our poor and middle-class houses would be built with all the appliances for domestic health and comfort which now are either done without or are subsequently added at great expense and trouble by the inmates themselves. We wish that someone had taken up this subject at the Congress.[93]

This remark was typical of the period. As women gained more and more recognition and confidence in design through their management of the home by "scientific" principles, they, like the physicians, were seen by an anxious public as alternative "designers" of domestic environments.

Women's organizations flourished. The National Housewifery Association was founded in 1881 or 1882. Like the Ladies' Sanitary Association, it began with solid upper-class backing and with the stated intention of improving the living conditions of the working class. Female education in domestic subjects was its major agenda: housework, cooking, child care, among other topics. The original founder, Miss Headdon, observed the "different phases of unhappiness springing from one source, – the thriftless ignorance of women."[94]

Domestic science was given the blessing of the medical profession on the grounds that a more scientific home would be a healthier home.[95] These changes in the status of domestic management occurred at a time of major improvements in the general education of English girls and women. In 1870 the Education Act had established the right of all English children to a formal education; by 1880, all children between the ages of five and ten years of age were required to go to school. Similar changes occurred in higher education. By 1870, the first women's college at Cambridge, Girton College, had opened its doors to students, though it was unrecognized by the university. Women were admitted to the University of London in 1878. Although debates raged about whether girls' education should differ from that offered to boys, the establishment of respected programs for girls, particularly at the university level, convinced people that women could contribute to society outside the home.

The invention of the new field of domestic science was part of a broader program to employ women in the late nineteenth century. A "surplus" of females – resulting from an imbalance in the number of men moving to the colonies, among other reasons – had reached seemingly insoluble proportions by 1891, when the census reported nearly 900,000 more women than men in England and Wales.[96] Ten years earlier there had been recorded 121 spinsters to every bachelor in London.[97] Many of these unmarried women, called "redundant" at the time, were forced to earn their own living. The new educational opportunities, including programs in domestic science, provided "professional" opportunities for the redundant spinsters. Domestic science was not threatening: women studying it did not put men out of work. Moreover, its subject matter seemed restricted to women's traditional work within the home: cooking, cleaning, and caring for the sick. Even the new field of hygiene, as we have seen, was considered a woman's version of science.

A major aspect of the discipline was the systematization of household cleanliness. This meant that women should follow a "routine" in keeping their houses clean. "Method and system," observed the house-cleaning expert Phyllis Browne, "are to household work what oil is to machinery – they make things go smoothly and easily." "System," she explained, "consists in having a clear understanding of what has to be done, when and how it is to be done, and arranging who is to do it."[98] Methods of house cleaning were equally important. Following the general scientific model, this meant the establishment of principles that were to be observed in the cleaning of a house. "There is a right way and a wrong way even of dusting a room or furniture," Browne asserted, and then explained at length to her female readership how to dust "correctly."[99] Again, the threat of sickness and death was upheld as the consequence of "incorrect" dusting: "Where dirt reigns, disease, misery and crime stand erect around his throne; liberty, progress, and enlightenment hide their heads in shame. All the great plagues which have destroyed human happiness, broken women's hearts and made children orphans, have held their carnival in the midst of dirt."[100]

Pointing to dirty houses (and, by implication, careless women) as the cause of illness was obviously not in itself a liberating factor for Victorian women. Through this kind of liability, however, women became "experts" on the design of houses. Women trained in the "principles" of hygiene spoke out publicly on the merits of various materials and designs, constructing a critical forum with which to consider the work of architects. In addition, women's accomplishments at home led directly to work in the supposedly public world of men. Having proven their gender-based competence in detecting faulty drains and poor ventilation in their own homes, women were among the first to be appointed sanitary inspectors of buildings as "health visitors" to the poor.[101] Frances Baker, a sanitary inspector for the district of Marylebone in London, inspected workshops as well as houses. In 1909 she registered and measured 153 workshops and re-inspected eighty-eight.[102] Most female building inspectors, however, focused on housing:

The women health visitors are appointed to visit from house to house under the directions of the medical officer of health, calling attention to the necessity for cleanliness of the house and its surroundings, giving advice as to the rearing of children and the nursing of the sick, distributing and explaining handbills on the prevention of infectious diseases, and doing all they can in other directions to help the people whom they visit to keep their homes in as healthy a condition as possible. They will urge on all possible occasions the importance of cleanliness, temperance, and thrift.[103]

Although many women volunteered their time as health visitors to the poor, some charged a fee for their services. Mrs Busset, of Busset and Company, for example, was a professional who specialized in domestic sanitation; her firm constructed furniture, woodwork and "other things that the average furnisher need not undertake."[104]

Women's familiarity with the architecture of home also facilitated their acceptance as professional "house agents." Miss Etta Nauen claimed that her success as a London estate agent in 1894 was due to advertising, though she suggested that the profession was well-suited to women:

As an occupation for women I think it excellent and women are eminently suitable as house agents; but if you ask me if I think it is likely to be a remunerative occupation to a large number of women taking it up now, I should hesitate to say "yes." I have been successful beyond my hopes, but then, you know, I am in the van; there is plenty of room in the van for others also, but they must have the necessary qualifications, which are, I think, tact, common-sense, and, certainly a business capacity. That is where I fear many women fail; they have wasted their life working in an amateurish kind of way.[105]

The "amateurish kind of way" to which Miss Nauen referred was a critical impediment to the acceptance of middle-class women as professionals in many fields outside the home. Critics objected to the idea of women receiving pay for their services; their objection was not that they considered women ineffectual.[106]

The overall tone of Victorian domestic advice literature implied that women could detect unsanitary work but could not undo or improve the mistakes supposedly made by builders or architects. Changes to the plans of the houses, at least in England, were beyond their immediate power, which many advisers suggested would be much improved if women were given the chance to design buildings. "Doubtless the great thing that strikes us when we are house-hunting is that if women architects could get employment houses would be far better planned than they are now," remarked Mrs Panton.[107]

The situation was very different in the United States. There women were encouraged to make extensive renovations to their homes, including substantial changes to the plans of their houses. In the name of domestic cleanliness, the American author Helen Dodd advised the wives of farmers to improve the arrangements of their houses to suit their own needs better. She told women to look critically at their houses and ask themselves whether the buildings really satisfied them rather than being

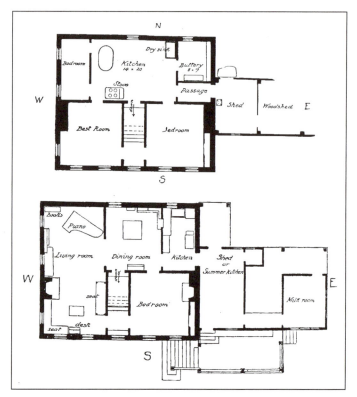

Figure 3.11
Renovations to a farmhouse to suit a farmer's wife (Dodd, *The Healthful Farm-house*, viii–ix) Courtesy of the Winterthur Library, Printed Book and Periodical Collection

designed to suit the rest of the family. Dodd set out some "principles of sanitation" for farmhouses which could be realized without employing skilled workmen; "any strong woman" could do the renovations, she said.[108] Dodd's instructions focused on changes to the interior arrangements of the houses without altering the exterior walls (fig. 3.11). For example, her renovated kitchen plan increased the direct light of both the kitchen and the dining room, as well as providing a more efficient work space in the kitchen.

E.C. Gardner's manual, *The House That Jill Built, after Jack's Had Proved a Failure*, also encouraged American women to modify their houses.[109] Using the narrative of a young married couple considering various arrangements of houses, Gardner conveyed to women standard architectural information on room composition, sanitary drainage, and decoration. Intended for three groups of people – those contemplating the purchase of a home, those wishing to improve their homes, and those who had suffered from living in homes based on errors in design – the book's title revealed the author's confidence in the design abilities of women.

No such books were written for English women, though women in Britain may have read the American literature. As noted above, their responsibilities appear to have been limited to the detection of faulty design and did not include the building's physical improvement. This was doubtless because the system of middle-class housing was far more standardized in England than in the United States; it was not necessarily a reflection of stronger feminist impulses among American women. The relationship of Victorian feminism and house design will be discussed further in chapter 5 of this study.

English novelists described women's familiarity with plumbing as a mark of newfound confidence. In *Pilgrimage*, for example, Dorothy Richardson described a woman's view of a Bloomsbury house in 1890:

The large dusty house, the many downstairs rooms, the mysterious dark-roomed vault of the basement, all upright in her upright form; hurried smeary cleansings, swift straightening of grey-sheeted beds, the strange unfailing water-system, gurgling cisterns, gushing taps and lavatory flushes, the wonder of gaslight and bedroom candles, the daily meals magically appearing and disappearing; her knowledge of the various mysteriously arriving and vanishing people, all beginning and ending in her triumphant, reassuring smile that went forward outside beyond these things, with everybody.[110]

As we saw at the beginning of this chapter, Mrs Plunkett's assignment of a "properly plumbed house" to "woman's sphere" in 1885 was undoubtedly accurate. Women actively participated in building construction and science through their regulation of healthy houses. Their own homes – particularly the drainage – were arenas through which they exhibited their mastery of these concepts, hence the name of the new field: "domestic science."

Equally important, however, was Plunkett's qualification of her statement that woman's sphere had many definitions. Although the new scientific and architectural expertise gained by women through sanitary science appear to be liberating, it set relatively rigid limits on their participation in health reform. Women were blamed for the persistence of disease among the middle class as well as for the unacceptable work of plumbers and architects. In addition to their role as regulators of healthy houses – as we will see in the next chapter – the close association of women and houses between 1870 and 1900 cast Victorian women into passive roles as the objects of scientific research. Like the service pipe, house drain, and ventilating pipe that defined woman's sphere, her body acted as both the protection against disease and the source of infection.

4 Childbirth at Home

The belief that the house and the body were inextricably linked, that ensuring the well-being of domestic spaces would ensure the health of the inhabitants of that space, and that this relationship between the house and the body should be regulated by women was never more evident than in the "architectural prescriptions" written by doctors for young married women in the late nineteenth century. In their observations on motherhood's spatial implications, social critics and medical experts articulated a clear conception of both the productive and the destructive powers of Victorian women.

The Victorian middle-class birthing experience was the time when women's bodies and domestic spaces intersected; birth itself was a transgression of the boundaries between the woman's body and the house as the child emerged from the womb. Childbirth was also a prime example of the provision of medical care within the middle-class house. Just as the sanitarians had exposed the inner workings of the house by breaking down the building's walls – in models such as the Insanitary Dwelling at the IHE and in the sectional illustrations in the popular press – the medical profession tried to dissolve the opaque barriers between the outside and inside of women's bodies in order to see, to explain, and to control women's health. Since the idealized domain of the middle-class Victorian woman was the house, it is not surprising that this breakdown took place in the context of domestic space: the lying-in room. More than an innovation of architectural convenience, the lying-in room was both a symbolic and a visible extension of the mother's body, an observable space through which doctors could expand the conceptual limitations of the body.

However, the doctors' attempt to control the relationship of women's bodies to the built environment began long before conception. Whereas potential mothers were told to frequent unconfined open spaces, as if in surrounding themselves by nature they, too, might become productive landscapes, pregnant women were advised to frequent confined controllable spaces, occupying an increasingly limited spatial sphere as they progressed through pregnancy. They were told to regulate their participation in the urban social realm – both for their own protection and for the protection of others around them – revealing the paradoxical position occupied by the Victorian woman in the middle-class house. As the regulators of healthy houses, women protected their families from infection and its associated evils; in childbirth, however, they became the source of such dangers.

The critical importance of the birthing space in the literature of Victorian health becomes clearer when one considers the central place that nineteenth-century society accorded to motherhood and the care with which the medical experts of the time sought to ensure the ideal conditions for middle-class childbirth. Few were more widely read than Pye Henry Chavasse, a Birmingham obstetrician, whose *Advice to a Wife* was the most popular work of medical literature written for women.[1] His writings reveal the simple conviction that the regulation of a woman's personal habits after puberty – diet, sleep, and social life – measured by the regularity of menstruation, ensured the healthiness of her womb and increased her potential for childbearing.[2] The "performance" of menstruation before marriage was a mark of health and happiness. Chavasse warned that "unless [menstruation] be in every way properly and duly performed, it is neither possible that such a lady can be well, nor is it at all probable that she will conceive. The immense number of barren, of delicate, and of hysterical women there are in England, arises mainly from menstruation not being duly and properly performed."[3] Regular menstruation was an achievement; the reward would be fecundity.[4]

The centrality of reproduction in women's lives was further underlined by the emphasis placed on their reproductive years.[5] True "womanhood" – the thirty years during which women could reproduce – was clearly demarcated by physiological changes. Menstruation, claimed Chavasse, was "the threshold, so to speak, of a woman's life," while menopause was the time when "she ceases to be after the manner of women."[6] A woman's reproductive years were also characterized by spiritual maturity. With the onset of puberty, Victorian experts marked "a change in the girl's religious nature."[7] Womanhood was, from their perspective, synonymous with potential motherhood.

Prescriptive literature, fiction, and other images accessible to women extolled the ideal that the only true measure of female happiness was a large family: "The love of offspring is one of the strongest instincts implanted in woman; there is nothing that will compensate for the want of children. A wife yearns for them; they are as necessary to her happiness as the food she eats and as the air she breathes."[8] Reproduction was the primary expression of female purpose, and the institution of marriage was structured, as it has been throughout history, to legitimate procreation.[9] Most middle-class women in the 1860s could expect to bear six children.[10] Of these, one or two would probably die during birth or soon after.[11] As historian Jane Lewis has remarked, "It was not uncommon for women in the nineteenth century to speak in the same breath of the number of children they had raised and the number they had buried."[12] Childbearing was not only an assurance of female happiness; it was also said to be a guarantee of good health. Single women were prone to more disease, most Victorian doctors claimed, and so were married women without children.[13] Indeed, pregnancy was upheld as a specific cure for a variety of illnesses.[14] Motherhood, therefore, was seen by both women and doctors as a form of preventive medicine.[15]

Like other physicians of his time, Chavasse explained reproduction to married women in ordinary, nontechnical language, chiefly by comparing them to aspects or elements of the landscape, most often to flowers or trees. "A wife," he wrote unabashedly, "may be likened to a fruit-tree; a child is its fruit."[16] Middle-class wives were told that they must "sow the seeds of health before [they could] reap a full harvest."[17] In the first year of marriage, women supposedly "la[id] the seeds of a future life of happiness or misery."[18] Children were thus seen as the natural product of women's bodies, and childbearing was treated as a biological imperative rather than as a socially conditioned choice.

The landscape analogy served to convince women that the preparation of their bodies for motherhood was a continuous one, rather than one that began with marriage. Like gardens, women's bodies had to be carefully tended from the earliest stages of life in order to produce beautiful and healthy plants. Childless women were described as "fruitless" or, more commonly, "barren." Chavasse elaborated on his agricultural metaphor when describing the childless: "We all know that it is impossible to have fine fruit from an unhealthy tree as to have a fine child from an unhealthy mother. On the one case, the tree either does not bear fruit at all – is barren – or it bears undersized, tasteless fruit – fruit which often either immaturely drops from the tree, or, if plucked from the tree, is useless."[19]

Barrenness was considered a uniquely female disease, whose origins were thought to lie in luxurious living and bad habits. Strictly medical origins were seldom considered, and the husband's fertility was simply not an issue. Barren women thus felt that they were denied children in punishment for improper behaviour – for deviating in some way from the productive state of nature into which they had passed at puberty. Barrenness was also considered to be peculiar to those segments of society living farthest from that state of nature: the urban middle and upper classes. Even in the early nineteenth century, many doctors noted that "we seldom find a barren woman among the labouring poor, while nothing is more common among the rich and affluent."[20] Hard-working women had more children, doctors claimed, suggesting that the supposedly idle lifestyle of the middle-class woman was the cause of her barrenness. "Riches and indolence are often as closely united as the Siamese twins," wrote Chavasse. "Rich and luxurious living, then, is very antagonistic to fecundity."[21] Diet, hard work, and a close relationship to nature were considered the foundations of working-class fecundity. If a woman had been married a year or two without conceiving, Chavasse suggested, "let her live, indeed, very much either as a poor curate's wife or as a poor Irish woman is compelled to live." This entailed a mostly vegetarian diet of milk, bread, and potatoes, and "no stimulants whatsoever."[22]

Chavasse's use of nature and landscape imagery with reference to human fertility went far beyond simple analogy. Because women were seen in both social and medical terms as passive, dependent figures, their bodies were thought to absorb the characteristics of their surroundings.[23] Thus, the spaces in which married women dwelt were capable of rendering them fertile or infertile. Like the fields of rural England, women could be cultivated to produce. It is not surprising, therefore, that doctors considered women in the city less likely to conceive than those living in the country. The reasoning was based on both social and biological grounds.[24] As innocuous a factor as the busy social schedule of a newly married city woman was liable to bring on exhaustion, thereby preventing conception. The very air in cities was unhealthy for women – both inside and outside buildings: "The air of an assembly or of a concert room is contaminated with carbonic acid gas. The gas-lights and the respiration of numbers of persons give off carbonic acid gas, which gas is highly poisonous ... The headache, the oppression, the confusion of ideas, the loss of appetite, the tired feeling, followed by a restless night – all tell a tale, and loudly proclaim that either an assembly or a concert room is not a fit place for a young wife desirous of having a family."[25]

Chavasse's prescription for such ills was equally predictable and equally informed by environmentally deterministic assumptions. In lieu of city streets, he recommended green fields as the best place for a young woman to walk. "Let her, if she can, live in the country," he advised. Simple exposure of the senses to the natural landscape was suggested as a cure *sui generis*. Chavasse's reminder that "the eye and heart are both gladdened with the beauties of nature" was explicitly linked to his belief that the womb would be likewise "gladdened" and made fertile.[26]

It was not only the air in the country that was thought to help women conceive. There was also the influence of the rural population, whose habits necessarily reflected the virtues of the rural environment. Indulgence was, by implication, targeted as a middle-class and exclusively urban phenomenon: "Hence it is that one seldom sees in cities, courts, and rich houses, where people eat and drink, and indulge in the pleasure of appetite, that perfect health and athletic soundness and vigour which is commonly seen in the country, in the poor houses and cottages, where nature is their cook and necessity is their caterer, where they have no other doctor but the sun and fresh air, and no other physic but exercise and temperance."[27]

Women could take long walks in the country, venturing farther from home without encountering threatening people or places. Particularly dangerous to a young mother, according to Chavasse, were working-class men. Not only were the places they worked – factories fired by coal – unhealthy environments for young females, but "the exhalations from the lungs and from the skin of the inhabitants, numbers of them diseased," tended to fill the atmosphere with impurities, hampering female fecundity.[28] As noted above, women needed open spaces in order to become pregnant; confined spaces worked against female fertility, the doctors claimed. Again, the reasoning behind their conclusions rested both on a specific fear of unhealthy air and on a more generalized – though not entirely separable – distaste for indulgent or unnatural habits. The house, even a country house, represented a threat to conception if it was full of "too many persons breathing the same air over and over again."[29] More-

over, confined spaces bred a kind of indolence that was not at all conducive to motherhood. This attitude was summed up by Dr Grosvenor:

Hot and close rooms, soft cushions, and luxurious couches, must be eschewed. I
have somewhere read, that if a fine healthy whelp of the bull-dog species were
fed upon chicken, rice, and delicacies, and made to lie upon soft cushions, and if,
for some months, he were shut up in a close room, when he grew up he would
become unhealthy, weak, and spiritless. So it is with a young married woman;
the more she indulges, the more unhealthy, weak, and inanimate she becomes –
unfit to perform the duties of a wife and the offices of a mother, if, indeed she be
a mother at all![30]

Conception marked the beginning of a major shift in a Victorian
woman's social status – from wife to mother.[31] The expectant mother was
different not simply for having "achieved" conception but for her new
ability to act upon – rather than simply absorb – the world around her.
The most striking difference between the doctors' advice to wives and to
mothers was in their appropriate spatial domains. No longer were open
spaces recommended; women in childbirth were totally confined. And
while potential mothers' bodies were understood in terms of gardens and
fields, the pregnant woman's body was a colonized space. Both categories
of women – like all people – were presumed to benefit from the salubrious effects of exercise and fresh air, but the prescription varied according
to the patient. The long walks that Chavasse had recommended as conducive to fertility were likely to cause "flooding, miscarriage and bearing-
down of the womb" in pregnant women. The expectant mother was
advised instead to take "short, gentle and frequent walks," and the attention that Chavasse and others devoted to her perambulation was far more
likely to take the form of prohibitions – against carriage rides, railway
journeys, and other strenuous forms of movement – than it was to encourage mobility in the city. In the ideal world imagined by Chavasse
and other Victorian doctors, pregnant women occupied an increasingly
limited spatial sphere as they progressed through pregnancy. Controlled
urban spaces, rather than the relatively untamed rural landscapes, were
better places for expectant mothers.

The few surviving sources that describe women's actual experiences of
pregnancy indicate that they did not always follow the narrow path the
doctors cut for them.[32] Jeanette Seaton, for example, attended twelve formal dinners between mid-May and early July 1892, and gave birth to a
daughter in October. Even two weeks before delivery she maintained her

usual busy schedule of calls, shopping, and theatre. Since she resided in Clapham, five miles from central London, and since her family was without a carriage, we can assume that she travelled on public transportation, ignoring the threat of miscarriage so vehemently expressed by most doctors.[33]

This insistence on maintaining the liberties afforded by childlessness is evident in the material culture of the period, particularly in the elaborate maternity dresses worn by middle-class women. Costume historian Zuzanna Shonfield has explained how the change in fashions for pregnant women from the "plain, everyday garments" of the 1860s to the more elaborate styles of the 1890s parallels the drastic drop in the birth rate in the final decades of the century. It is likely, says Shonfield, that the woman of the 1890s "took her role as mother less for granted than she would have done earlier in the century. The lace and ribbons of her maternity garments may have been a way of asserting that she continued to see herself as a seductive bride rather than as a staid expectant mother."[34] The same evidence could be interpreted, however, as a widespread acceptance of pregnant women in the so-called public sphere as women simply ignored the advice of their doctors and maintained their regular schedules.[35]

Successful or not, Victorian doctors attempted to limit the kinds of space frequented by pregnant women because they believed that external environmental conditions were inextricably linked to the womb. We have seen how Chavasse and others believed that women wishing to become pregnant could, through their behaviour and the spaces with which they surrounded themselves, become the willing receptors of a benevolent landscape. Expectant mothers were urged to exercise similar power; they too, said the doctors, could so position their bodies in spaces that they would profoundly affect the success of their pregnancies.

Even the diagnosis of pregnancy presented Victorian doctors with the problem of detecting an essentially interior condition from the exterior, underlining the impermeability of the boundary between women's bodies and the outside world of men. Until the 1880s, fetal movement, or "quickening," was considered the only sure sign of pregnancy. Quickening came from the ancient idea that the fetus was suddenly infused with life. Although Victorian doctors claimed that they no longer believed in quickening as evidence for pregnancy, they trivialized the period of pregnancy preceding fetal movement, endowing the event itself with ritual significance.[36] Quickening was important to doctors because it represented the mother's awareness of the new life growing inside her body and also because it marked the ascent of the womb into the belly, followed immediately by a noticeable increase in the mother's size. The life inside her began to occupy space outside the regular confines of her body and became correspondingly more real.

Doctors tried desperately to identify symptoms of pregnancy visible outside the women's body. W.F. Montgomery, author of the classic *Exposition of the Signs and Symptoms of Pregnancy*, maintained that changes in the follicles on a woman's breasts indicated pregnancy.[37] Chavasse held that a pretty woman would suddenly become plain during the early months of pregnancy; but as her time advanced, she would resume her former "pristine comeliness."[38] The doctors' sense of exclusion from the inner workings of female reproduction is clearly expressed in the ways they classified the signs and symptoms of pregnancy. "Presumptive" signs included the cessation of menstruation, the occurrence of morning sickness, a craving for unusual food, and quickening. "Objective" or "positive" signs were those that could be positively observed and identified by the doctor, such as the increased size of a woman's body and the detection of a fetal heartbeat. Doctors were quick to cite instances in which women had erred in the self-diagnosis of pregnancy.[39] Montgomery said that women were likely to lie about pregnancy, and he boasted that he had felt a fetus before its mother, with his hand. He told stories of unwed mothers who had denied their pregnancies even when the baby's feet had appeared. Most Victorian doctors, however, readily admitted the fallibility of their methods. As Montgomery acknowledged, for physicians the diagnosis of pregnancy could "give rise to great embarrassment."[40]

The relationship of pregnant women to their surroundings was complicated by the fact that their minds appeared to play a powerful intermediary role between the outside world and their wombs. The "maternal impressions" theory held that the character of the developing fetus was affected not only by the general health of the mother but also by her thoughts and feelings.[41] Until the mid-nineteenth century, the state of a woman's mind, pregnant or not, was most commonly cited as the chief cause of congenital malformations.[42] Although most doctors in the second half of the century questioned the nature of the connection between the mind and the womb, they clearly did not reject it altogether, for they nearly always included detailed accounts of such occurrences in their books for women. In the early 1890s, for example, Dr C. Lloyd Tuckey told mothers that this "old subject" was "surrounded with mystery even today."[43] The most common story was that a pregnant woman's desire for unusual food would cause an image of the food type to be imprinted on the skin of the baby. But although doctors repeated such stories, they consistently refuted the "impressions" theory. For instance, after describing how a pregnant woman had given birth to a child missing a hand after seeing a one-armed beggar during her fifth or sixth month, Dr Thomas Bull suggested that Victorian medical science need offer no explanation, and he quoted a Dr Turner of 1723 who had said, "How these strange alterations should be wrought, or the child cut, wounded, or maimed, as if the same was really done with a weapon, whilst the mother is unhurt, and merely by the force of the imagination, is, I must confess, above my understanding; but it is a fact, undeniable." Nevertheless, Bull suggested that the malformation was a mere coincidence.[44]

The doctors were equally unwilling to accept the opposing position – that the environmental experiences of a woman had no effect on the fetus inside her; they thus insisted on the need to protect women from emotional disturbances of any kind. In the interests of protection, the doctors clearly appreciated the opacity of the woman's body in acting as an impermeable boundary between the outside world and the inner environment of the uterus. The pregnant woman's body, it seemed, acted as a necessarily thick layer of insulation around the baby. In view of this perception of women's bodies as protective shelters for their tiny inhabitants, it is not surprising that the French term for pregnant, *enceinte*, meaning walled or enclosed, was preferred by many doctors in England.[45] The word "confinement," one expert noted, limited "the view at once to the earthly and material part of maternity; and not only that, but it dwells on the pains and discomforts attending child-birth, and accentuates them in the mother's mind."[46]

Victorian doctors revealed, time and again, their frustration with the basic fact that pregnancy – as well as other female ailments – was beyond their sight. They could not control what they could not see, they implied, echoing the sanitarians' attitude to domestic architecture. Just as the sanitarians had dissolved the walls of the house, the medical profession tried to break down the opaque barriers between the outside and inside of women's bodies by confining the pregnant woman to an easily controllable and observable environment (fig. 4.1).

The architecture of confinement was realized through the refurbishing of an ordinary bedroom in the house.[47] This birthing room, or "lying-in room" as it was commonly called, accommodated the mother, her attendant, and the baby, from the onset of labour until one month after delivery. This was the time believed necessary for the womb to return to its normal size and for the body of the newly delivered mother to be "purified" of the illness and dangers associated with childbirth.[48] The prepara-

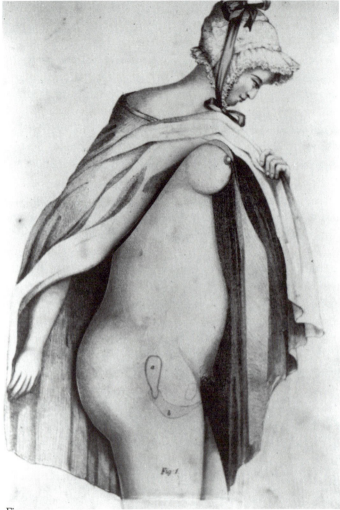

Figure 4.1
Illustration of a pregnant woman (Spratt, *Obstetrical Tables*, 1833) Courtesy, Royal College of Midwives, London

tion of the lying-in room began long before the expected date of birth, coinciding with other social and economic contracts made outside the home. As soon as a woman suspected that she was pregnant, she was advised to employ a "monthly nurse" to attend her during both childbirth and lying in. The lying-in room and the monthly nurse were expressions of the special status accorded to childbirth within the Victorian household. Pregnancy was seen not as an illness but as an altered condition.[49]

The lying-in room was thus clearly distinguished from the sickroom that was such a common feature of Victorian middle-class houses. Similarly, the monthly nurse was a different person from the "sick nurse" who was employed by a family to attend members while they were ill. A woodcut after David Wilkie shows the affectionate relationship between a newly delivered mother, her monthly nurse, and a young infant (fig. 4.2).[50]

From the perspective of the doctors, the health of the house, like the woman's own physical health, was solely the pregnant woman's responsibility. Expectant mothers were urged to check the sanitary state of their houses as soon as they realized they were pregnant, particularly its ventilation and drainage. "Let a lady look well to the ventilation of her house," was the advice of many Victorian doctors.[51] "It is an absolute duty," warned Florence Stacpoole in 1889, lecturer to the National Health Society, "for every woman who is expecting to become a mother to do her best to keep the air of the house she lives in as pure as possible."[52] Sensitive as they considered the state of pregnancy, and overly protective as they were of the expectant mother's emotional state, experts insisted that pregnant women inspect the chimneys and unstop the drains of their houses. The house of the pregnant woman thus became an extension of her body. Careful regulation of house ventilation, for example, was believed to enrich the blood of pregnant women, "who are already in a weakened state."[53] Stacpoole told her readers that with the invention of the microscope, it had been discovered that the pregnant woman's blood was weaker than usual. "The chief thing that helps to make rich blood is *pure air!*" she explained.[54] Pregnant women were urged to follow the instructions for room ventilation promulgated by the National Health Society:

There is a very simple plan advocated by the National Health Society by which rooms may be always ventilated without letting in a draught (for it should be remembered that ventilation and draught need not mean the same thing). The plan is to place a piece of wood which has been made to fit exactly into the window sash, and which should be about three inches in depth, into the lower sash, the lower frame of the window is then shut down upon this, and so a space is left *between* the two sashes, which causes no draught, but allows a gentle current of pure air from the outside to circulate in the upper part of the room, and at the same time the occupants are not chilled, even if the weather is cold.[55]

Unventilated rooms poisoned the tiny lives growing inside the womb, Victorian women were told: "You who breathe such air, breathe in what

Figure 4.2
The monthly nurse (woodcut after D. Wilkie, 1840) Wellcome Institute Library,
London

is poisonous, and this poison is racing through your blood into every
limb in your body with every breath you draw!"[56] Like her own physical
health, the condition of a woman's home depended on the care with
which she maintained it. This was also the case, as we have seen, with
the houses of women who were not pregnant. "If you want a thing done
well, do it yourself,' is an old saying, and if you are going to have new
drains put into a house, inspect the work at every step," advised the editor of *Baby*, a journal for young mothers.[57]

The preparation for lying in, the construction of its "architecture," was also the pregnant woman's responsibility. The lying-in rooms were a conspicuously separate world from the setting that accommodated normal family life, typically requiring elaborate planning, alterations to the functions of rooms, and the acquisition of material goods intended specifically for lying in – much as was done for the sickroom. Doctors usually recommended a large bedroom or two adjacent rooms with an interior connection; in no circumstances were these room to communicate through the main hallway of the house. Of four house plans drawn by the obstetrician W.S. Playfair showing the rooms occupied by his patients during lying in, three had internal connections between the bedroom (where childbirth supposedly took place) and an adjacent dressing room. This presumably allowed the young mothers to move freely between the two spaces without entering the circulation corridor (figs. 4.3 and 4.4). Childbirth and lying in thus occupied a large area of the house, within an essentially independent precinct.

For this reason, the back of the house was the preferred location for the lying-in room. The typical Victorian house, as we have seen, was planned with the public rooms at the front of the building.[58] These were often associated with men's activities. The rear of the house was quieter as well; traffic on the street might disturb the young mother in childbirth. The tranquillity of the lying-in room was particularly important in large towns, insisted Catherine Gladstone, who authored an important book on the lying-in room for the International Health Exhibition in 1884. "We cannot say too much upon the subject of perfect quiet; it is all-important," she stressed. "Care should be taken to prevent the rattling of windows and blinds."[59] Since even the sound of footsteps could be injurious to a woman in childbirth, Gladstone recommended laying strips of carpet on the floor to absorb sounds, and she advised the use of "noiseless crockery" in the lying-in room.[60]

It was equally important for the lying-in room to be well removed from "all bad smells" in the house.[61] This fear of noxious gases, as we have seen, reflected a central point of debate in the Victorian discussion of the spread of diseases both before and after the formulation of the germ theory. However, bad smells could be useful warnings of danger. "Verily the nose is a sentinel!" Chavasse explained. "It is doubtless, then, admirably appointed that we are able to detect 'the well-defined and several stinks.'"[62] As such "stinks" were usually emitted from the kitchen and sanitary facilities, the lying-in room was, ideally, isolated from these functions and located above the ground floor. "The usual bedroom need

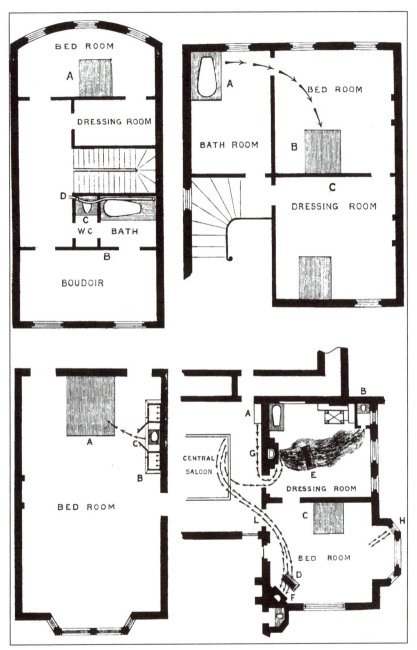

Figures 4.3 and 4.4
Plans of lying-in rooms drawn by W.S. Playfair (*Lancet*, 5 Feb. 1887, 252–3) Courtesy of McGill University Libraries, Montreal

not be resorted to," explained author-decorator Jane Ellen Panton, "and great care should be taken that the event takes place in the sunniest and most cheerful room in the house."[63] The season in which the birth would occur, according to Panton, should be a major factor in the choice of a lying-in room. She advised women to pick a room from which the sunset could be viewed or, in the case of a summer baby, from which one could watch the sunrise.

Women were encouraged to "review the house, and choose the room which best agrees with these conditions," assuming personal responsibility for the establishment of the birthing space within the architecture of the house.[64] The choice of room was not to be taken lightly, doctors insisted; the decision was to be made "with previous thought."[65] If a furnished house was rented for the confinement, as was often the case when aristocratic women came to London from the country to give birth, its "history" should be researched, particularly the history of the bed.[66] The doctors warned that women in childbirth could be infected by the beds in which other women in childbirth had died.[67] Again, this illuminates the widespread uncertainty over the spread of disease years after the formulation of the germ theory. In their advice concerning both illness and childbirth, the experts insisted that "things" – furniture, clothing, books, letters – could spread fever and infection.

Not surprisingly, then, women were responsible for the alterations made to the room in anticipation of childbirth. Early in the pregnancy the doctors gave the mothers-to-be detailed lists of special things to acquire for the lying-in room. These lists were remarkably consistent and included clothing, linen, bedbaths, bedpans, and large items of furniture that were intended to facilitate "confinement" for an entire month (fig. 4.5). Wealthier women purchased portable beds just for the occasion, rupturing the "symbolic connection between sexual intercourse and birth which would have been more evident had the marriage bed been used for both purposes," as childbirth historian Judith Lewis has noted.[68] This special furniture and the new arrangement of the room served to differentiate childbirth from everyday life. The newness also ensured that the furniture and accoutrements had not been used previously by women giving birth.

Like the healthy maintenance of the house in general, women's responsibility for the architecture of confinement meant that any problems during childbirth or lying in were the result of their own negligence; both the house and the woman were scapegoats for the inability of medical experts to explain the mysteries of reproduction – and for any profes-

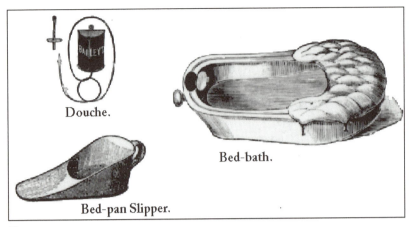

Douche.

Bed-bath.

Bed-pan Slipper.

Figure 4.5
Objects for confinement (Westland, *The Wife and Mother*, 52–3) Courtesy of the British Library, London

sional incompetence of the doctors. Furnished "only with what is absolutely necessary," the ideal lying-in room of the late nineteenth century contained a single bed, with "neither curtains nor valance," placed in a position that allowed the woman in labour to be helped (and reached) from all sides – that is, not up against a wall.[69] An iron bedstead was recommended by most doctors.[70] To make it easier for the doctor to reach the woman, the bed was often raised – in advance of delivery – about a foot above the floor by positioning blocks of wood under the posts.[71] A few chairs, a table for dressings, and another to hold the washbowl completed the furniture of lying in.

Lay advisers stressed that the room should resemble a sitting room rather than a bedroom so that the woman's friends would feel welcome to visit her.[72] It would help the young mother see her condition as different from an illness, said Panton, if the lying-in room was "made as pretty, convenient, and as unlike the orthodox sick-room as can be managed."[73] The room was to be thoroughly cleaned just before the woman's confinement, with "none of the heavy work done by the mother."[74] This process included washing the walls, cleaning everything in the room including the backs of pictures on the walls, hanging new curtains, dusting the light brackets, and thoroughly beating the carpets.[75] Some doctors even suggested covering the rugs in the area of the bed with several layers of newspaper and then further protecting them with old sheets.[76]

The doctors' advice to women on the details of childbirth gave a fairly precise picture of when, where, and how the major characters might move through the various rooms of the house as the time of delivery approached. The Leeds physician Henry Allbutt provided a particularly vivid rendering of the "choreography" of childbirth in *The Wife's Handbook* (1877). Complete separation from the family took place with the onset of labour. As the pains increased, the monthly nurse (who was already resident in the house) and the mother retreated to the lying-in room and the doctor was summoned. The bed, probably acquired for the occasion, was then specially prepared for the birth. The various authors gave detailed instructions on how the sheets should be arranged so that the bed would "run no great risk of being soiled" and would be "guarded" by a macintosh or waterproof sheet.[77]

As labour progressed, the furniture of the room was used by the woman to alleviate her pain and discomfort. Leaning on the foot of the bed or the back of a chair provided comfort for her. As the baby emerged, the woman was advised to get into the bed and press her feet against a towel that had been fastened to its foot. If there was any possibility that the delivery would take place before the arrival of the doctor, the woman was advised to be in bed lest the child fall on the floor and be killed.[78] Yet despite all this precision of detail, spelled out by Allbutt, Chavasse, and other doctors in their predictions of what might occur in a typical delivery, the process remained essentially unpredictable. The "reckoning," or estimation of the delivery date and the duration and difficulty of labour, was in Victorian times virtually impossible to predict, as it still is today.[79]

The isolation of the lying-in room did not only provide a controlled environment in which the newborn child could begin life; it served another purpose too. The very things that were purposely excluded from the birthing space and were perceived as dangerous to the mother in delivery were also produced inside this protected space. Women in childbirth produced noises and smells. More serious still was the fact that women in childbirth were believed actually to generate disease. The architecture of lying in, in its posture of isolation within the house and its distinct material culture, was as much a way of protecting the family from the woman in childbirth as of isolating her from the family. The special furniture, the newspapers on the floor, and the spatial separation of the lying-in room from the other rooms in the house were ways of sequestering and controlling the polluting power of women's "interiors."

This belief that women in childbirth actually fouled the environment they occupied was in fact common to many cultures. Childbirth historian Ann Oakley has explained that the persistence of this belief in small-scale traditional societies is part of a larger belief system that sees "the reproductive powers of women" in general as dangerous. "The parturient woman," says Oakley, "is subject to a host of regulations which control and isolate her act of birth, so that the rest of society is not contaminated by it."[80] Although the isolation of middle-class mothers in Victorian London was less extreme than the groups studied by Oakley, the process was identical. Removed from the family at the onset of labour and sequestered in a room or suite of rooms that were completely separate from all other spaces in the house, the newly delivered mother became part of an easily controllable environment and was thus seen as less threatening to other family members and to society in general.

The initiative taken by women for the architectural arrangements surrounding birth and their accountability for this architecture reveal the paradoxical situation of women in the late-Victorian home. By seeing women as "pollutants," medical experts expected them to secure the safety of other family members by "cleaning" their houses and isolating their bodies. This was undoubtedly a natural extension of the mid-century notion of the evangelical mother, the "angel in the house" who was responsible for purifying the family in moral terms. The paradox was most clearly articulated during pregnancy and childbirth. As late as the 1890s, the Victorian woman, like the house itself, was considered a factor of disease, not only through her own carelessness or ignorance – as many medical experts suggested – but simply through the enigma of her capacity to reproduce. The view of pregnancy as an "infective malady," as Oakley has elaborated, is the reason why maternity hospitals developed entirely independently from hospitals for the sick. It was not because of the dangers posed to pregnant women – as is commonly assumed – but because of the dangers women posed to those already vulnerable through illness.[81]

Predictably, entry to the lying-in room was restricted. The doctor and monthly nurse were often the only attendants to childbirth. Sometimes the woman's mother or a married friend was present, though Chavasse recommended that if the young woman's mother was likely to depress rather than cheer her daughter, she should remain in another part of the house.[82] Husbands were permitted in the lying-in room only for a short time after delivery and only if "the soiled clothes have been put out of the way."[83] Chavasse was clearly more concerned about the harmful effects of the clothing on the man than the danger of his presence on the newly delivered woman.

Even the presence of the doctor in the lying-in room was not wholly recommended. "It is neither necessary nor desirable for a medical man to be much in a lying-in room," Chavasse stated. "It is better, much better that he retire in the day-time to the drawing-room, in the night season to a bedroom, and thus to allow nature time and full scope to take her own course without hurry and without interference, without let and without hindrance. Nature hates hurry, and resents interference."[84] Privacy during labour was also a noted class distinction among women. Working-class mothers frequently invited crowds of neighbours and friends to their lying-in rooms, thus overheating the room and supposedly slowing the process of labour.[85]

The sounds accompanying childbirth also could be disturbing to family members. "During the pains the breath should be held, and the woman must refrain from crying out," instructed Allbutt.[86] Another doctor noted that because of the "tearing or cutting" nature of pain experienced in the advanced stages of labour, "the woman generally cries out, and is very restless, tossing about the bed in an uneasy manner."[87] William Gladstone, when recording in his diary the birth of his son in 1840, remarked on his wife's lack of cries: "[Catherine] has been most firm and gallant, altho not only Lady W[enlock] and Lady B[raybrooke] (the only friends who have been in the house) but Dr L[ecock], encouraged her to scream."[88]

Some women gave birth in silence, particularly those who were not afforded the luxury of space in which to express pain. So quiet was Mary, a servant employed by Thomas and Jane Carlyle, for example, that when she gave birth in a small closet off the dining room in the Carlyles' terraced house in Chelsea, her presence went unnoticed by those in the dining room. "While she was in labour in the small room at the end of the dining-room," reported Jane Carlyle, "Mr. Carlyle was taking tea in the dining-room with Miss Jewsbury talking to him!!! Just a thin small door between!" Thomas Carlyle went upstairs, and the newborn baby was removed from the house wrapped in linens.[89]

The smells of women's bodies were also noted by observers of Victorian childbirth. In particular, the odour of the afterbirth was consistently described as unpleasant. Chavasse recommended that the monthly nurse burn it immediately, but only "after all the servants are gone to bed" – probably for fear that it might infect them rather than because of any unpleasantness the smells might cause.[90] The discharges from women's bodies for up to two weeks after childbirth were also described as having "in some cases a disagreeable odour."[91] In lying-in hospitals, the bloody discharges of women's bodies supposedly "filled the air with noxious smells" and was likened by physicians to the fumes emanating from garbage-strewn streets.[92]

Another reason why Victorian childbirth was spatially "confined" was that it often resulted in death, obviously a frightening sight for the woman's husband or for other children in the family. In the late nineteenth century, one in 120 women died in childbirth.[93] Death following childbirth was among the most unpredictable illnesses at the time; even seemingly healthy women developed sudden high fevers and died within days of delivery. The source of their condition, which acquired the general label of puerperal or childbed fever, remained a mystery to British doctors for most of the century. The only certainty was that the death rate at home was better than that in the lying-in hospitals used by working-class mothers. Uncertainty over the spread of puerperal fever underlined the continuing need for the spatial confinement of women recovering from childbirth.

The international professional debate revolved around whether the fever originated in the body, the room, or the attendants to childbirth. Although the Viennese doctor Ignaz Semmelweis had proved in 1847 that puerperal fever was transmitted by the hands of doctors, his theory was bitterly opposed by the profession and was long ignored in England.[94] Oliver Wendell Holmes had reached precisely the same conclusion in the United States as early as 1843.[95] Doctors in both Europe and America, however, insisted that they helped women in labour, and they looked desperately for other explanations for the fatal illness.

The lying-in room and the middle-class house were easy targets in view of the general belief of the Victorian medical profession in the power of environments to spread illness. More than twenty-five years after Semmelweis's discovery, W.S. Playfair wrote an influential article in the *Lancet*, in which he published the four house plans already mentioned, tracing the paths which he believed had been taken by sewer gas to the beds of parturient women (see fig. 4.4). In spite of the fact that Playfair's patients had been safely sequestered from the circulation spaces in their houses, they had nonetheless contracted puerperal fever. The article contains no reference to Semmelweis; it treats the house itself as the agent of fever.

Playfair illustrated his theory by describing the death of a friend's wife. The young couple had moved into their new house a year earlier, believing that the sanitary state of the building had been carefully checked. The main drain of the house, however, was found to be in an insanitary condition. More serious still was the location of the water-closets and soil pipe in the middle of the house, precisely where the house-doctors had warned people to avoid placing these facilities. Playfair blamed the woman's death on this close connection between the rooms. "The boudoir, where the patient chiefly lived, and the w.c. were practically in one," the doctor remarked.[96]

By mapping the flow of the disease from the architecture to the woman's body using traditional modes of architectural representation, Playfair deflected the blame for puerperal fever from his own profession – whose members were actually spreading the disease – and placed it on the builders and plumbers:

Increased attention on the part of the profession may do something, but not much, for the demon plumber is abroad, and one may rest in fancied security that proper care has been taken, while the carelessness of a single workman may render all our precautions useless. The whole system of closet and water arrangements in modern towns lends itself so easily to faulty construction that defects are not astonishing, and I believe that nothing but such a provision will teach builders and plumbers the importance of their work.[97]

T. Pridgin Teale published a similar account in his popular book, describing the house of a physician whose wife had been infected by puerperal fever (fig. 4.6). After the sanitary defects in the house had been discovered and corrected (the lavatory in a dressing room adjacent to the lying-in room had been directly connected to a soil pipe), "the lady recovered without a drawback."[98]

Beneath the doctors' shifting of professional blame lay a set of philosophical assumptions that were, as we have seen, common to the practice of medicine in their time. The physicians' insistence on the complete culpability of faulty construction techniques – on the architecture of the house – reveals their fundamental faith in visible, tangible explanations for internal states, even though there was already evidence to the contrary. The conditions that Playfair prescribed for the lying-in room represented an attempt to create a perfectly controlled, visible environment – one that controlled the invisible, internal environment of the womb. Catherine Gladstone went so far as to call attention to the new demand for plumbers in childbirth: "It is within our own experience that a distinguished physician insisted on the presence of the plumber to remedy a defect in the lying-in room, even though labour had already begun."[99]

The doctors' emphasis on the house as the agent of disease reveals the medical profession's assumption that women themselves were the source of illness. The architecture of the lying-in hospital provides further evi-

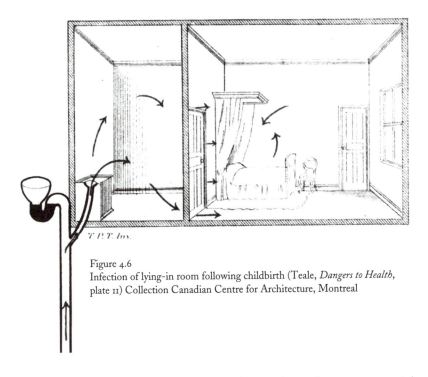

Figure 4.6
Infection of lying-in room following childbirth (Teale, *Dangers to Health*, plate II) Collection Canadian Centre for Architecture, Montreal

dence for this belief. Beginning in the late eighteenth century, special maternity hospitals were constructed in Britain to provide an arena for the teaching of obstetrical medicine, which was distinguished as a separate field of medicine, as previously noted, because of the potential danger of its patients to the rest of society. As medical historian Gail Pat Parsons has explained, the high death rates at these lying-in hospitals convinced physicians and other medical experts of the dangers of women's bodies during childbirth and suggested that newly delivered mothers could "manufacture puerperal fever at will."[100]

In view of these assumptions, it is not surprising that Victorian physicians feared that they themselves would become infected, with consequent damage to their medical practice. Parsons's research has shown how many Victorian doctors were forced to modify their behaviour and even abandon their private practice when they appeared to play a "carrier" role in the spread of childbed fever. For example, physician Robert Storrs "changed [his] clothes, and used every means ... to prevent ... spread" among his patients, who were dying inexplicably from puerperal fever. He abandoned his practice and embarked on a trip, supposing a poison "clung to [him]."[101]

A woman's slow and controlled release from the lying-in room to the other parts of the house was further evidence of these fears. The process was closely tied, in the minds of doctors, to the return of the woman's womb to its normal size. "Remember that the usual and normal time that nature takes to recover the elasticity of all the parts concerned in child-birth is a month," experts warned, "and that till all the contractions have taken place, and this elasticity is restored, it is not safe for her to go downstairs."[102] Chavasse permitted the woman in recovery to enter the drawing room after two weeks, depending on its proximity to the lying-in room.[103] Doctors warned women that if they did not stay long enough in the lying-in room, their bodies would remain in an "enlarged state."[104] Or they might suffer from "falling of the womb" and be unable to bear more children.[105] The rooms of the house outside the well-defined limits of the lying-in room were closely associated with the state of the mother's reproductive organs and the likeliness of their infecting other members of the family. Thus, the amount of time that had elapsed since the birth determined when and where newly delivered mothers could enact their post-partum lives. A rare image shows a young mother being visited by three female friends in the parlour of her home soon after childbirth. Obviously still recovering from the event, she rests in an upright armchair with her feet on a pillow while her friends, standing, admire the baby (fig. 4.7).

The end of "the month" saw the full return of the middle-class woman to normal life, a change that corresponded in the Victorian imagination with the return of the woman's womb to its regular size and shape. At this time, she could once again share a bedroom with her husband; the new baby would be moved into the nursery. The temporary alterations made to the bedroom would be undone. The transition made by the child from the carefully regulated womb to the house would now be complete.

The woman's release from the house, however, was only allowed after the ceremony of "churching," in which she publicly thanked God in church for her safe delivery. Her body was then considered "purified." She could now resume normal sexual relations with her husband, and the monthly nurse would be dismissed.[106] The spatial and economic implications of childbirth, as we have seen, were directed almost solely from what was perceived to be happening inside the woman's body. "No time is lost in the long run by this period of perfect repose before taking up the duties of life again," advisers to women insisted. "Nature, society and religion all sanction it, nay, require that till 'the days of her purification are ended' she shall be secluded from the world."[107]

Figure 4.7
Visit to the young mother (*Queen* 75 [1884]: 33) Courtesy of the Board of Trustees of the Victoria & Albert Museum

According to evidence in the women's press, women viewed this "seclusion from the world," "confinement," or "retirement" very differently from the way the medical experts saw it. Both Jane Ellen Panton and Eliza Warren recalled their own experiences of childbirth when giving advice to young women. These recollections, unlike the doctors' prescriptions, were unhampered by a sense of duty. "Naturally these times are looked forward to with dread by all young wives," asserted Panton. She called the lying-in room a "temporary prison."[108] From her perspective, the spatial isolation of women in childbirth and recovery represented a form of compensation (from men to women) for the burden of producing children:

If only I can get one of the male sex to believe that we do sometimes want a little of his freedom, a little of his powers of money-making, a little of his ability to take a holiday unhaunted by never-ceasing dreads and fears of what awful ends the children are coming to at home in our absence, I shall not have lived in vain, particularly if at the same time he takes the double burden on his own shoulders, when his wife has presented him with a small son or daughter, and takes care that not even a whisper of the cook's wickedness passes the bedroom door, until Materfamilias is able to bring her mind upon a matter that can, no doubt, be explained as soon as the feminine intellect grapples with it.[109]

Panton wrote candidly of her personal feelings and experiences, admitting that a new baby was nothing but "a profound nuisance": "It howls when peace is required, it demands unceasing attention, and it is thrust into Angelina's arms and she has to admire it and adore it at the risk of being thought most unnatural, when she really is rather resenting the intrusion, and requires at least a week to reconcile herself to her new fate."[110] Panton warned young mothers "not to trust entirely to the doctor's recommendation" but rather to trust "her mother's advice."[111]

Women writers associated the spatial separation of parturient mothers and their babies with women's relative power in the family. Whereas, at mid-century, mothers, nurses, and babies had remained together in the lying-in room for the entire month after delivery, most babies born later in the century were removed from their mothers immediately after delivery. Again, this came as much from fear of the mother infecting the child as from the need for the mother to have complete rest in recovery. "At least two rooms, *en suite*, and each with a separate entrance are necessary," stated Catherine Gladstone, "one for the patient, the other for the nurse and baby."[112] Eliza Warren attributed the poor health of her son to the fact that he had remained too close to her after birth. The infant had slept on an improvised bed – two pillows on an armchair – next to his mother's bed. As soon as the nurse left, Warren had taken the child in her arms and stuffed him with food. She had even slept with him in her arms. "My boy had mastered me," she admitted in retrospect. The problem with Warren's son, according to a neighbour, was that he had been "too much in the arms already."[113]

Suckling the newborn had traditionally been a reason for the newly delivered mother to keep the baby in her room and even in her bed. However, the advent of artificial food in the second half of the nineteenth century changed everything. After about 1870, artificial baby food was considered superior to breast milk. "Science," it was believed, could correct the imperfections of breast milk, which formerly had been considered the most "natural" food for babies. Artificial food and special containers designed to hold it meant that women could depend on others to feed their babies and could therefore enjoy uninterrupted sleep after delivery and have long periods alone. Following scientific principles, the new baby bottles were much more predictable than women's breasts. The "Thermo-Safeguard Feeding Bottle," for example, had a thermometer embedded in its glass, allowing mothers and nurses to ascertain the exact temperature of its contents. The bottle also had a register that measured the amount of food consumed by the baby (fig. 4.8). Temperature and quantity, of course, were impossible to regulate in the mother's body.[114]

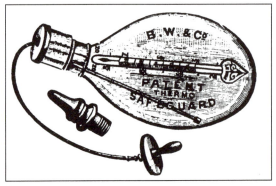

Figure 4.8
"Thermo-Safeguard Feeding Bottle" (Chavasse, *Advice to a Mother*, advertisement) Collection of A. Adams

Furthermore, said the women, the spatial separation facilitated by the advent of artificial food made them better mothers. If a mother could "depend on her 'cow,'" noted Panton, her "baby becomes a pleasure instead of a nuisance."[115]

By the 1920s, the rituals of middle-class childbirth had been completely moved from home to hospital.[116] The period from 1870 to 1900 is therefore an illuminating index of notions of power and control over bodies and domestic space before the "obstetrical takeover" of childbirth documented by Oakley and other historians of medicine. Women's power in the home during these three decades, paradoxical as it was, must have hindered the control sought by physicians over reproduction. As long as the mysteries associated with the spread of infection remained unexplained, women and houses were held responsible.

5 Domestic Architecture and Victorian Feminism

In the last chapter we saw how the rituals associated with Victorian childbirth affected the ways in which rooms in the middle-class house were perceived, and how this in turn enforced new relationships between rooms (and people) because of what was believed to be happening inside the woman's body. Improvements in the social status of Victorian women also changed the ways in which both domestic and urban spaces were perceived and controlled. Indeed, the spatial relationships among women and between mothers and children were significant issues in Victorian feminism, largely as a result of a fiery critique of the Victorian house in the women's press during the period 1870–1900.[1]

This chapter explores four effects of a distinctly feminist perspective of the home: the separation of mothers and their children in the typical middle-class house; a "feminine" understanding of the house boosted by the rise of interior decoration as an appropriate occupation for middle-class women; the construction of purpose-built housing for women in London; and, finally, the acceptance of women as professional architects in England. The ways women reformed space – by making changes in the functions of rooms, by the manner in which space was depicted and described, and in their new professional role as designers – call for a fresh look at the "woman question." The house, like the vote, was a highly charged political issue as well as a significant instrument of Victorian feminism.

The feminist reform of domestic architecture began with a fairly comprehensive critique of the middle-class house. As early as the 1860s, descriptions of London houses in the women's press were filled with despair:

The orthodox London house now constructed for the use of the middle classes, consists of two underground kitchens, and on the ground floor two gloomy parlours, one for structural reasons generally smaller than the other. After these come two flights of from twenty-four to twenty-eight stairs, conducting to two drawing-rooms over them, of the same grand pianoforte shape; another staircase, and two sleeping apartments; another staircase, and two more; and then, if the house be a large one, another climb, and perhaps another, conducts us to one or two upper couples of rooms, perhaps, however, subdivided by lath partitions into three or four cupboards for servants' sleeping apartments.[2]

Passages like these illuminate the two features of middle-class domestic architecture on which feminist criticism focused: the impact of house design on women's health, and the effects on motherhood of the English system of compartmentalized rooms that were accessible only from a corridor. By suggesting that the overall design of the house was more suited to men's lives than to their own needs, Victorian feminists encouraged women to undo or improve – as best they could – the numerous mistakes of the architect or builder. Reformed domestic space was thus a direct expression of women's power.

In view of the authority gained by women in the health movement as "regulators" of household systems, it was predictable that the feminists' initial criticism of the house would be that it was unhealthy. For example, they said that the amount of stair climbing required in the management of the typical English household was "injurious" to women's bodies. In fact, the usual reason cited in the women's press for the "ruined constitutions and shortened lives among working women" as well as among "an immense upper class" was the amount of stair climbing demanded of women by the arrangement of houses:

All physicians agree in declaring the exercise of stair-mounting to be most injurious to women; their testimony is almost unanimous as to the mischief it causes to the female constitution, for we never met a physician who did not counsel about every other of his patients to avoid the fatigue of ascending stairs. Reflecting on the necessary mounting and remounting of stairs for all women engaged in household work, or even in higher life superintending their nurseries, we are tempted to exclaim in despair, Who then can be cured?[3]

The typical house was also undesirable because of the dangers the stairs posed to young children, the noise resulting from stair climbing, and the greater number of servants required by the design. The actual number of steps in the English house was typically counted out in the women's press as if readers were unaware of the precise number:

These houses contain on an average from seven to ten flights of stairs – the number of steps is proportioned somewhat irregularly, but there are generally from twelve to fifteen steps from the kitchen to the dining-room, and from twenty to twenty-five from the dining to the drawing rooms; twenty-five to twenty-eight from drawing-room to the first floor of sleeping-apartments, and from sixteen to twenty-two from that to the second; then, if the house be a good-sized one, twelve to sixteen more, and then twelve more to the last floor. Thus we have from seventy-three or eighty-five steps to ninety or a hundred and fourteen in a single house.[4]

So debilitating to mistresses and their servants was the design of the "stair-containing house" that critics compared the conditions to those of prisons – except that in prisons, they said, the authorities had a more enlightened view of the impact of "stair-mounting" on women: "Medical men are so well agreed that it is unfit for women, that the treadmill has been discontinued in our prisons for female convicts. Nevertheless, every private house contains in its staircases a small treadmill in effect, for the benefit of the household, and especially the servants.[5]

The second aspect of middle-class houses that was of particular concern to the women's movement was the compartmentalized arrangement of rooms. Compounded by the vertical distance of the stairs, this plan was considered especially detrimental for women with children, who complained that they could neither see nor hear their children in other rooms in the house: "She has to leave her children in her second-floor room while she prepares her dinner in the underground kitchen, and she 'never knows if she shall hear the baby cry or not,' to quote the words of a poor young mother who had essayed the comforts of such a home, and who further told us that she had to toil again and again up the staircase to attend to her children, and then return to her work below."[6]

Women thus presented their critique of the house on the grounds that the house itself was unhealthy – and this did not only mean bad drainage and unventilated spaces. In feminist terms, the "arrangement" or design of the house was the cause of their poor health. The young mother quoted above, for example, claimed that after two years "her chest was weak, and the steep flights of stairs grew daily more painful to her," rather than pointing to the effects of the house's design on her ability to perform as a mother.

As a result, many English mothers looked with envy to the continental plan, which accommodated an entire family on a single floor, with rooms opening up onto one another (as in the typical Parisian apartment) rather than opening from a single hall. English women remarked how this arrangement allowed French mothers to hear and see their children in other rooms; they could be with them and yet apart from them at the same time, perhaps reading, writing letters, or visiting with a friend while their children played in a nearby room. Most appealing in the single-floor Parisian apartment was the total absence of stairs.

Although open-plan, single-floor houses had been constructed in Edinburgh, they were virtually unknown in London, where the system of land tenure inherited from the great estates had favoured large developments of terraced housing, built to nearly identical plans.[7] Two single-floor housing blocks had, however, been constructed in London by the 1860s, and both were immediately hailed in the feminist press as healthier, more comfortable, and more economical for women than the usual type of London house. One of these projects, in Finsbury, housed twenty working-class families, and the feminists who visited it in 1864 remarked on a "sensation of space and airiness," which they had "never before met in the houses of the poor."[8]

A similar twelve-roomed house at Victoria Street and Ashley Place convinced the feminists of the advantages of the plan for middle-class householders as well. The group of women journalists who toured the building found the spatial flow between rooms particularly attractive: "Once inside, we were tempted to believe ourselves back in some old country mansion, so comfortable did the long quiet passages, with suites of rooms opening one into another, as seen through the half-open door, appear.[9] Although the families living in the building had no access to a square or garden, they appeared "highly content," according to the journalists.[10] The project contained apartments varying in size from six to twenty rooms grouped around a central hall. The women visitors noted that the number of servants required in these dwellings was half as many as the same families had employed in "an ordinary *staircased* house."[11]

In addition to the need for fewer servants, the women noted the reduction in noise and the even temperature of the hall and rooms as a result of the arrangement of contiguous spaces. "There is the power to place three or more bedrooms close together," they remarked, a feature that allowed mothers to hear their children during the night. The apartments were supposedly cleaner than typical London houses because the doors opened to an interior corridor rather than to the inclement London weather. This arrangement also provided security in the building, allowing a woman more freedom: "When she desires to go out she can lock the door, and leave the key with the porter, confident that all is safe, for no backdoor or unguarded area offers an entrance to vagrants and pilferers."[12]

The late-nineteenth-century feminist press was explicit in its association of house plans with the value of women's work. A "great evil of modern life," one journalist explained, was that most educated women became "unproductive labourers." Implying that the blame lay with the architecture of houses, she continued: "Any system of house-building which would make [their work] more respectable and convenient would be valuable."[13] Although the feminists believed that the open plan on a single floor would provide "a great comfort to all women," it was apparently unacceptable to middle-class men: "We have heard almost every lady who has lived abroad commending the single-floor houses of the continent as being more comfortable to them than the narrow, staircased London houses. We do not recollect one single lady proving an exception to the rule, but occasionally they answer, 'Oh, it is very convenient, but Mr – (her husband) did not like it as well.'"[14]

Male critics associated the continental plan with the seemingly promiscuous lifestyle of the Parisians. The French tradition of interconnected rooms *en suite* was interpreted in England as "an affront to common decency," particularly the Parisian custom of using a bedroom as an extension of the drawing room.[15] "A French family may not care at all for privacy," reported the *Building News* in 1857, "[they] may see nothing objectionable in thoroughfare rooms – in having bed-chambers not only adjoining to and immediately communicating with sitting-rooms, but inaccessible except by passing through the latter. Of course, they do not feel incommoded, or they would not put up with such highly objectionable arrangement of plan. Put up with it, however, they do; and their doing so does not say much for their refinement."[16] Other common criticisms of the Parisian apartment included the lack of individual streetdoors and the sharing of public stairs, a situation that was exacerbated by the mix of classes in Parisian apartment buildings.[17] By focusing on the loss of control resulting from the Parisian plan, English men overlooked the advantages of multipurpose rooms for child care.

A journalist in the *Morning Advertiser*, however, suggested that the adoption of flats in England might enhance the institution of marriage. And on at least two occasions in the 1870s the *Architect* published plans of flats, urging their adoption by the middle class (fig. 5.1).[18] These plans

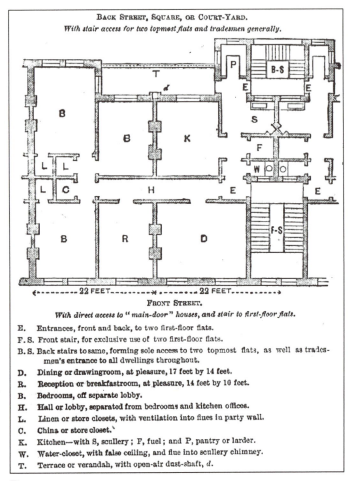

BACK STREET, SQUARE, OR COURT-YARD.
With stair access for two topmost flats and tradesmen generally.

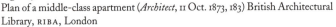

FRONT STREET.
With direct access to "main-door" houses, and stair to first-floor flats.

E. Entrances, front and back, to two first-floor flats.
F.S. Front stair, for exclusive use of two first-floor flats.
B.S. Back stairs to same, forming sole access to two topmost flats, as well as tradesmen's entrance to all dwellings throughout.
D. Dining or drawingroom, at pleasure, 17 feet by 14 feet.
R. Reception or breakfastroom, at pleasure, 14 feet by 10 feet.
B. Bedrooms, off separate lobby.
H. Hall or lobby, separated from bedrooms and kitchen offices.
L. Linen or store closets, with ventilation into flues in party wall.
C. China or store closet.
K. Kitchen—with S, scullery; F, fuel; and P, pantry or larder.
W. Water-closet, with false ceiling, and flue into scullery chimney.
T. Terrace or verandah, with open-air dust-shaft, *d*.

Figure 5.1
Plan of a middle-class apartment (*Architect*, 11 Oct. 1873, 183) British Architectural Library, RIBA, London

differed substantially from the Parisian model in that the apartments were designed to have completely separate rooms on a single floor. Nevertheless, the *Morning Advertiser*'s reporter saw clear advantages for women in the proposed buildings:

There is a great advantage to a family in having all the rooms it occupies on one floor. Less fatigue is incurred in passing from room to room than in running up and down stairs; and as a large amount of labour is thus saved, a smaller number of servants is required to attend to the wants of the family ... The wife would therefore be more like the mistress of her home than many a wife is at present; she would be able to watch and to protect her children more effectually against such accidents as arise from the ignorance or neglect of nurses.[19]

The reporter saw advantages for men, too: "We have no hesitation in saying that if houses were built in London on the plan *The Builder* has suggested, a great many professional men with limited incomes, who do not marry at present because they believe their incomes are insufficient to keep up suburban houses ... would be lured from their cosy little 'dens' or chambers ... and speedily converted into happy and comfortable Benedicts."[20] In fact, though, as architectural historian John Burnett has noted, the use of the middle-class flat in London was mostly limited to families without children.[21]

Women who dared to criticize English domestic architecture also called for an overall reduction in the size of houses, citing a direct connection between the design of their homes and women's power. "The introduction of servants' help and modern improvements into our dwellings," said Rachel B. Gleason in 1898, "seems to have multiplied and complicated domestic duties, so that women are more worn and worried than when they did their own work, and spun, wove, made, and mended for the whole family." Consequently, she said, "As the first step toward diminishing family expenses and domestic duties, let us have a small house."[22]

English feminists looked with envy at the lives of American women, whose relative freedom they attributed both to smaller families and to more advanced household technology.[23] Frances E. Willard, in speaking to the Chicago Women's League, forecast that "numberless invaluable appliances would be given to blocks of houses" in the ensuing decade, and she suggested that Pullman should apply the comforts of train cars to home life. "If men had been worried as women have by household affairs," she argued, "they would long ago have settled the whole by forming syndicates."[24]

A marked reduction in household labour was not the only reason feminists favoured small houses; they also recognized the inverse relationship between house size and the proximity of a mother to her children. "The nurseries," explained author-decorator Jane Ellen Panton, "are so far off that the mother scarcely ever climbs up to them, and in consequence has her children downstairs with her in and out of season, until they gradually absorb the grown-up atmosphere and become little prigs who care nothing for a romp."[25] Panton was quick to blame builders and architects for the unfortunate situation of women, pointing again to the English system of separate rooms as the main problem. The use of female design consultants – even unpaid ones – could only improve the relationship of houses to domestic life, she said: "All too often one is compelled to have the infant in one's room because of the absurd way in which our houses are arranged, and I do wish architects and builders ... would consult a jury of matrons, even if they will not consult their wives alone, before they set to work to give us any more houses, for really they are one and all ignorant of the commonest principles of their art as regarded from a purely feminine point of view. Why won't they recollect that one or two rooms should lead out of each other?"[26] Panton encouraged women to insist on purpose-built nurseries, to rise up against "the 'demon builder,' the cause of so very many of our domestic woes and worries," reminding them that it was demand that created supply.[27] Women, she implied, affected demand.

Panton's call for a "feminine point of view" in architecture was nevertheless not loud or powerful enough to change the well-established system of development in London. While women noted improvements in both the underground railroad system and the installation of telegraph wires in the world's largest city, they remarked that "no corresponding improvement has taken place in the dwellings of which the metropolis is composed."[28] The plans of houses designed after 1870 did not reflect changes in the status of women in the late nineteenth century; rather, the new womanhood "adjusted" the old houses by segregating children and hiring a specialist to care for them and by demanding furniture and materials that were easier to clean.

These changes in the "fit" of family life to typical middle-class houses are evident from modifications in the ways rooms were used as the century progressed, mostly as a result of women's "rearrangement" of room uses. Earlier in the nineteenth century, children had had the run of the entire middle-class home. They played in the parlour; some even slept in rooms that were seemingly intended for adult uses – for example, the dining room and drawing rooms. In the eighteenth century, the novelist and adviser to women, Maria Edgeworth, had insisted that babies sleep in the living room so that they would grow accustomed to the noise of the sewing machine and the sound of voices.[29] Similarly, children's occupation of public rooms in the early Victorian house was seen as a way of acculturating them to adult life.

It also reflected the methods of child care that were popular at the time. Experts at mid-century had emphasized the closeness of the mother-child bond in successful parenting. The phrenologists George and Andrew Combe, for example, whose ideas were the foundation of most of the child-care books of the time, described a mother's power in terms of her ability to stimulate the thirty-five "powers and organs" of the mind which they had isolated. Different characters, they believed, could be developed by the different degrees to which these faculties were stimulated. "Their supposed ability to influence the relative development of these powers and organs by applying the right stimuli," observed historian Christina Hardyment, "gave mothers some of their new sense of power." Ideally, this meant that mothers would spend as much time as possible with their children, since stimulating the correct parts of a child's mind was a long and tedious process. Andrew Combe emphasized the exclusiveness of the mother's responsibility for the child in the formation of moral and intellectual character: "To her exclusively the infant looks for that cherishing and affectionate care which its tender and delicate frame requires; and to her the child directs every appeal whether of kindness or suffering, in the full confidence that she will be ever watchful for its happiness and relief, and that from her a look or a cry will procure the requisite sympathy or aid. She alone it is who provides its nourishment, regulates its exercise, and watches over its slumbers."[30] Combe's scheme for the "ever watchfulness" of mothers depended on physical proximity: on the mother sleeping with her baby for its first six weeks of life, and on children appropriating the drawing room as their major play space in the house.

Evangelicalism, too, had positioned the mother in a room with her children by reinforcing the importance of spaces shared by mothers and children. This powerful movement within the Church of England, which had attempted to abolish slavery and to reform British morals, had projected a new ideal of family life between 1780 and 1820, positing woman as a domestic being and highlighting her role as mother. "God has thus given her all the power," the Rev. John Abbott told his readers, "that she may govern and guide them as she pleases."[31] Religion as a part of daily life was the central concern of evangelical domestic ideology. The house was thus the setting for a truly religious and moralistic existence, which was managed almost exclusively by mothers.[32] Patricia Branca, Christina Hardyment, and other historians of motherhood have noted how mid-century mothers raised their children almost single-handedly; relatively few middle-class families employed nursemaids to care for their children at that time. Just under 40,000 nursemaids served 150,000 families classified as upper-middle class in 1851. "The picture," explained Hardyment, "is not one of general remoteness of mother from child."[33]

As a result of these beliefs, public rooms in the early Victorian house were the setting of intense interaction between mothers and children. The parlour was the place for family prayers; as a kind of secularized temple, it was under the complete control of the wife and mother. Mid-century advice books for women nearly always show mothers supervising their children's activities in the drawing room.[34] Evangelical texts, too, told of mothers disciplining their children in the parlour, reinforcing its significance as the centre of maternal power.[35]

A lapse of evangelical power after mid-century made this form of space sharing in the middle-class house inconceivable. Late-Victorian children were banished from adult spaces in the home and given their own private domain. "Children had once mingled freely with adults in the public life-style of the Middle Ages, but now they became more and more excluded from adult life," historian Susan Lasdun has explained. "Both the growing concept of class, which by the eighteenth century precluded mixing outside one's own, and the strict moral code by which many parents sought to raise their children prohibited the free intercourse that children had hitherto enjoyed."[36] Images of late-nineteenth-century parlours are thus very different from the illustrations at mid-century. Typically, they show special occasions, such as Christmas or birthdays, with the nanny in the background, suggesting that the children's occupation of adult space requires her supervision (fig. 5.2).

"I can assure you, she's quite a parlour-child," said an elderly man of his spoiled granddaughter in the final years of the nineteenth century. Parlour-children were those who had spent too much time with adults. Author Jennie Chappell described this phenomenon – the result, apparently, of the lack of separate rooms for children:

I knew a parlour-child some years ago. She was an only child, as such usually are, and her mother, belonging to the middle class but with aspirations superior to her station, endeavoured to bring her little girl up to be a sort of human non-such ... There was no spare room in the house to which she might repair ... When not at school, she was constantly in the parlour in a state of hush and re-pression ... She grew up round shouldered, short-sighted, anaemic, and a martyr to 'nevers'; developing, when she grew old enough to reason, an abiding resent-ment at the training which had undermined her health in the process of making her a parlour-child.[37]

Rather than regarding children's occupation of rooms such as the parlour as a measure of intimacy between mothers and children or as a space in

Figure 5.2
Family in a drawing room (*Queen* 82 [1887]: 834) Courtesy of the Board of Trustees of the Victoria & Albert Museum

which women might set an example for their children, experts after 1870 saw such interaction as dangerous and unhealthy. It too closely resembled working-class living conditions. Even more to the point, it denied women's need for space of their own – which was increasingly being seen as a necessary accoutrement of modern motherhood – and thus foreshadowed by several decades Virginia Woolf's association of women's power with exclusive space.[38]

The spatial separation of mothers and children paralleled substantial improvements in the status of women. Progress in girls' education in the 1870s has already been mentioned; in 1869 the Municipal Franchise Act extended the vote in local elections to women taxpayers (though universal female suffrage was not gained in England until 1928). Two years earlier, in 1867, the first parliamentary debate on female suffrage had been held, though it had failed to gain support. The first Woman's Suffrage Bill, in 1870, likewise failed, but a widespread recognition of the rights of married women to own and control their own earnings and possessions was gained by the first Married Women's Property Act of 1870, though it disappointed many feminists. These political victories – monumental as they were – were not the only form of Victorian feminism. In houses all over London, middle-class women exerted their newly attained power in more private ways – by separating themselves from their children in the home.

After 1870, children occupied a completely separate spatial realm in the Victorian house: the nursery. In fact, there had been rooms set aside for children long before the nineteenth century; many medieval houses contained a "nurcerie," as did most grand houses in the eighteenth century. Historian Jonathan Gathorne-Hardy states that there were "nurcerys" as early as the thirteenth century, though these probably accommodated both women and children, rather than children exclusively.[39] In the nineteenth century, children became essential (rather than incidental) occupants of the house. "What gave [Victorian family quarters] their peculiar Victorian character," explains historian Mark Girouard, "was that they were designed for husband, wife and children, not just for husband and wife."[40]

A complete separation of parents and children was ideal. "To keep the children out of the adults' way was the really vital consideration in planning the nursery department," according to historian Jill Franklin.[41] Even Henry James promoted the separation of English children from their mothers. "The whole of the nursery quarters are isolated, as they should be, and served by a separate corridor,"[42] the American novelist remarked of Crathorne Hall. Hermann Muthesius, in his penetrating analysis of the English house, observed that British nurseries were so separate that a visitor might not even notice that the family included children. "They are strictly segregated geographically as well as ... organisationally," the German author added, "for the nurseries are always in a remote part of the house (in a side wing or on the top floor) and the children and their nurses are looked after quite separately from the kitchen upwards. The children remain separate members of the household until adolescence."[43]

Muthesius's description of the children's quarters as "from the kitchen upwards" was extremely perceptive. Since the children's spaces were increasingly segregated from the more public spaces in the Victorian house, they encroached on parts of the building that traditionally accommodated servants. While the rise of a specialist servant, the nanny, to care for children clearly paralleled the spatial separation of children from their mothers, many historians have seen architecture as the agent of change. "Plainly, until her kingdom had been firmly marked out, until her territories were sufficiently numerous for her to become a force in the land, the Nanny could not come into her own," asserts Gathorne-Hardy, assuming that the architectural changes preceded and even facilitated social transformations.[44]

This spatial separation of women and children in the final decades of the century was also facilitated by the fact that there were fewer children than before. Beginning about 1870, the middle-class birth rate in England dropped dramatically. Historians disagree on the role women played in this development. J.A. Banks, whose *Prosperity and Parenthood* was among the first to name a single cause for the change, argued that the economic depression of the 1870s caused couples to limit the size of their families in order to maintain the standard of living to which they had grown accustomed in the prosperous 1850s and 1860s. Others have seen the change in the birth rate as a result of the relative scarcity of domestic servants in the late nineteenth century. The increased availability of both contraception and abortion during the period has also been suggested.[45]

Perhaps the ways in which rooms in the home were used also convinced couples to limit the number of children they produced. The notion that a certain distance between mothers and children should be maintained at home – a space that served to distinguish middle-class motherhood from working-class motherhood and at the same time allowed women to pursue other interests – may have contributed to this dramatic drop in the middle-class birth rate. Baby bottles, perambulators, nannies, and nurseries were part of an elaborate material culture developed to bridge this growing space between mothers and children.[46]

Remote though it often was, the Victorian nursery was an essential part of even the smallest middle-class house after 1870.[47] Like the lying-in room, it was usually completely invisible in the architectural drawings, depending largely on women's allocation and rearrangement of an ordinary bedroom for children's special use, rather than on special planning on the part of the architect.[48] Eliza Warren's small house always contained a nursery for her eight children – even though the family had to forfeit a sitting room – so that the children could be kept from "rambling all over the house from attic to kitchen."[49]

More often the nursery was at the top of the house. Panton perceptively remarked that the location of most nurseries in London was evident from the street by the presence of barred windows: "I am not in the least exaggerating when I say that, especially in London, the very top rooms in a tall house are those set aside for the little ones. Pass along any of our most fashionable squares and thoroughfares, and look up at the windows. Where are the necessary bars placed that denote the nurseries? Why, at the highest windows of all. My readers can notice this for themselves, and say whether I am right or wrong."[50]

The preference for rooms at the top of the house satisfied the call for "remoteness" recommended by many experts and obviously justified the employment of a nanny, but it also reflected the late-nineteenth-century practice of giving children the "best" rooms in the house. Panton advised young mothers to allocate the "best room" in the upper part of the house, as near as possible to the mother's room.[51] The allocation of prime space in the house may have served to alleviate maternal anxiety from handing over the children to nannies; but as Franklin has noted, it also represented major changes in attitudes towards childhood. Late-nineteenth-century children were seen less as tiny versions of adults and more as "young creatures with a charm of their own."[52] Childhood was regarded as an especially vulnerable time in life, as it is today, when temperament, habits, and even taste were formed. The "best rooms" were thus seen as a wise investment in the children's future.

Many of the assumptions made about the power of domestic space on individuals recovering from illness were also applicable to the design of nurseries, presuming again that well-designed spaces fostered the healthy development of the inhabitant of that space. "The pages of Nature's secret book have been opened," exclaimed Lady Cook in 1897, echoing Chadwick's statements of more than fifty years earlier, "and have proved that the processes of evolution are very largely dependent upon the conditions of the environment."[53] "To have good and healthy children," warned Panton, "it is positively necessary to have good and healthy nurseries."[54]

Advice on the design of nurseries thus ranged from predictable recommendations for plenty of sunlight, fresh air, and "cheerful and pretty" surroundings, to objects and furnishings intended to serve less physical, didactic functions.[55] The Victorian nursery was a "lesson-ground" for "ladies and gentlemen in embryo."[56] The pictures on nursery walls, which were believed by many experts to exert an enormous influence on young children's thoughts, acted as a potent form of "silent teaching." "A child's mind is a curious thing," Panton instructed her female readers, "and receives certain memories in the shape of pictures." She recommended carefully chosen photographs and etchings, intending to instil "lesson[s] or pleasant stories," rather than pictures discarded from other rooms in the house.[57] The expression of "good taste" in the nursery would thereby instil in developing children a lasting appetite for similar objects. "By giving the dear things nice surroundings," explained Panton, "you do your best to insure nice tastes."[58]

The same counsel of "careful choice" directed the acquisition of nursery furniture. Experts warned mothers to avoid furnishings that had been discarded from other rooms and to purchase furniture that was specifically made for the nursery. The consistency of this warning in the women's literature could mean that many women continued to furnish children's rooms with adult furniture from the rest of the house. By the 1890s, however, Heal's and similar furniture stores were offering middle-class consumers a full line of nursery furniture, as well as accessories such as nursery crockery, pictures especially for children's rooms, and small-scale chairs and dressers.[59] Like the special furniture acquired for childbirth, nursery furniture expressed the vulnerability and singularity of childhood. The size of the nurseries was another point of concern among women. Most advisers suggested at least 1,000 cubic feet for each child. Mary Blanchflower's nursery was fifteen feet by twelve feet, which she considered small.[60]

Among architects, the appropriate spatial relationships between women and children were less clear. Robert Kerr, the author of a major book on house planning, advocated a significant separation of mothers and children, insisting that "the main part of the house" should be "relieved from the more immediate occupation of the Children." On the other hand, his contemporary, J.J. Stevenson, thought that the nurseries should be close to the mistress's bedroom, "for no superiority in nurses can supply a mother's oversight."[61] Kerr also admitted that a mother needed "a certain facility of access" to her children. According to him, this degree of separation was a clear mark of class: "In other words, in a house where the children are supposed to be placed under the care of less experienced and responsible attendants, the Nurseries, although still kept apart, ought to be so placed as to be under the immediate supervision of the mother, both by day and by night; secondly, in houses where superior servants are to be calculated upon, the care of the mother has only in a small degree to be provided for."[62] In spite of his relegation of children to the care of servants, Kerr's view remained conservative. "This is a maxim of English house-building," he concluded, "that no English mother, even a duchess, will confide her children wholly to other hands than her own."[63]

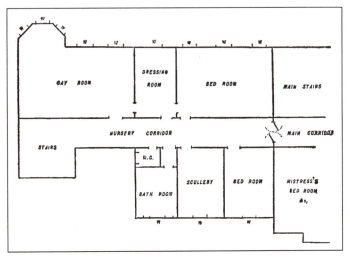

Figure 5.3
Plan of a nursery wing (Murphy, *Our Homes*, 87) Collection Canadian Centre for Architecture, Montreal

The difference between the ideal nurseries imagined by experts and the nurseries commonly found in middle-class houses was clearly considerable; most authors went to great lengths to describe the former and then suggested ways in which their recommendations could be applied to the latter. Some authors even suggested the construction of new nursery wings, with separate stairs and corridors especially scaled for children (fig. 5.3). "A stair arranged for adult legs is steep and toilsome to little ones," reminded one specialist.[64] Placed near the parents' bedroom, the ideal nursery wing was at the very least a "room apart" and a "delightful retreat," emphasizing its separateness from the rest of the house.[65]

The need for separate nurseries gave middle-class women the chance to alter what they saw as the poor arrangements of their houses. Many mothers cut doors through the interior walls in frustration over the compartmentalized arrangement of the house. "A small doorway was cut," reported Blanchflower, "to allow mother and nurse to pass easily from one room to another, without carrying baby through the passage way." If women constructed new connections between their rooms and those of their children, they were warned to include in their renovations one of the "clever padlock bolts, insuring perfect privacy when desired."[66]

The ease with which childless couples lived in the same type of house as that designed for families with children was further evidence to feminists of the poor fit between the English house and domestic life. Some houses were even blamed for childlessness. Jane and Thomas Carlyle were the oft-cited example; their home in Chelsea for thirty-eight years was a traditional English terraced house.[67] Panton and many other observers of the built environment saw the Carlyle home as both the source and the reflection of the Carlyle's unhappy relationship, stemming, of course, from their ill health. "The hideous paper and paint ... the dark windows ... all accounted to me for a great deal of Mrs Carlyle's ill-health and low spirits," stated Panton, "and for a vast quantity of Mr Carlyle's dyspepsia and ill-tempered behaviour."[68] The Carlyles could not even agree on the benefits of fresh air. Thomas Carlyle liked plenty of fresh air in the house, while his wife complained constantly of drafts. "As he never takes cold himself," Jane Carlyle said of her husband, "he can't be made to understand how sitting between two open cross windows, at midnight, in an east wind, should not be excessively bracing and healthy for me."[69] Their unhappy, unconsummated marriage was well known in the 1880s.[70] Like the houses of childless couples such as the Carlyles, houses designed for bachelors always included provision for children. In this way, bachelors' houses were no different from traditional houses, as if accommodating a childless lifestyle might prevent one from having children.[71]

The banishing of children from adult spaces in the middle-class home also meant, as Leonore Davidoff, Judith Neiswander, and others have noted, that houses could be on view to other adults more often than before.[72] At the same time the home, particularly the parlour, became more closely associated with the personality of the wife and mother. As we have seen, after 1870 advisers to women urged their readers to take control, to make decisions, and to arrange their houses in ways that satisfied their own needs. This gave rise to several new occupations for middle-class women, including interior decoration and architecture, but it also represented the association – seldom explicated at the time but widely understood – that control over domestic space represented a form of feminism.[73]

Panton, whose ideas we have heard throughout these chapters, was not a feminist in the modern sense; that is, she did not support equal rights for women. Like Catharine Beecher in the United States, she did not believe in women's higher education or that women should vote. In fact, she worried about anything that would take women out of the home; the solution to the restrictions on women's power, which clearly concerned her, was family limitation – consciously limiting the size of one's family – and she saw reformed house plans as a step towards this goal.

The major lesson of Panton's work is that nineteenth-century feminism meant far more than suffrage. She advocated feminism in a spatial sense by suggesting that Victorian women take control and manage space in their homes. "One's personal tastes were not consulted when one was put in the world," she said of being a woman, "and whether one hates it or not, does not alter the fact that a woman's sphere is domestic, more or less." A woman did little to help the female cause, she said, by "clapping on the breeches which don't fit and in which she looks hideous and indecent, and becoming that strange creature," the suffragette. "Women in the open market; women on platforms; women demanding equal rights to discuss disgusting subjects in public with men, all these will disappear and they will once more reign in their own kingdom, the realm of home."[74] Instead of suffragism, Panton advocated a much more private form of feminism: family limitation. Particularly concerned about the plight of daughters, she supported state interference to force men to support their unmarried daughters. Alternatively, she said, insurance companies might develop schemes to protect young women.[75]

Women's arrangement and decoration of their houses, according to Panton, was another way ordinary middle-class women expressed female power. The "feminine point of view" of architecture was the way in which domestic space was described and illustrated by the "lady decorators." These women depicted model houses by making perspective drawings, which required less technical knowledge than the traditional architectural drawings of plans, sections, and elevations. The perspective drawings encouraged confidence in women by showing how spaces might look if their advice was followed (fig. 5.4).

This "feminine," perspectival view was in marked contrast to the "scientific" sectional approach espoused by the building-doctors discussed in chapter 2. While the physicians' sectional drawings and models of houses emphasized the separate parts in the functioning of the whole house and the connections of the house to the outside world, the perspectives that appeared in the women's press represented a less fractured view of the home, creating the illusion of a whole. As doctors attempted to disassemble the female body – to study and differentiate its parts – in order to explain physiology and disease, women reassembled domestic spaces, as if to reconstitute the surfaces, planes, textures, surfaces, and colours of rooms lost during its scientific dissection. The feminist perspective, in this respect, overlapped with the way an architect-sanitarian such as Robert Edis described his model room at the International Health Exhibition as a "complete and indivisible thing," rather than as a collection of

Figure 5.4
Perspective view of a middle-class drawing room. (Garrett, *Suggestions for House Decoration*, facing 62) British Architectural Library, RIBA, London

"isolated articles."[76] Exterior views of architecture rarely appeared in the women's press.

Decoration was also likened to areas where women's authority was already established, such as fashion and hair design.[77] "Furniture is a kind of dress, dress is a kind of furniture, which both mirror the mind of their owner," stated Mary Eliza Haweis in *The Art of Decoration* (1881). As if subscribing to the feminine reliance on the perspective, she boosted confidence in her readers by reminding them that "a room is like a picture."[78]

This notion of the interior "perspective" was widely used by English department stores, which in the 1860s and 1870s began to exhibit "model rooms." Like the perspective drawing, these displays offered female

Figure 5.5
Typical model room (Heal and Son collection, 1894) Archive of Art and Design,
London

viewers a fairly precise view of how particular pieces of furniture, fabrics, and other objects would look in their homes (fig. 5.5). As early as the 1860s, Heal and Son, purveyors of bedroom furniture, showed "three or four suites, in different colours, placed in separate compartments in their extensive show rooms, so that customers may see the effect as it would appear at their own houses."[79] London stores published special guides for women to accompany their "fitted rooms," and these advice books nearly always included perspective views of the model rooms. It is impossible to know whether the rise of the perspective in the women's press inspired the commercial use of the model room or whether this display technique encouraged the use of perspective in women's magazines. What is certain is that the model room and the perspective drawing became popular around the same time and that both were intended to appeal to women.

"Fitted rooms" were also standard attractions at public exhibitions in the late nineteenth century.[80] As we saw in chapter 1, the International Health Exhibition (IHE) of 1884 included several model rooms.[81] Most of them were contributed by London furniture stores. For instance, there was a room furnished by Messrs Jackson and Graham of Oxford Street, which was arranged by the prominent London architect, Robert Edis (see fig. 2.3); Heal and Son also contributed a small bedroom to the exhibition (see fig. 3.10). These rooms were featured in the coverage of the IHE in ladies' magazines and in furniture-trade journals but were barely mentioned in the architectural press, a fact that underlines their appeal to women.[82]

In this way the decorators, department stores, and exhibitions inspired a form of "spatial feminism" by encouraging women to view their houses critically and to rearrange them to suit their needs. Many "lady decorators," of course, saw the profession of interior decoration as a more direct extension of women's struggle in the public world of politics, education, and urban reform. The hosting of feminist meetings in private houses (which themselves were exhibitions of their mistresses' interest in decoration) caused the line between women's public and private lives to be irreparably blurred. Haweis, for example, often opened her house, Queen House on Cheyne Walk, to public view for meetings with distinctly feminist agendas.[83] To a large audience gathered in her drawing room in 1892 she proposed the resolution that women have the right to direct parliamentary representation. Under the name of the Central National Society for Women's Suffrage, the feminists met "in the pretty rooms of this most artistic house."[84] In this same drawing room Haweis conducted a series of lectures entitled "At Homes in Chelsea." In addition to well-known male lecturers, the speakers included three women: Sarah le Grand, Mrs Humphry Ward, and Lady Jephson.[85]

Similarly, the drawing room of political activist Emmeline Pankhurst's "large, old-fashioned but comfortable" house on Russell Square was the regular location of feminist meetings: "It was impossible to look at Mrs Pankhurst's earnest face and hear her eloquent, burning words and not feel she was an enthusiastic believer in her own sex and their rights. She is deeply interested in this question, and holds large drawing-room meetings, where may be heard many of the foremost women speakers." Pankhurst, too, was "an authority on decoration" and was employed with Emerson and Company on Regent Street.[86] In this capacity, she "placed artistic furniture within the reach of the large number of those English people, who possessed only of small means, have hitherto been unable to beautify their homes," as well as employing a large number of women.

It is no coincidence that many ardent feminists were interested in interior decoration. The Haweis and Pankhurst drawing rooms, frequented by those working on "women's questions," must have served as subtle evidence of the compatibility of women's political duties and domestic duties; house decoration was of service to the women's movement, rather than forcing suffragists to neglect their homes and families. At the end of an interview in her drawing room, Mrs Pankhurst's four children and husband burst through the door. "Does this not prove conclusively,"

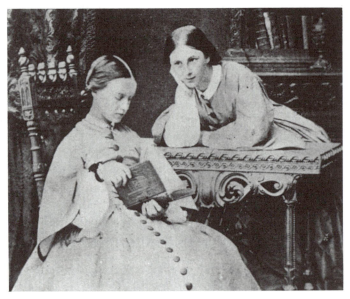

Figure 5.6
Portrait of Millicent and Agnes Garrett (Strachey, *Millicent Garrett Fawcett*, facing 16) Courtesy of McGill University Libraries, Montreal

asked her husband, "that neither business nor politics can in any way take from all that we desire and look for in the wife and mother?"[87]

Agnes and Rhoda Garrett, the first professional decorators in England, had equally close links to mainstream feminism.[88] As sister and cousin to two of the most visible and active feminists in the Victorian women's movement, they were well connected within London's growing network of professional women. Agnes Garrett was the sister of Millicent Garrett Fawcett, the pioneer in the struggle to gain the vote for British women, and Elizabeth Garrett Anderson, the first woman physician in England (fig. 5.6).[89] Both Agnes and Millicent Garrett had been active in John Stuart Mill's campaign for women's suffrage.[90] This "good connection," coupled with "honest good work," contributed to the cousins' immediate success in the new field of house decoration, noted Agnes Garrett in 1890.[91]

The Garretts' book, unlike Haweis's and Panton's, was limited to advice on house decoration.[92] Their feminist political connections brought them several major commissions. In addition to work at the new women's colleges at Oxford and Cambridge (of which no record has survived), they designed the furniture for Standen – Philip Webb's house for the

Beale family – in 1892–94.[93] Mrs Beale was related to Dorothy Beale, principal of Cheltenham Ladies' College, a celebrated girls' school founded in 1853. In the early 1870s, Agnes and Rhoda Garrett also decorated the home of Elizabeth Garrett Anderson and her husband.[94] The two Garrett decorators thus made no secret of their feminist political agenda. Rhoda Garrett worked with Josephine Butler on the repeal of the Contagious Diseases Acts, which "marked a new and more particular specification of sexuality within sanitary discourse."[95] She was pictured in the *Graphic* in 1874 wearing the costume of a "platform woman."[96] The Garretts spent considerable time with the Fawcetts and the Andersons. "The three households were in constant communication," noted Ray Strachey in her 1931 biography of Millicent Garrett Fawcett.[97]

The Garretts worked in the modes we have already identified as feminist. Their book, *Suggestions for House Decoration* (1876), contained six interior perspectives illustrating their advice. They designed a model bedroom for the Paris Exhibit of 1878; and after Rhoda's death (in 1882), Agnes contributed a model boudoir to the Bristol Exhibition of Women's Industries of 1885.[98] Their Paris exhibition – and presumably much of their other work – outraged male critics. The author and decorator Lewis F. Day was their most outspoken critic. He called the furniture in the Paris bedroom "clumsy and tasteless," "with no trace of art in it and no particular evidence of taste." "As a room it is passable," he allowed, but "as an exhibition it is rather ridiculous." Day made no effort to conceal the sexist basis of his criticism. The Garretts' display in Paris, he said, was proof of "how little is enough to satisfy the ambition of lady-decorators."[99]

The "containment" of decoration within the home was a significant factor in the gendering of the Victorian house. As the house decoration and the perspective view increasingly came to be associated with women in the 1870s and 1880s, the design of domestic interiors in general also came to be regarded as women's domain. "The architectural house-decorator does for the inside of a house exactly what the architect does for the outside," was a typical explanation of the interior decorator's responsibilities.[100] This notion of the woman arranging and even designing the interior of her home was relatively new. As Neiswander has noted, books on domestic architecture at mid-century rarely mentioned the interiors of houses, suggesting by their silence that rooms were consistent with the architectural style of a building's exterior. Most books on houses written in the 1850s were intended for architects or labourers. None was intended for women.

With the vast literature produced for women on house interiors after about 1870, a division of the house along gendered lines occurred.[101] Women's predilection for decoration fitted well with Victorian theories of sexual difference, which claimed that because of the smallness of their brains, women were better at arranging or finishing work started by men rather than initiating the work themselves. "Her intellect is not for invention or creation, but for sweet ordering, arrangement, and decision," stated John Ruskin in *Sesame and Lilies*.[102] But more important for the women's cause was the nonthreatening nature of this "interior" occupation. Critics of Victorian feminism claimed that involvement in politics or business would make women masculine.[103] A cartoon by Linley Sambourne in *Punch*, "A Troubled Dream of the Future" (fig. 5.7), illustrated the fears of antisuffragists that women politicians would even dress as men. The accommodation of suffragist meetings in drawing rooms, the presence of loving children and husbands during interviews with the feminist press, and the obvious interest of some feminists in decoration must have done much to defuse Victorian antisuffragism. While the "empire of woman [was] no longer the empire of the hearth," this did not mean she had necessarily lost interest in that hearth.[104]

Millicent Fawcett, throughout her long campaign for suffrage, stressed how women's experiences in the home – "the motherhood of women" – was a good reason in favour of enfranchisement: "If men and women were exactly alike, the representation of men would represent us; but not being alike, that wherein we differ is unrepresented under the present system. The motherhood of women, either actual or potential, is one of those great facts of everyday life which we must never lose sight of. To women as mothers is given the charge of the home and the care of the children ... We want the home and the domestic side of things to count for more in politics and in the administration of public affairs than they do at present." Fawcett held that extending the vote to women would "strengthen true womanliness in women" (for example, women would be good economists because of their experience as homemakers) and that what made a woman a "useful member of society in [her] private life" would make her excel in "public duties."[105] The visibility of the suffragettes' homes and their apparent interest in decoration undoubtedly reinforced this point of view.

Although feminists were restricted from the practice of architecture – which presumably meant the design of exteriors – they played an active role in the construction of several entire buildings in London. Together with James Beale (of Standen) and another lawyer, John Westlake, Agnes

Figure 5.7
Cartoon of a suffragist (*Punch*, 14 June 1884, 279) Courtesy of McGill University Libraries, Montreal

Garrett was influential in the formation of a limited company for the erection of housing for women. The Ladies' Residential Chambers Ltd., as it was called, was the second company formed for this purpose.[106] A third company, the Ladies' Residential Chambers Company, was formed in 1891.[107] These companies constructed at least three large blocks of housing in London for middle-class women.[108] The first project, the Ladies' Residential Chambers on Chenies Street, opened in 1889 (figs. 5.8 and 5.9). Designed by architect James McKean Brydon, the building contained "distinct sets of rooms, each having its own front door." Each flat consisted of two or three rooms in addition to a pantry. Kitchen and dining facilities, however, were shared, allowing women to enjoy the

Figure 5.8
Perspective of Chenies Street Ladies' Chambers (*Builder*, 9 Nov. 1889, facing 332)
Collection Canadian Centre for Architecture, Montreal

"advantages of co-operative housekeeping."[109] Also in 1889 the foundation stone of Sloane Gardens House was laid in London's Lower Sloane
Street. The largest of the three projects, it was intended to house 150
women.[110] Three years later the York Street Ladies' Chambers opened its
doors to middle-class women (figs. 5.10 and 5.11). As in the Chenies
Street project, the tenants were expected to dine communally, "with club
conveniences." Designed by architects Balfour and Turner, the York
Street project was planned to have sixty sets of rooms.[111]

The construction of these buildings marked an enormous victory in
the nineteenth-century women's movement. First, it acknowledged in
real ways the need to accommodate unmarried, independent women, a
group that occupied a larger proportion of the population than ever before. Second, it recognized that the design of traditional middle-class
housing did not suit the needs of single women. By 1881 London had
461,593 spinsters to its 380,763 bachelors. While there were 121 spinsters
to every 100 bachelors in the metropolis, the rest of England and Wales
had a ratio of only 102 spinsters to every 100 bachelors. "London is the

Figure 5.9
Chenies Street Ladies' Chambers today (A. Adams)

best place for the unemployed female," observed Allerdale Grainger in an analysis of the census returns of 1881.[112] Finally, the design and construction of purpose-built housing offered women a safe and protected environment in the unpredictable city, thwarting fears about the chastity of independent, professional "ladies."

Many of these women, forced to support themselves financially, worked as teachers, nurses, and in other professional capacities. The "life of a bachelor girl in a big city" became associated with diverse professions: "Opposite her is a medical student, and by her side a teacher in one of the girls' public day schools. The woman with the thin, worn face, in the well-cut black dress, is the head of a department in a great drapery house, and the curly-haired, round-face girl next her is studying at the Guildhall School of Music. Farther on is a lady in a sage-green dress, and

Figure 5.10
York Street Ladies' Chambers (A. Adams)

with somewhat rampant locks, who draws for the illustrated papers. There are journalists and nurses and girl-clerks by the dozen."[113] The demand for women's housing, "a new problem," became "a side issue of the vexed Woman's Question."[114]

The architects of the Chenies Street Ladies' Chambers, the York Street Ladies' Chambers, and Sloane Gardens House met the challenge of housing independent women in different ways. Brydon's Chenies Street project represented the most conventional solution. Apart from the shared dining room in the basement (and the absence of individual kitchens), these ladies' chambers were simply ordinary flats, each containing two or three rooms and a pantry. Providing "an excellent combination of privacy and co-operation," the arrangement of the building allowed each tenant to hold keys to the main door and to her own apart-

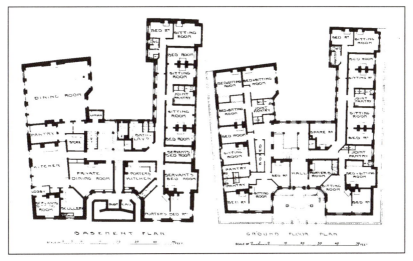

Figure 5.11
Plan of York Street Ladies' Chambers (*Architectural Design*, May–June 1978, 357) Collection
Canadian Centre for Architecture, Montreal

ment. Service was controlled by the individual tenant. She could hire a
servant at a fixed hourly rate or make her own weekly or monthly arrangements.[115] The architectural press pointed to the hall and stone staircase, "both lined to a height of about 5 ft. with glazed pattern tiles."[116]

The design of Balfour and Turner's York Street building was much less
conventional, offering various types of accommodation for women.
Some units were to be shared by two or three women, and while some
units were simple bed-sitting rooms, others contained two bedrooms,
two sitting rooms, and a shared pantry. This arrangement, termed "co-
flatting," was deemed less successful than the more private, individual-
ized units of Brydon's project. "This system of sharing," observed a critic,
"introduces an unnecessary additional complication in life."[117]

Sloane Gardens House, which was intended for women earning far
less than the tenants in the other two projects, consisted almost exclusively of bed-sitting rooms. The dining room operated on the "restaurant
principle," and bathrooms were managed on a "penny-in-the-slot principle." There were, in addition, drawing, reading, and music rooms for the
use of the tenants. Alice Zimmern, who authored an extensive article on
the projects in 1900, considered that this arrangement provided "the
greatest happiness of the greatest number."[118] All three of these London
projects echoed the proposals for "feminist apartment hotels" made by
Charlotte Perkins Gilman in the United States.[119]

An influential fourth project (which was never constructed) was described by Gilbert Parker, a Canadian, at the International Women's Congress in 1889. Parker's scheme was planned for 400 women and was expected to "bear some resemblance to Sloane Gardens House," though it would be "larger and cheaper." English women were shocked to hear that the rooms would not have fireplaces – "that Englishwoman's palladium, the individual hearth." The building was to have three different kinds of accommodation: 70 double-bedded rooms, 50 large single ones, and 280 small rooms.[120]

These housing projects are evidence of a complex feminist network that was in operation within the British architectural profession by the 1870s. While John McKean Brydon was designing the Chenies Street Ladies' Chambers, he was also working on another major public building for women, the New Hospital for Women on Euston Road (fig. 5.12).[121] This building presumably followed sanitary standards, the design committee having benefited from "the advice and co-operation of Miss Florence Nightingale and Sir Douglas Galton on sanitary and other arrangements."[122] The commission for both the housing project and the hospital – which was later called the Elizabeth Garrett Anderson Hospital – probably came to Brydon through personal and professional connections with the Garretts, who had apprenticed under him.[123] The success of this "architectural feminism" depended to a large extent on the public and private lives of the so-called Queen Anne architects.

In 1867, Brydon had moved to London from Glasgow, where he had been an assistant to architect John James Stevenson. Flora and Louisa Stevenson, the architect's sisters, were active in the women's movement in Scotland.[124] In addition, a close family friend of Stevenson, J.G. Skelton Anderson, married Elizabeth Garrett in 1871. From that moment on, the women's cause had faithful and powerful architectural allies.[125] Eustace Balfour – of Balfour and Turner – was the brother of Arthur J. Balfour, Britain's prime minister from 1902 to 1905; his sister, Eleanor Mildred Balfour, or Mrs Sidgwick, was the well-known advocate of women's higher education, who was principal of Newnham College, Cambridge, from 1892 to 1910. Eustace Balfour had apprenticed with Basil Champneys, the architect of Newnham College, before setting up his own practice in 1879.[126]

Both the New Hospital for Women and Newnham College represent the culmination of several of the themes considered in this study. Although Brydon's hospital was obviously a public building, its architectural imagery was clearly drawn from the realm of private, middle-class

Figure 5.12
Elizabeth Garrett Anderson Hospital (A. Adams)

domestic architecture; it resembled a large house. Like other buildings in the Queen Anne style, the new hospital was constructed of brick. It consisted of three interconnected sections, as if it occupied several existing houses rather than being purpose-built. The steeply pitched gabled roofs, elaborately carved tall chimneys, and projecting bay windows (which are somewhat altered today) also contributed to the "domestic" character of the architecture.

The architect of Newnham College, Cambridge (fig. 5.13) – another significant public building, in that it was the second women's college at the university – employed a similar architectural language. Like the hospital, the college was built on a characteristically domestic scale, appearing more as a conglomeration of houses than a massive new institution. Designed by Champneys from 1874 to 1910, the college was largely the result of the efforts of Millicent and Henry Fawcett to integrate women into Cambridge University.[127]

Figure 5.13
Newnham College, Cambridge University (A. Adams)

This appearance of domesticity was common to many other new women's institutions, for example, Somerville College and Lady Margaret Hall at Oxford, Girton College at Cambridge, and the School of Medicine for Women in London.[128] As Deborah Weiner has pointed out, the Queen Anne style was also adopted for the new London board schools, following the passage of the Education Act of 1870.[129] Like the role of the middle-class house in Victorian feminism, the appearance of the house played a subtle but significant part in the acceptance of the architecture of social re-form in the public landscape. Edward Robert Robson, the schools board's chief architect, even referred to the board schools as "homes of educa-tion."[130] Queen Anne architecture was seen as purposefully feminist be-cause both the building types and the architects – through their association with well-known Victorian feminists – were seen as embodying this notion of "feminine regulation."[131] Like the sickroom, the lying-in room, and the healthy house, buildings such as the New Hospital for Women and Newn-ham College were manifestations of a distinctly feminist material culture.

The step from architecture *for* women to architecture *by* women was much larger than most feminists imagined and was facilitated to some ex-tent by the association of Queen Anne architecture with feminist issues. In 1898 Ethel Charles became the first woman member of the Royal Insti-tute of British Architects (RIBA). Two years later her sister, Bessie Charles, also became an architect.[132] As early as 1874, however, the architect E.W. Godwin had stated a case for "lady architects": "A young man, or youth, is 'made' an architect by being allowed to study under an architect in his office for three, four, or five years ... His sister may be better qualified for an architectural student than he: may have the power of design in her: may have a special eye for colours, or at any rate greater power of adaptability. I see nothing to stay the exercise of these powers. I know of nothing that could impede her progress as an architect ... The right sort being found, there is before her a wide field of usefulness."[133] Panton, too, had frequently stated that houses would be truly improved only when women were permitted to become architects. "I suppose we must await our lady architect before these [improvements] are universal, or before we get a really perfect house, from a woman's point of view at least."[134]

The feminist inclinations of Queen Anne architects extended far beyond their network of family and friends and beyond the isolated pleas for women architects. Many of the drawings produced by the Queen Anne architects show how both the sanitarians' ideas and the "feminine" point of view had affected architectural representation as early as the 1870s. A drawing by Godwin, for example, of an unidentified house from as early as 1871 can be seen as a hybrid of several modes examined in this study (fig. 5.14). The section – an unusual drawing to show a scheme of interior decoration – was reminiscent of Teale's drawing of healthy houses; conspicuously absent, of course, are any graphic indications of the circulation of deadly gases in the rooms of the house. Godwin's house is healthy. In addition, a woman appears in the drawing as a vital part of the decorative scheme of the house. Godwin's house is politically progressive. Finally, the ease with which the drawing could be read – relative to typical sectional drawings, which were much more technical – reflected the same spirit of accessibility as the model rooms featured at public exhibitions and department stores.[135]

The eventual acceptance of women architects in England at the turn of the century was based on their proven abilities in the two social debates examined in this study: sanitary reform and social reform. The association of "successful" professional women with the early housing projects undoubtedly helped their case as well. Ethel and Bessie Charles, for example, lived in Balfour and Turner's York Street Chambers.[136]

It is often assumed that the history of women and architecture in England began with Ethel Charles's acceptance by the RIBA in 1898. However, both the women's press and the built environment provide ample evidence that women's manipulation of space began long before then, in the ways they adjusted their houses to fit modern motherhood, the feminization of interior decoration, and the construction of purpose-built

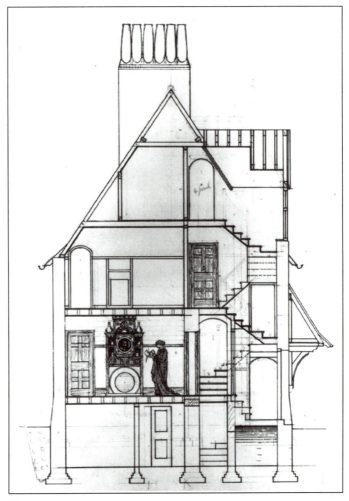

Figure 5.14
House section by E.W. Godwin. Drawings Collection, RIBA, London

housing for women. The turn of the century, in fact, marked the end rather than the beginning of a period when women enjoyed considerable control over the domestic spaces they inhabited. Largely as a result of reforms enacted by doctors and women, architects reappeared on the scene as the century drew to a close, functioning as designers of everything that women had been encouraged to oversee for three decades: interior design, furniture, and in some cases even dress. As the control of domestic space, particularly interior decoration, returned to men's control, English women returned to motherhood.[137]

Conclusion

The close association of houses, bodies, and women in England was short-lived – approximately thirty years – but it was profound. The end of the story occurred around the turn of the century, when Mrs Plunkett's call for women and plumbers to do their whole duty was realized, at least in England. Contrary to her prediction, however, the need for doctors continued. By 1900, many of the ideas about domestic architecture that had emerged as aspects of health reform and feminism in Britain were incorporated into architect-designed houses and neighbourhoods. Doctors returned to treating people's bodies separately from their houses; and women, denied their role as inspectors and designers of domestic architecture, returned to motherhood.

Most twentieth-century houses were smaller than their predecessors, and the rooms were less segregated and specialized. In the first decade of the new century, the English-speaking world witnessed the meteoric rise of the "bungalow," a fairly compact house with a remarkably open plan and little or no provision for servants.[1] Bungalows featured kitchens that were integral parts of the major living spaces rather than being separate rooms in the back. They represented a less formal, more natural, and decidedly healthier way to live.

The home economics movement, as it developed in the early twentieth century, revisited many of the ideas that had first been suggested by sanitary science. It recommended the planning of kitchens, in particular, on scientific principles. But its importance as a link between efficient house planning, science, and women's power extended far beyond the rearrangement of kitchens. The little material that has survived illuminating the response of girls and women to the rationalization of their houses through home economics classes is extremely telling with regard to architecture. Home economics instruction involved an enormous amount of information on the process of building construction, and the students did not simply absorb this architectural education passively; they applied their knowledge in the design of buildings.[2]

As the century progressed, the middle class in large cities increasingly found the apartment house an acceptable place to call home. Some apartments had combined dining and living rooms, a pairing of functions that was to become a standard feature of middle-class houses a half-century later. Apartments were particularly attractive to women, as many scholars have noted, because of the ease with which they could be maintained and the cooperative nature of their planning.[3] These profound changes in middle-class domestic life have been variously attributed by architectural historians to the impact of modernism, the revolutionary ideas of heroic architects, and even the lack of servants for the middle class.[4] In North America, they have often been read as hallmarks of the Progressive era. The seeds of a more rational, healthier middle-class house, however, were perceptible in the literature of health reform and feminism long before the turn of the century.

The medical and feminist sources on domestic architecture reveal as much about what the English middle-class house in the final decades of the nineteenth century was *not* as they do about its real position in social change. For example, the house was *not* a safe, protective shelter, removed from a dangerous and unpredictable Victorian city. Between 1870 and 1900, middle-class houses were considered much more poisonous and dangerous than public spaces or working-class neighborhoods, the subject of earlier reforms. The continued spread of disease even after the development of the germ theory was conveniently blamed on both architecture and women as doctors expanded their professional territory. Public health was debated in the language and culture of architecture, explicitly in places such as the International Health Exhibition of 1884 (where the supposedly typical middle-class house was portrayed as a hodgepodge of sanitary errors) and implicitly in the reform and regulation of ordinary houses.

Alternative sources to those traditionally used in architectural history also reveal the fiction of the middle-class home as a "separate sphere," which presumes that it was antithetical to women's political struggles in the nineteenth century. This ideology of separate spheres still forms the basis of most interpretations of late-nineteenth-century housing. But as a different approach reveals, the house played a major role in Victorian feminism as a place where women proved their readiness for changing ideals and exhibited their competence as mothers, managers, and healers; the house offered opportunity, rather than being an institution that confined women or limited their power.

In particular, women's mastery of domestic architecture in health reform laid the groundwork for their entry into the profession as architects, and it may have facilitated the acceptance of women physicians, too. It certainly strengthened the general feminist cause in Britain. There is also some evidence that the links made by feminists between women's emancipation and plumbing occurred simultaneously on an international scale and may have been even more explicit in the United States. During her speech at the 1882 conference held at Greenwood Lake, New Jersey, the feminist reformer Isabella Beecher Hooker urged the large crowd of suffragettes assembled before her to master the plumbing systems in their houses. Perhaps encouraged by her half-sister, Catharine, whose interests in technology, feminism, and housing had inspired her own design of the American Woman's Home thirteen years earlier, Mrs Hooker saw the relation between feminism and plumbing quite clearly. It was her own practice, she admitted, to inspect the work of a plumber "until she understood every point of it."[5]

Primary sources on the history of medicine and women show that improvements in domestic architecture were not the innovations of Victorian architects, who actually played fairly subordinate roles in the reform of houses based on health and women's concerns; they were, rather, the achievements of medical experts and women. This realization should cause architectural historians to re-examine the so-called reform styles of the late nineteenth century, the Arts and Crafts movement, the Queen Anne style, and the Aesthetics movement. Traditional art and architectural histories have described the architects involved in these efforts as "progressive," suggesting that their inclination to design clothing, textiles, furniture, and other household artifacts was a mark of their growing power. As we have seen, many of these areas had been the responsibility of middle-class women decades earlier.

Indeed, evidence in both the women's press and the medical press locates architects far from the cutting edge of reform. Their penchant to reclaim the domestic interior and its associated decorative arts as the province of the house architect in the final years of the last century was really a futile attempt on the part of a profession desperate to regain the

Figure 6.1
Architect G.G. Hoskins confronted by a sewer rat (Hoskins, *An Hour with a Sewer Rat*) Courtesy, Hagley Museum and Library

home as its exclusive professional turf; British architects, such as Godwin and Charles Rennie Mackintosh, for example, renewed and re-emphasized their role as artists in these movements, having lost the battle to be seen as scientists. Architect George Gordon Hoskins published *An Hour with a Sewer Rat* in 1879. This humorous book told of a late-night visit paid to his office by a sewer rat, who proceeded to instruct the architect on the subject of house drainage (fig. 6.1). "I dare say you know more about sewer rats than sewers," said the rodent to the perplexed architect.[6]

Because of the tension between medical and architectural professional responsibilities, it fell to women to regulate, control, and reform the late-nineteenth-century house. As doctors disassembled the middle-class house in their popularized sectional drawings, women reconstituted its ailing parts in the practice and literature of feminism, enclosing and protecting the home. In this process, they blurred the boundaries between the private and public spheres. As a profession, architects never fully regained the middle-class house as their exclusive province.

Further study of other social issues may uncover additional incidents of women gaining responsibility for particular spaces as male professionals fought for control. Later in the century, for example, housing and interior design became a recognized "ghetto" for women architects (along with historic preservation), as male architects struggled once again to redefine the profession. And in North America at least, even the nature of women's bodies, particularly the design of their clothing and their supposed need for separate sanitary facilities, were suggested as reasons to exclude them from professional schools of architecture.[7]

Perhaps, in the end, the health movement and the women's movement were simply two aspects of a larger phenomenon in the late nineteenth century which assumed a new relationship of women to their things and especially to their houses. Whether it was the choice of a career in the newly feminized field of interior decoration, the inspection of faulty drainpipes, the rearrangement of a bedroom for a sick child, confinement during childbirth and recovery, or the overt criticism of her house, the Victorian middle-class woman assumed a new level of responsibility for the relationship of bodies and space. This action was often, though not always, on the advice of a medical expert. Architects reacted rather than acting; they participated at the end of a well-established reform movement rather than initiating reforms through their architecture as we have been led to believe.

In this century, the hospital has taken over from the home as the main site of middle-class health care. Further study of the relations of bodies and buildings through the arrangement of the urban hospital may show that this same attitude of female regulation persisted beyond 1900, albeit in a new form. The siting of nurses' residences and maternity hospitals in relation to general hospital buildings, for example, suggests that a careful degree of separation was maintained between women and the centre of health-care institutions in the early twentieth century, much as the lying-in room was isolated in the Victorian middle-class house.[8] In other words, women workers and patients in the twentieth-century hospital are still understood in Mrs Warren's terms as being simultaneously a blessing and a curse.

The boundaries between domestic architecture and social institutions in the late nineteenth century were much more fluid than the ubiquitous "separate spheres" theory has allowed us to explore. In some cases this ambiguity is in fact the key to the true meaning of the buildings with regard to gender issues. The architecture of small urban hospitals – for example, Brydon's Elizabeth Garrett Anderson hospital of 1889–90 – has been completely overlooked in the literature on hospital history. Too modest to merit the scholarly attention given to large urban institutions, this early hospital for women had a distinctly domestic appearance. Covered porches, bay windows, and small rooms helped to mask the scientific processes that were enacted inside its brick walls and perhaps eased the general transition of women into the city. The building's houselike appearance, too, in addition to its role as an expression of female power, was an illustration of the gradual movement of health care out of the home. Were early-twentieth-century hospitals simply containers for medical technologies or were they themselves "machines for healing," like the Victorian house? Schools, libraries, clubs, colleges, and convents are now attracting serious scholarly attention as evidence of this "deflation" of the middle-class house in the twentieth century.[9] Each of them accommodated a function or functions that had previously taken place at home. Architecture is indeed a lucid illustration of this important transformation.

Doctors and architects also continued to compete as expert designers of hospital environments well into the twentieth century. In 1916, Sir Henry Burdett commented to the American Hospital Association on the lack of progress made by the architectural profession in the design of hospitals. He suggested that "a reduction in the evils and disappointments now experienced when buildings are completed" could be avoided by working directly with a physician in the design process.[10]

Issues of gender illuminate the essentially *public* nature of domestic architecture.[11] As we have seen, the final three decades of the nineteenth century were a time of intense turmoil and experimentation, when professional and political power were argued in architectural terms. Houses, bodies, and women were vital parts of that debate, rather than being passive recipients or mere reflections of social ideals.

Notes

INTRODUCTION

1 Warren, *How I Managed My Children*, 7.
2 Jane H. Walker, *Handbook for Mothers*, 1.
3 Panton, *Kitchen to Garret*, 39.
4 On architectural and urban history, see Burnett, *Social History;* Clark, *American Family Home;* Forty, *Objects of Desire;* Girouard, *Sweetness and Light;* Handlin, *American Home;* Jeffrey, "The Family as Utopian Retreat"; Wright, *Moralism and the Model Home.* On the cults of domesticity and true womanhood, see Ryan, *Empire of the Mother;* Smith-Rosenberg, "Female World of Love and Ritual"; Welter, "Cult of True Womanhood."
5 Houghton, *Victorian Frame*, 343.
6 Houghton cited Ruskin's lecture "Of Queen's Gardens" as "the most important single document I know for the characteristic idealization of love, woman, and the home in Victorian thought" (ibid., 343).

CHAPTER ONE

1 This description of the Old London Street at the International Health Exhibition is based on observations reported in "The International Health Exhibition," *Builder,* 3 May 1884, 601–2; "The Health Exhibition," *Builder,* 17 May 1884, 687–8; Hart, "International Health Exhibition"; Sala, "Health Exhibition"; *International Health Exhibition Official Guide,* 45–50; and Galton, "International Health Exhibition."

2 *Illustrated London News*, 2 Aug. 1884, 94.

3 *Art Journal*, n.s., 4 (1884): 161.

4 *Illustrated London News*, 2 Aug. 1884, 91.

5 *International Health Exhibition Official Guide*, 7.

6 Health exhibitions had already been held in England in conjunction with the annual meetings of the Social Science Association, beginning with Leeds (1871), followed by Norwich (1873), Glasgow (1874), Brighton (1875), and Liverpool (1876). The Sanitary Institute held a similar exhibition in 1879. See Hart, "International Health Exhibition," 35.

7 Ibid.

8 For information on Chadwick's career, see Briggs, "Public Opinion"; Finer, *Life and Times*; and R.A. Lewis, *Edwin Chadwick*.

9 Chadwick, *Report*, 369.

10 This act established a Central Board of Health for five years. Towns with a particularly high mortality rate were required to establish their own boards of health and appoint medical officers. It was not until the act of 1875, however, that these requirements were enforced. After 1875, all towns were required to appoint a medical officer of health and to supply their inhabitants with clean water, proper drainage, and sewerage.

11 Walvin, *Victorian Values*, 34.

12 Goubert, *Conquest of Water*, 42.

13 The IHE produced twenty-eight handbooks and hosted thirty-six lectures and fourteen conferences. These were recorded in twenty volumes of reports. See *Health Exhibition Literature*.

14 *International Health Exhibition Official Guide*, 11.

15 No traces of the IHE have survived on the site. Today the grounds are occupied by Imperial College of Science and Technology, which was established in 1907 through the federation of the Royal College of Science, the Royal School of Mines, and City and Guilds College. See "Imperial College of Science and Technology," in Weinreb and Hibbert, eds., *The London Encyclopaedia*, 405. For a detailed account of the history of the Royal Horticultural Society garden, see Sheppard, ed., *Survey*, 124–32. The area behind the Royal Albert Hall also had been used by the International Medical & Sanitary Exhibition of 1881. See *International Medical & Sanitary Exhibition Official Catalogue*.

16 For a description of the vendors along Exhibition Road in South Kensington, see *Architect*, 23 Aug. 1884, 114. The statistics on visitors were reported in *Architect*, 8 Nov. 1884, 296.

17 "Our Insane-itary Guide to the Health Exhibition," *Punch*, 14 June 1884, 277.

18 *Architect*, 23 Aug. 1884, 114.

19 For further information on the international pavilions, see *Architect*, 23 Feb. 1884, 129–30. The entry to the Belgian pavilion was illustrated in the *Illustrated London News*, 2 Aug. 1884, 108; outside dining and a stand offering mineral waters were adjacent to the pavilion.

20 Other health exhibitions also featured water fountains illuminated with coloured light. See "The Manchester International Health Exhibition," *Sanitary Record*, 10 May 1895, 1613.

21 On the proliferation of fountains in public space as symbols of what he called the "conquest" of water, see Goubert, *Conquest of Water*, 79–82.

22 *Illustrated London News*, 2 Aug. 1884, 106.

23 Hart, "International Health Exhibition," 55; *International Health Exhibition Official Guide*, 56.

24 *International Health Exhibition Official Guide*, 56.

25 *Journal of the Society of Arts*, 28 Nov. 1884, 41.

26 *International Health Exhibition Official Guide*, 56.

27 Hart, "International Health Exhibition," 40, 55–6.

28 *Journal of the Society of Arts*, 28 Nov. 1884, 55.

29 "Our Insane-itary Guide to the Health Exhibition," *Punch*, 28 June 1884, 309.

30 Francis Smith, *People's Health*, 229–38. For a detailed account of Snow's discovery, see Cosgrove, *History of Sanitation*, 91–8. For an explanation of how cholera was actually transmitted, see Sheppard, *London 1808–1870*, 247–8. See also Longmate, *King Cholera*.

31 Cosgrove, *History of Sanitation*, 104–5.

32 Brack, "Architecture of Health."

33 The Metropolis Local Management Act of 1855 had a dual mandate. It was to create many other district boards of works, which were to look after the construction and maintenance of local sewers, and to form the Metropolitan Board of Works to build a general system of main drainage. See A.F. Green, "London's Drainage," 149.

34 Sheppard, *London 1808–1870*, 284.

35 A.F. Green, "London's Drainage."

36 "The Metropolitan Main Drainage," *Illustrated London News*, 19 Feb. 1859, 173; "Main Drainage of the Metropolis," *Illustrated London News*, 27 Aug. 1859, 203.

37 Goubert, *Conquest of Water*, 61–7.

38 A.F. Green, "London's Drainage," 149.

39 "The Metropolitan Main Drainage," *Illustrated London News*, 19 Feb. 1859, 173.

40 "New Inventions: The Hercules Street-Cleansing Machine," *Sanitary Record*, 15 Feb. 1890, 402.

41 There are no extant images of this building; it was described in the *International Health Exhibition Official Guide*, 44.

42 *Builder*, 17 May 1884, 688.

43 "Our Insane-itary Guide to the Health Exhibition," *Punch*, 9 Aug. 1884, 65.

44 Ibid.

45 *Builder*, 17 May 1884, 688.

46 It was recommended to visitors that they first visit Old London Street, then proceed to the Prince of Wales's and water companies' pavilion. See *International Health Exhibition Official Guide*, 13.

47 *Builder*, 3 May 1884, 601.

48 This may have been due to restraints of the site, but it was also completely consistent with other nineteenth-century exhibitions. Burton Benedict has described this common technique of "miniaturization" in the construction of models of cities, parks, and streets at world's fairs as a way of impressing the public and expressing control of the simulated environment. See Benedict, *Anthropology of World's Fairs*, 17.

49 "Our Insane-itary Guide to the Health Exhibition," *Punch*, 2 Aug. 1884, 49.

50 *Builder*, 17 May 1884, 687.

51 *International Health Exhibition Official Guide*, 3.

52 The scale of the exhibits, according to visitors, was also extremely ambiguous. Although details of the houses were represented full-size, the rooms themselves were noticeably smaller than those typically found in houses matching their external appearances. See *Builder*, 16 Aug. 1884, 221.

53 No illustrations of the models have survived. Visitors noted, however, the resemblance of the houses to Dr T. Pridgin Teale's illustrations in *Dangers to Health*. Although the houses are described in the *International Health Exhibition Official Guide* (53), a lengthier description appeared in the *Guide to the Sanitary and Insanitary Houses*. Unfortunately, the British Library's copy of this guide was destroyed in the bombing of London in World War II; the library retains a microfilm copy.

54 *Builder*, 16 Aug. 1884, 222.

55 "Our Insane-itary Guide to the Health Exhibition," *Punch*, 16 Aug. 1884, 82.

56 Ibid.

57 "The Sanitary and Insanitary Dwellings," *Architect*, 23 Aug. 1884, 116.

58 Pasteur, Lister, and Koch pioneered the germ theory independently. Pasteur, in 1864, proved that disease was caused by bacteria; Joseph Lister pioneered antiseptic surgery in 1865; in 1882, Robert Koch isolated the bacteria that

caused tuberculosis and cholera. For a review of pre-Victorian theories of disease, see Temkin, *Double Face*, 456–71.

59 On the social and cultural implications of the miasma theory, see Hamlin, "Providence and Putrefaction," 381–411.

60 A third theoretical position, identified by medical historian George Rosen as "limited" or "contingent" contagionism, held that contagia existed but depended on favourable atmospheric conditions for transmission, combining ideas from the other two theories. See Rosen, "Disease, Debility, and Death," 635.

61 Nancy Tomes has noted the turn from public to domestic architecture in her analysis of the American sanitarians. See Tomes, "Private Side," 5.

62 The sanitary reform of working-class housing in nineteenth-century England has been the subject of many fine studies. See Briggs, *Victorian Cities;* Burnett, *Social History of Housing;* Daunton, *House and Home;* Dyos and Wolff, eds., *Victorian City;* Gaskell, *Model Housing;* Gauldie, *Cruel Habitations;* and Sheppard, *London 1808–1870.* On the impact of photography on urban reform, see Blau, "Patterns of Fact."

63 Stefan Muthesius claims that this change occurred with the near death of the Prince of Wales in 1871, supposedly as a result of faulty plumbing. See Stefan Muthesius, *English Terraced House*, 55.

64 Many historians have identified the urge for self-improvement or self-help as a major force in nineteenth-century middle-class society. See Briggs, *Victorian People*, 116–39; Houghton, *Victorian Frame*, 237–9. On the idea of self-help in health reform, see Morantz, "Health Reform and Women."

65 The death rate decreased steadily each decade. See Rosen, *History of Public Health*, 339.

66 Haley, *Healthy Body*, 5, 10–11.

67 Rosen, *History of Public Health*, 294. François Delaporte has explained how "living space" in this way became "causal space," as the dwelling actually seemed to create the conditions facilitating the spread of disease. See *Disease and Civilization*, 85–6.

68 On the development of ventilation systems in public buildings, see Bruegmann, "Central Heating," and Forty, "Modern Hospital."

69 For an extensive discussion of the American reaction to sewer gas, see Handlin, *American Home*, 457–9. See also Tomes, "Private Side," 509–10.

70 The Building Act of 1875 stipulated that water closets must have at least one exterior wall with a window. See Stefan Muthesius, *English Terraced House*, 58.

71 See, for example, "Sewer Gas: Controversies Concerning It and New Means of Disposing of It," *Sanitary Record*, 2 June 1894, 761–2.

72 "Sewer Air," *Sanitary Record*, 22 Dec. 1894, 1266.

73 Richardson, "Health in the Home," 9–10. "Continued fever" was a name used for many types of "fever" that were undistinguished until later in the century. See Rosen, "Disease, Debility, and Death," 630.

74 See Dr Stirling, "Healthy and Unhealthy Homes," *Sanitary Record*, 15 Dec. 1894, 1251. Today we know that tuberculosis is spread by respiration directly from one person to another or by drinking infected milk.

75 Galton, "Warming and Ventilation," 485.

76 Ibid., 497.

77 This is an excerpt from Rhoda Broughton's *Come Up as a Flower* (1867), as cited in Brightfield, "Medical Profession," 254.

78 For a lengthy discussion of arsenical papers and the associated illnesses, see Morris, "Arsenic in Wall-papers."

79 A.W. Stokes, public analyst to Paddington, Bethnal Green, and St Luke, for example, claimed that those who avoided wallpaper were equally at risk because wall paint also contained lead and arsenic. Stokes said that 10 per cent of the wallpapers he tested contained arsenic. See Stokes, "Arsenic in the Home."

80 See Teale, *Dangers to Health*, plate 51.

81 This story is recounted in ibid., plate 30.

82 Conventional views of the history of medicine cite 1880 as a watershed between the older theories and the germ theory. See Tomes, "Private Side," 513. The architectural evidence also affirms the findings of Parsons, who argued that only élite medical professionals followed a single theory of disease transmission while ordinary practitioners often subscribed to several theories. See Parsons, "British Medical Profession," 138–50.

83 Temkin, *Double Face*, 469–70.

CHAPTER TWO

1 This re-enactment of Teale's lecture, "Healthy Houses," delivered at the IHE on 24 June 1884, is based on a review in the *Builder*, 5 July 1884, 10.

2 Teale, *Dangers to Health*, 5. The flaws in the Insanitary Dwelling at the IHE were apparently similar to Teale's plate, for a journalist in the *Builder* suggested that Teale's diagrams would have strengthened the lessons intended by the models. See "The Sanitary and Insanitary Houses at the Health Exhibition," *Builder*, 16 Aug. 1884, 222.

3 Teale, *Dangers to Health*, 6.

4 Ibid., 5.

5 There is some evidence that a similar struggle was enacted between American physicians and architects. See, for example, comments on the ignorance

of architects in the *Sanitary Engineer*, 14 Dec. 1882, 27, and the *Sanitarian* 19 (Aug. 1887): 107–14.

6 *Dictionary of National Biography*, s.v. "Parkes, Edmund Alexander."

7 The museum was an important locale for the dissemination of sanitary knowledge. See *Parkes Museum of Hygiene International Medical and Sanitary Exhibition Official Catalogue*, 141–3, and "The Parkes Museum," *Architect*, 19 July 1884, 43.

8 This was noted by Lloyd G. Stevenson in "Science Down the Drain," 1.

9 W.P. Buchan, "Recent Improvements in House Drainage," 157.

10 Lord Stanley, *Transactions of the National Association for the Promotion of Social Science* (1857), 41, noted in Wohl, *Endangered Lives*, n.p.

11 The spatial and environmental aspects of Victorian medicine were particularly evident in the increased use of maps in nineteenth-century public-health reports. See Elliot, *City in Maps*, 78–81, and Jarcho, "Yellow Fever."

12 The plans, sections, and descriptions of these houses were published in Drysdale and Hayward, *Health and Comfort*.

13 The germ theory was explained in popular literature in many different ways, some of which included disguised versions of the older theories of transmission. See McClary, "Germs Are Everywhere."

14 Dixon and Muthesius, *Victorian Architecture*, 68.

15 Plunkett, *Women, Plumbers, and Doctors*, 203.

16 Teale, *Dangers to Health*, plate 19.

17 Sociologist Magali Sarfatti Larson has identified the "negotiation of cognitive exclusiveness" as a distinctive characteristic of nineteenth-century professionalism. See Larson, *Rise of Professionalism*, 15–18, 30–31. For a discussion of how nineteenth-century American architects fitted Larson's model of professionalism, see Upton, "Pattern Books," 112–14.

18 "Medical Officers of Health v. Sanitary Engineers and Architects," *Sanitary Record*, 16 July 1888, 10–11.

19 Benjamin Ward Richardson, "Health in the Home," 5.

20 Teale, *Dangers to Health*, 8.

21 Maguire, *Domestic Sanitary Drainage*, 2.

22 Benjamin Ward Richardson, *National Health*, 47.

23 Poore, *Dwelling House*, 2.

24 Ibid., 11–12.

25 Eassie, *Sanitary Arrangements*, 13.

26 Bledstein, *Culture of Professionalism*, 88.

27 For a discussion of how nineteenth-century American architects used "science" to further their professional status, see Upton, "Pattern Books."

28 Benjamin Ward Richardson, "Health in the Home," 1.

29 "The Physiological Effect of Light," *Sanitary Record*, 15 June 1891, 621.

30 "Report of the Lancet Special Commission on the Relative Efficiency and Cost of Plumbers' Work," *Lancet*, supplement, 4 July 1896, 71–99.

31 Plunkett, *Women, Plumbers, and Doctors*, 95.

32 Stefan Muthesius, *English Terraced House*, 55; Tomes, "Private Side," 530.

33 Hellyer, *Plumber and Sanitary Houses*, 1.

34 "Report of the Lancet Sanitary Commission on the State of Londesborough Lodge & Sandringham, in Relation to the Illness of H.R.H. the Prince of Wales," *Lancet*, 9 Dec. 1871, 828–31.

35 "The Death of the Prince Consort," *Lancet*, 21 Dec. 1861, 599.

36 "Report of the Lancet Special Commission on the Relative Efficiency and Cost of Plumbers' Work," *Lancet*, supplement, 4 July 1896, 72.

37 "The Plumber," *Sanitary Record*, 23 Sept. 1893, 157.

38 Hellyer, *Plumber and Sanitary History*, 8.

39 "The Plumber," *Sanitary Record*, 23 Sept. 1893, 158.

40 "The Education of Plumbers," *Sanitary Record*, 16 March 1891, 461.

41 "The Plumber and His Prospects," *Sanitary Record*, 23 March 1895, 1484. For an interesting discussion of issues debated before the bill, see "The Registration of Plumbers," *Sanitary Record*, 15 July 1887, 1–2.

42 "Report of the Lancet Special Commission on the Relative Efficiency and Cost of Plumbers' Work," *Lancet*, supplement, 4 July 1896, 73.

43 Teale, *Dangers to Health*, n.p.

44 Bledstein, *Culture of Professionalism*, 100.

45 Branca, *Silent Sisterhood*, 66.

46 Bledstein, *Culture of Professionalism*, 100. At the same time, physicians expanded their professional territory into the business of selling patent medicines by claiming "scientific prowess." See Branca, *Silent Sisterhood*, 67–8.

47 "The Sanitary Inspector," *Sanitary Record*, 2 Sept. 1893, 116. The Sanitary Inspectors' Association was founded in 1883. See "Sanitary Inspectors' Association," *Sanitary Record*, 23 March 1895, 1492. The constitution of the Northern Sanitary Association of Scotland and England was quoted in Plunkett, *Women, Plumbers, and Doctors*, 101.

48 "The Sanitary Inspector," *Sanitary Record*, 2 Sept. 1893, 115. For detailed information on the nature and processes of sanitary inspection, see Thomson, "The Inspection of Plumber-work," 377.

49 The exhibition of Sanitary and Insanitary Dwellings, however, was organized by a committee that included at least two architects, and the general design was the work of architect J.R. Roberts. See "The Sanitary and Insanitary Houses at the Health Exhibition," *Builder*, 16 Aug. 1884, 221.

50 T. Roger Smith, "A Public Health Exhibition," 3.

51 "What Is a London House?" *Architect*, 4 Dec. 1880, 347.

52 "The Sanitary and Insanitary Houses," *Lancet*, 16 Aug. 1884, 297.

53 "The Sanitary and Insanitary Dwellings," *Architect*, 23 Aug. 1884, 116.

54 "What Is a London House?" *Architect*, 4 Dec. 1880, 347.

55 Ibid.

56 "Medical Officers of Health v. Sanitary Engineers and Architects," *Sanitary Record*, 16 July 1888, 11.

57 Neiswander has pointed out that Edis "came closest to the sanitarians." See Neiswander, "Liberalism, Nationalism and the Evolution of Middle-Class Values," 109.

58 For general information on the career of Robert W. Edis, see Neale, "Architect Presents Arms" and "Robert William Edis." On Edis's contribution to the World's Columbian Exposition in Chicago, see Sandweiss, "Around the World in a Day."

59 See Godwin, *Dress in Its Relation to Health and Climate*. Godwin, like Edis, was extremely interested in furniture and decoration. This is evident from his letters, held at the National Archive of Art and Design, and also from his numerous publications. As a major figure in the Aesthetic Movement, his commissions reflected these interests. See Aslin, *E.W. Godwin*.

60 In Shirley Forster Murphy's collection of papers by sanitarians, Edis's is entitled "Internal Decoration."

61 His ideas were "so frequently published" that a major journal on furniture design expressed no need to review them in its coverage of the IHE. See "The Health Exhibition – Continued," *Cabinet Maker and Art Furnisher*, 1 Aug. 1884, 21.

62 Others who perhaps also acted in this capacity were the engineer Douglas Galton, an important authority on hospital design, and Henry Roberts, the designer of working-class housing based on sanitary principles.

63 "The Building of London Houses," *Architect*, 23 Feb. 1884, 129.

64 "About to furnish" was a common reference in the nineteenth-century to young couples setting up their first home.

65 "The Health Exhibition – Continued," *Cabinet Maker and Art Furnisher*, 1 Aug. 1884, 22.

66 "At the Health Exhibition," *Cabinet Maker and Art Furnisher*, 1 July 1884, 2.

67 An analysis of Hygeia is presented in Cassedy, "Hygeia."

68 Benjamin Ward Richardson, *Hygeia*, 19, 24. A revised version of Richardson's address was reprinted as "A City of Health," in the *Sanitarian* 4 (Jan. 1876): 24–30, and 4 (Feb. 1876): 68–76. At precisely the same time, the influential suburb of Bedford Park in west London was being constructed with houses without basements. See Girouard, *Sweetness and Light*, 160–76.

69 Benjamin Ward Richardson, *Hygeia*, 20.

70 Ibid.

71 Ibid., 21.

72 Ibid., 22.

73 Ibid., 46.

74 Ibid., 30.

75 Poore, *Dwelling House*, vi.

76 Ibid., 13.

77 A perspective and plans of this convalescent home are illustrated in ibid., 16.

78 Ibid., 44–5. This idea resembled American sanitarian George Waring's proposal for a dry-earth-closet system to fertilize the householder's property. See Handlin, *American Home*, 459–65.

79 Poore, *London*, 37–8.

80 Ibid., 38–9.

81 Ibid., 46.

82 Ibid.

83 Poore, *Dwelling House*, 5–6.

84 Ibid., 6.

85 Handlin cited Fowler as one of the first Americans to articulate the advantages of concrete. See Handlin, *American Home*, 288.

86 Ibid., 289–90.

87 Fowler, *Home for All*, 12. Andrew Jackson Downing's books, such as *The Architecture of Country Houses*, suggested this same idea. For an insightful essay on the relationship between the architectures of Downing and Fowler, see Creese, "Fowler and the Domestic Octagon."

88 Handlin, *American Home*, 288.

89 For biographical information on the Fowlers, see "Fowler, Orson Squire," *Appletons' Cyclopaedia of American Biography* (New York: Appleton 1888), 2:517–18, or his entry in the *Dictionary of American Biography*, s.v. "Fowler, Orson Squire."

90 Fowler, *Home for All*, 98. Frederick's diagrams are in Handlin, *American Home*, 422–3.

91 "A Model House," *Queen* 86 (July–Dec. 1889): 212.

92 Their ideas were also noted in the American press. See "The Ventilation of a Doctor's House," *Sanitary Engineer*, 8 March 1883, 315. Hayward's own house is cited as "The Octagon" on Grove Street in *The Homoeopathic Medical Directory* of 1868. Perhaps this was a reference to its Fowler-inspired form.

93 This was referred to as a "whole-house treatment" in Eassie, *Sanitary Arrangements*, 152.

94 Drysdale and Hayward, *Health and Comfort*, 53.

95 This description, from Inman's *Preservation of Health*, 27–8, was cited in Drysdale and Hayward, *Health and Comfort*, 54.

96 The house was on the east side of Grove Street in Liverpool.

97 Drysdale and Hayward, *Health and Comfort*, iv.

98 Ibid., 12.

99 Ibid., iii.

100 Ibid., 59.

101 *The New Encyclopaedia Britannica*, 15th ed., s.v. "Homeopathy."

102 See Nicholls, *Homoeopathy*, 133–64.

103 *Homoeopathic Medical Directory of Great Britain and Ireland*, 121.

104 Nicholls, *Homoeopathy*, 181.

105 Haley, *Healthy Body*, 69, 4.

106 See *Baby* 3 (Dec. 1889–Nov. 1890): 3–4, 29–30, 55, 78–9, 102–3, 129, 150–1, 173–4, 199–200, 222–3, 244–7, 269–71.

107 "Ventilation," *Baby* 3 (Oct. 1890): 244. See also the illustrated article "Respiration," in *Baby* 3 (July 1890): 175.

108 See advertisement in Dodds, *Health in the Household*, n.p.

109 Wood-Allen, *Marvels*, 15.

110 Ibid., 4.

111 See Davison, "City as a Natural System."

112 Benjamin Ward Richardson, "Health in the Home," 28.

113 For a brief history of water supply in English cities, see Stefan Muthesius, *English Terraced House*, 55–62.

114 Banner, *Wholesome Houses*, 90.

115 "Architects' Conference at the Health Exhibition," *Architect*, 12 July 1884, 23–4.

116 The papers were published in the IHE literature. See "Health in the Dwelling," *The Health Exhibition Literature*, vol. 2.

117 Ibid., 328.

CHAPTER THREE

1 Plunkett, *Women, Plumbers, and Doctors*, title page.

2 Ibid., 94. Plunkett's book revealed both the new roles for women created in the Domestic Sanitation Movement and the widespread influence of the British building-doctors in America. Published in New York in 1885, Plunkett's book contained several illustrations copied directly from Teale. See, for example, her fig. 28.

3 Ballin, "Health in Our Homes," 3.

4 "Domestic Economy," *Englishwoman's Review*, 15 Aug. 1877, 350.

5 For an analysis of the literature and language of separate spheres, see Kerber, "Separate Spheres." See also McDowell, "City and Home."

6 Men supposedly operated in both spheres. See Davidoff and Hall, "Architecture of Public and Private Life," 326. On the link between gender and anti-urban trends in British planning, see Davidoff, L'Esperance, and Newby, "Landscape with Figures."

7 There are exceptions to this in recent literature. See Poovey, *Uneven Developments*, 1–23; Blackmar, *Manhattan for Rent*, 126–38; Davidoff and Hall, *Family Fortunes*, 357–96; Ryan, *Women in Public*, 58–94.

8 Many historians rely on the pattern of forces described by Philippe Ariès in "The Family and the City" and *Centuries of Childhood*.

9 Jane Lewis, *Women in England*, x.

10 Blackmar, *Manhattan for Rent*, 110.

11 Panton, *Way They Should Go*, 165.

12 Sarah Ellis, *Wives of England*, 129.

13 There is a huge literature on Victorian women in England. The major studies that subscribe to the "separate spheres" model include the following: Branca, *Silent Sisterhood;* Dyhouse, *Girls Growing Up;* Gorham, *Victorian Girl;* Jane Lewis, *Women in England;* Jane Lewis, ed., *Labour and Love;* Vicinus, *Independent Women;* Vicinus, ed., *Suffer and Be Still* and *Widening Sphere.*

14 The first women's suffrage committee was formed in 1866; women taxpayers voted in local elections in 1869, following the Municipal Franchise Act. It was not until 1928 that the Equal Franchise Act allowed all women over twenty-one to cast votes. See Holdsworth, *Out of the Doll's House*, 12–13.

15 The first woman architect in Britain, Ethel Charles, was accepted by the Royal Institute of British Architects in 1898, just three years before Queen Victoria's death. See Lynne Walker, "Women and Architecture," 99.

16 Davidoff, "Mastered for Life."

17 Davidoff, *Best Circles*.

18 On the department store as an institution designed to appeal to women, see Benson, *Counter Cultures*.

19 Ryan, *Women in Public*, 59.

20 This question has not been explored fully by historians because of a dearth of sources. Studies that begin to address men's influence at home include Mangan and Walvin, eds., *Manliness and Morality*.

21 The major text advising women how to decorate dining rooms was Martha Jane Loftie, *Dining-Room*. On the history of the dining room, see Clark, "Vision of the Dining Room"; on dining rooms in aristocratic houses, see Franklin, *Gentleman's Country House*, 48–51.

22 Garrett and Garrett, *Suggestions for House Decoration*, 28.

23 Most Victorian books on house planning described men's rooms this way. For a typical example, see Kerr, *Gentleman's House*, 101–10, 129–38.

24 For an analysis of the gender divisions of a house plan published by Robert Kerr, see Matrix, *Making Space*, 64–7.

25 See Kerr, *Gentleman's House*, 125; Hermann Muthesius, *English House*; J.J. Stevenson, *House Architecture*, 2: 57; Harris, "Cultivating Power."

26 Kerr, *Gentleman's House*, 124.

27 Audsley and Audsley, *Cottage*, 24.

28 Kerr, *Gentleman's House*, 119.

29 Ibid.

30 Hermann Muthesius, *English House*, 85.

31 Garrett and Garrett, *Suggestions for House Decoration*, 28.

32 Ibid., 56.

33 Blackmar, *Manhattan for Rent*, 128.

34 Bourdillon, *Women as Healers*, 17.

35 Lesley Hall, *Hygeia's Handmaids*, 21.

36 On scientific theories of sexual difference in general in the nineteenth century, see Jane Lewis, *Women in England*, 83–92.

37 Ibid., 174. Lewis referred to Celia Davies, "Making Sense of the Census."

38 Cited in Morantz-Sanchez, "Female Student Has Arrived," 63.

39 Benjamin Ward Richardson, "Woman as a Sanitary Reformer," 190.

40 Jane Lewis, *Women in England*, 91.

41 Barbara Ehrenreich and Deirdre English have noted how the germ theory became a doctrine of individual guilt. See Ehrenreich and English, *For Her Own Good*, 74–5.

42 "Reviews," *Sanitary Record*, 15 Jan. 1887, 335.

43 For a typical article, see "Going Over the New House," *Baby* 3 (Dec. 1889): 129.

44 Teale, *Dangers to Health*, plate 5.

45 Ballin, "Health in Our Homes," 3.

46 Maguire, *Domestic Sanitary Drainage*, 194–5.

47 See Teale, *Dangers to Health*, plate 3. For the candle test, see plate 18.

48 Ibid., plate 18.

49 Ballin, "Ventilation, Lighting, Warming, Furnishing," 271. On arsenical wallpapers in general, see Morris, "Arsenic in Wall-papers."

50 A test devised by F.F. Grenstted, for example, required only an ordinary gas jet. See "Test for Arsenic in Wall-paper," *Sanitarian* 18 (May 1887): 425.

51 These appeared in *Baby* 3 (Dec. 1889–Nov. 1890). A similar series appeared in the *English Woman's Journal*. See "Modern Housebuilding," *English*

Woman's Journal 10 (Feb. 1863): 399–404, and "House Building," ibid., 12 (Feb. 1864): 27–30, 341–7.

52 Gulick, "The Home Maker," 64.

53 On physicians blaming women for having poor health, see Branca, *Silent Sisterhood*, 66.

54 This process was expounded by William Dean Howells in his novel *A Hazard of New Fortunes* (1890), in which Mrs March, exposing her "female instinct for domiciliation," led her husband on a lengthy search for lodgings in New York.

55 Plunkett, *Women, Plumbers, and Doctors*, 10.

56 Lindsay Granshaw has explained how general cleanliness and antisepsis were seen as two distinct methods. See Granshaw "Upon this Principle I Have Based a Practice."

57 Connor, "Listerism Unmasked," 236–8.

58 See, for example, Richardson's suggestions in "Light in the Sick-room," and the advice of American physician F.C. Larimore, "Hygiene of the Sick-room."

59 Barker, *Bedroom*, 94–5. Books on bedrooms typically included entire chapters on how to transform them into sickrooms. See, for example, ibid., 94–109.

60 Gladstone, *Healthy Nurseries*, 124–5.

61 MSA and MRAS, *Grammar of House Planning*, 38.

62 Marion Sambourne's diaries were analysed in Nicholson, *Victorian Household*. For this photo and the description of Maud's illness, see ibid., 46. Today the Sambourne house appears much as it did in the late nineteenth century. It is operated as a house museum by the Victorian Society.

63 See chap. 11, "The Sick Room," in Panton, *Nooks and Corners*.

64 Barker, *Bedroom*, 97–8.

65 Charlotte Perkins Gilman, *The Yellow Wallpaper and Other Writings*, 3–4.

66 Allen, *Building Domestic Liberty*.

67 Catherine J. Wood, "The Sick-room and Its Appliances," 179.

68 On the "atmosphere of constant crisis," see chap. 2, n17. These titles are reproduced from Ehrenreich and English, *For Her Own Good*, 157.

69 Neiswander, "Liberalism, Nationalism and the Evolution of Middle-Class Values," 107–9.

70 An illustration and description appeared in Galton, "The International Health Exhibition," 294–5.

71 For a characteristic article from the Victorian women's press, see "Hints on Home Nursing," *Young Woman* 1 (Oct. 1892–Sept. 1893): 415–16.

72 This typical advice for the management of a sickroom is extracted from Chavasse, *Advice to a Mother*, 215–20.

73 Morantz, "Making Women Modern," 493.

74 "Ladies' Sanitary Association," *Englishwoman's Review*, 15 March 1882, 136–7.

75 Some of these lectures were reviewed in "Sanitary Lectures," *English Woman's Journal* 31 (1 Sept. 1860): 46–54. On the international contributions of the LSA, see "The Ladies' Sanitary Association," *Englishwoman's Review*, 15 May 1876, 221–2. By 1860, the LSA had produced 76,500 tracts; by 1861, the number had increased to 138,500. See "The Third Annual Report of the Committee of the Ladies' Sanitary Association," *English Woman's Journal*, 1 Dec. 1860, 236–41; "Fourth Report of the Committee of the Ladies' Sanitary Association," ibid., 1 May 1861, 192; and "The Ladies' Sanitary Association," *Baby* 6 (Dec. 1892–Nov. 1893): 153.

76 "The Ladies' Sanitary Association," *English Woman's Journal*, 1 April 1859, 84.

77 "Second Annual Report of the Ladies' National Association for the Diffusion of Sanitary Knowledge," *English Woman's Journal*, 1 Aug. 1859, 387.

78 See ibid., 380–7. By 1860, formal ties with the EWJ had been severed; see "The Third Annual Report of the Committee of the Ladies' Sanitary Association," *English Woman's Journal*, 1 Dec. 1860, 238–9.

79 "Ladies' Sanitary Association," *Englishwoman's Review*, 15 March 1882, 136.

80 Roberts's major books were *The Improvement of the Dwellings of the Labouring Classes* (1850), *The Model Houses for Families* (1851), and *Essentials of a Healthy Dwelling* (1862). On Roberts's houses at the Great Exhibition, see Gaskell, *Model Housing*, 19–23; on his association with the society, see Foyle, "Henry Roberts, 1802–1876" 5–8.

81 The lectures were reviewed in "Sanitary Lectures," *English Woman's Journal*, 1 Sept. 1860, 46–54.

82 Ibid., 53.

83 "Domestic Hygiene," *Sanitary Record*, 1 Dec. 1892, 263.

84 Ibid.

85 Hellyer, *Plumber and Sanitary Houses*, 11.

86 Benjamin Ward Richardson, "Woman as a Sanitary Reformer," 190.

87 Bohun, "Back to the Home," 182.

88 Ehrenrich and English, *For Her Own Good*, 141–81.

89 Gulick, "The Home Maker," 64.

90 Browne, "The Profession of Housewifery," 223.

91 Beecher, "Method and Regularity in the Home," 51.

92 A report on the entire conference was published in "Domestic Economy," *Englishwoman's Review*, 15 Aug. 1877, 347–55.

93 Ibid., 354–5.

94 Mrs Mallet, "National Association for Housewifery," 7.

95 Ehrenreich and English, *For Her Own Good*, 156.

96 Morgan-Brown, "What the Census of 1891 Tells Us," 683.

97 Grainger, "Census Statistics as Indicative of the Employment of Women in London," 64.

98 Browne, "House-cleaning," 870.

99 Ibid., 875.

100 Ibid., 869.

101 See "Women as Official Inspectors: English Experience," *Sanitarian* 32 (May 1894): 437–43; "Women Sanitary Inspectors," ibid., 43 (July 1899): 70–1. On American women as inspectors, see "The Sanitary Inspectress and Her Maid," ibid., 44 (Jan. 1900): 34–9. On the steps performed by both male and female inspectors in England, see "House Inspection," ibid., 10 (Feb. 1882): 156–61.

102 Cited in Bourdillon, *Women as Healers*, 31.

103 Rachel Montgomery, "Careers for Women," 200.

104 *Englishwoman's Year Book* (1909), 68.

105 "A Woman House Agent," *Woman's Signal*, 30 May 1895, 338.

106 See Day, "The Woman's Part in Domestic Decoration," 457–63.

107 Panton, *Kitchen to Garret*, 4.

108 Dodd, *Healthful Farmhouse*, 3.

109 Gardner, *House That Jill Built*.

110 Dorothy M. Richardson, "Interim," in *Pilgrimage*, 2:428. For a detailed analysis of the relationship of fictional spaces to real-world architecture in eighteenth- and nineteenth-century England, see Tristram, *Living Space*.

CHAPTER FOUR

1 This book appeared in new editions until 1925. In *Kitchen to Garret* (181), Panton referred to it as a "necessary possession" for young matrons. On the popularity of Chavasse's book in general, see Attar, *Household Books*, 48; Hardyment, *Dream Babies*, 42–3; and Dwork, "Victorian Child Care."

2 Chavasse, *Advice to a Wife*, 87. The interdependence of Victorian women's physiological, mental, and emotional states as measured through their menstruation has been discussed at length in Shuttleworth, "Female Circulation."

3 Chavasse, *Advice to a Wife*, 86.

4 The notion that failure to menstruate was a sign of illness predated the nineteenth century. See Martin, *Woman in the Body*, 31.

5 See Smith-Rosenberg, "Puberty to Menopause."

6 Chavasse, *Advice to a Wife*, 88, 109.

7 Solis-Cohen, *Woman in Girlhood*, 103.

8 Chavasse, *Advice to a Wife*, 8.

9 *Etiquette of Love*, 95.

10 Brookes, "Women and Reproduction," 152; Weeks, *Sex, Politics, and Society*, 45. In the mid-1870s the fertility rate of births was 156 per 1,000 women in the childbearing age group of fifteen to forty-four; by 1901 it had fallen to 114. This rate included all women, regardless of class. See F.M.L. Thompson, *Rise of Respectable Society*, 53. For useful graphs showing statistical change over time, see Oakley, *Captured Womb*, 295–307.

11 It is impossible to estimate the average number of deaths per family, since most deaths were unrecorded. See Oakley, *Captured Womb*, 32, 296. Death rates varied dramatically between urban and rural districts in England. For contemporary reactions to the statistics, see Leared, "Infant Mortality and Its Causes," 173–83; and "Infant Mortality," *Englishwoman's Review*, 15 Jan. 1895, 31–4.

12 Jane Lewis, *Labour and Love*, 3.

13 Brookes, "Women and Reproduction," 151.

14 W.F. Montgomery, *Signs and Symptoms of Pregnancy*, 25; Stacpoole, *Advice to Women*, 57.

15 Ann Douglas Wood has shown how nearly all female diseases in the nineteenth century were thought to originate in the womb or from behaviour that was distinctly unfeminine. See Wood, "The Fashionable Disease."

16 Chavasse, *Advice to a Wife*, 3.

17 Ibid., 3–4.

18 Black, *Young Wife's Advice Book*, iii.

19 Chavasse, *Advice to a Wife*, 3.

20 Buchan, *Domestic Medicine*, 341–2; see Attar, *Household Books*, 43.

21 Chavasse, *Advice to a Wife*, 21.

22 Ibid., 22.

23 While puberty made boys stronger, it was thought to render young girls more dependent on others. See Smith-Rosenberg, "Puberty to Menopause," 26. This is also reflected in the language commonly used to describe menstruation; menstruating women were often characterized in the nineteenth century as "unwell" or "poorly."

24 Many other doctors noted that menstruation began earlier in girls who lived in cities. See, for example, Black, *Young Wife's Advice Book*, 5. Black also remarked that menstruation occurred earlier among working-class girls, "where the whole surroundings are more conducive to the development of a healthier and a hardier frame." See also Solis-Cohen, *Woman in Girlhood*, 101.

25 Chavasse, *Advice to a Wife*, 17.

26 Ibid., 19–20.

27 From the essay by Dr Grosvenor, "Essay on Health," quoted in ibid., 20.

28 Ibid., 19.

29 Ibid.

30 Ibid., 20.

31 For an interesting analysis of how Victorian maternity clothes expressed this change in status from wife to mother, see Hoffert, *Private Matters*, 32–7.

32 Hoffert found no evidence to support the claim made by many historians that American women restricted their social activities during pregnancy. See ibid., 26–30.

33 Shonfield, "Expectant Victorian," 38.

34 Ibid., 37.

35 On the impact of dress reform in general, see Roberts, "Exquisite Slave."

36 The pre-quickening period was also differentiated in law. The Ellenborough Act of 1803 said that any person causing miscarriage in a woman before quickening should be charged with felony and imprisoned up to fourteen years; the same offence after quickening was punishable by death. See W.F. Montgomery, *Signs and Symptoms of Pregnancy*, 75–90.

37 Ann Oakley has noted that Montgomery took no less than 492 pages to describe the symptoms by which a doctor might diagnose pregnancy. See Oakley, *Captured Womb*, 19.

38 Chavasse, *Advice to a Wife*, 121.

39 An oft-cited example was the story of Queen Mary, who stated that she had felt fetal movement and sent dispatches of the news of an heir to foreign courts. See W.F. Montgomery, *Signs and Symptoms of Pregnancy*, 77.

40 Ibid., 81.

41 See Ballantyne, "A Series of Thirteen Cases of Alleged Maternal Impressions," 1025–34.

42 Oakley has pointed out how Geoffrey Saint-Hilaire's research in the early nineteenth century caused doctors to question the maternal impressions theory. Saint-Hilaire noted that unmarried women did not produce more children with birth defects. See Oakley, *Captured Womb*, 24.

43 Tuckey, "Maternal Impressions, and Their Influence on the Offspring," 287–8.

44 Bull, *Hints to Mothers*, 43.

45 Chavasse used the term *enceinte* interchangeably with "pregnant" throughout *Advice to a Wife*; he said that it came from *incincta* or "unbound." See Chavasse, *Advice to a Wife*, 125.

46 O'Neill and Barnett, *New Life*, 15.

47 On the arrangement of bedrooms in American houses, see Cromley, "Sleeping Around," 1–17.

48 This was marked by the "churching" of the mother and the christening of the child. There is some debate among scholars whether "purification" (and the assumption that women were contaminated) was explicitly stated in the ceremony. Judith Schneid Lewis claims that churching was more a ceremony of thanksgiving than purification (*In the Family Way*, 201–2). Edward Shorter discusses the idea of contamination in *A History of Women's Bodies*, 288–9.

49 Oakley, *Captured Womb*, 14.

50 Nearly all the authors of advice manuals to women stress the special qualifications and characteristics of monthly nurses. See Beeton, *Beeton's Book*, 1020–2; Baker, *Companion to the Lying-in Room*.

51 Chavasse, *Advice to a Wife*, 129.

52 Stacpoole, "Maternity Readings for Mothers' Meetings," 4.

53 Stacpoole, "Maternity Readings," 8.

54 Stacpoole, "Maternity Readings for Mothers' Meetings," 4.

55 Stacpoole, "Maternity Readings," 8.

56 Stacpoole, "Maternity Readings for Mothers' Meetings," 4.

57 Ballin, "Drainage," 150.

58 Black, *Young Wife's Advice Book*, 51. The preference for confinement at the rear of the house was disconcerting to later authors, who noted that the modern flat was not arranged in this manner. See Fox, *Mother and Baby*, 24.

59 Gladstone, *Healthy Nurseries*, 144. The use of noiseless blinds was also recommended by Fox (*Mother and Baby*, 25).

60 Gladstone, *Healthy Nurseries*, 144.

61 O'Neill and Barnett, *New Life*, 42.

62 Chavasse, *Advice to a Wife*, 130.

63 Panton, *Way They Should Go*, 36.

64 O'Neill and Barnett, *New Life*, 42.

65 Black, *Young Wife's Advice Book*, 50.

66 For further information on upper-class women going to London to give birth and the political implications of London births, see Judith Lewis, *In the Family Way*, 157–61.

67 O'Neill and Barnett, *New Life*, 92.

68 Judith Lewis, *In the Family Way*, 162.

69 Jane H. Walker, *Handbook for Mothers*, 98–9.

70 Bigg, *Wife's Health*, 62.

71 Wheeler, *Before the Baby Comes*, 90.

72 Panton, *Way They Should Go*, 36.

73 Panton, *Kitchen to Garret*, 180.

74 Fox, *Mother and Baby*, 25.

75 Ibid.

76 Wheeler, *Before the Baby Comes*, 89.

77 Gladstone, *Healthy Nurseries*, 145.

78 Allbutt, *Wife's Handbook*, 20.

79 Most of the manuals included elaborate tables for reckoning. See Chavasse, *Advice to a Wife*, 181–4, for a typical example.

80 Oakley, "Wisewoman and Medicine Man," 32.

81 Ibid., 33.

82 Chavasse, *Advice to a Wife*, 220.

83 Ibid., 211. There is evidence that Victorians may have ignored this advice and that some husbands may have attended childbirth. See Hoffert, *Private Matters*, 75–7.

84 Chavasse, *Advice to a Wife*, 207.

85 Black, *Young Wife's Advice Book*, 49.

86 Allbutt, *Wife's Handbook*, 21.

87 Black, *Young Wife's Advice Book*, 56.

88 The diary entry was reproduced in Francis B. Smith, *People's Health*, 59.

89 This story was recounted in Holme, *Carlyles at Home*, 8.

90 Chavasse, *Advice to a Wife*, 232.

91 Ibid., 242.

92 Parsons, "British Medical Profession," 141–2.

93 Gladstone, *Healthy Nurseries*, 142.

94 See Semmelweis, *Etiology*. It is interesting that opponents to Semmelweis's conclusions pointed to other environmental conditions to explain the decrease in mortality rates following his introduction of chlorine handwashing. See DeLacy, "Puerperal Fever," and Parsons, "British Medical Profession," 138–50.

95 Holmes published his observations in *The New England Quarterly Journal of Medicine and Surgery* (April 1843), reprinted in his collected *Medical Essays*, 103–72.

96 Playfair, "Defective Sanitation as a Cause of Puerperal Disease," 252.

97 Ibid., 254.

98 Teale, *Dangers to Health*, plate 11.

99 Gladstone, *Healthy Nurseries*, 44.

100 Parsons, "British Medical Profession," 141; she cited James Young Simpson's *Selected Obstetrical and Gynaecological Works* (1871).

101 Parsons, "British Medical Profession," 142–3.

102 O'Neill and Barnett, *New Life*, 50.

103 Chavasse, *Advice to a Wife*, 251.

104 *On the Evils Resulting from Rising Too Early after Childbirth*, 17.

105 Chavasse, *Advice to a Wife*, 245.

106 *Mother's Home-book*, 29. The ritual of churching was usually followed by the christening of the child. A similar tradition in Hebrew law prohibited women from entering holy places for thirty-three days after giving birth to a son or for sixty-six days after the delivery of a daughter. See note 48.

107 O'Neill and Barnett, *New Life*, 50.

108 Panton, *Kitchen to Garret*, 180. Her autobiography is *Leaves from a Life*.

109 Panton, *Kitchen to Garret*, 184–5.

110 Ibid., 182.

111 Ibid., 181.

112 Gladstone, *Healthy Nurseries*, 145.

113 Warren, *How I Managed My Children*, 10–12.

114 The design of baby bottles was much improved after the invention of the rubber teat in 1845; still, many of them were impossible to clean inside. In 1900, the Allenbury feeder, the first bottle with a teat and valve, superseded all others. See *Collection of Feeding Bottles*, 3.

115 Panton, *Kitchen to Garret*, 163.

116 Hospitalization of middle-class women was more common in the United States than in England in the 1920s, but the number of hospital births in England grew steadily between the wars. See Carter and Duriez, *With Child*, 140–6.

CHAPTER FIVE

1 The "women's press" in this case refers to popular journals for women, with and without feminist associations. The major feminist journals included the *English Woman's Journal*, the *Englishwoman's Review*, the *Woman's Herald*, *Woman's Signal*, *Women's Penny Paper*, and the *Young Woman*. Nonfeminist journals in this survey were the *Queen* and the *Englishwoman's Domestic Magazine*.

2 "Modern Housebuilding," *English Woman's Journal* 10 (Feb. 1863): 399.

3 "House Building," *English Woman's Journal* 12 (Feb. 1864): 27.

4 "Modern Housebuilding," 399–400.

5 "House Building," 28; "Modern Housebuilding," 400.

6 "House Building," 26–7.

7 On the planning of nineteenth-century London, see Olsen, *Town Planning in London*. For an analysis of the development of the terraced house form, see Stefan Muthesius, *English Terraced House*.

8 "House Building," 28.

9 Ibid., 28–9. This Victoria Street building was probably the experimental apartment house often referred to in the professional architectural press. It was built by a Mr Mackenzie, according to the *Builder*, and designed by Henry Ashton. See Burnett, *Social History of Housing*, 209–10, and "London Middle-Class Dwellings," *Architect*, 8 April 1871, 184. Another apartment building commonly cited was Mall Chambers in Kensington, which seems to have been built on an open plan and was supposedly an example of "how not to do it." See "London Middle-Class Dwellings," *Architect*, 1 April 1871, 168. For general information on middle-class apartment buildings, see Dixon and Muthesius, *Victorian Architecture*, 69.

10 "House Building," 29.

11 "Modern Housebuilding," 401.

12 Ibid., 402–3.

13 Ibid., 404.

14 "House Building," 30.

15 Olsen, *City as a Work of Art*, 123.

16 As cited in ibid., 118.

17 See "London Middle-class Dwellings," *Architect*, 8 April 1871, 184; "Houses in Flats," *Architect*, 20 Sept. 1873, 141.

18 Burnett claimed that the *Builder* was "alone in advocating [flats] as a solution to the problem of urban sprawl." See Burnett, *Social History of Housing*, 209.

19 These comments from the *Morning Advertiser* were reported in "Homes for the Middle Classes," *Builder*, 22 Jan. 1876, 82.

20 Ibid.

21 Burnett, *Social History of Housing*, 210.

22 Gleason, "Household Cares," 342. On the relationship of household technology and the oppression of women, see Cowan, *More Work for Mother*, Davidson, *A Woman's Work Is Never Done*, and Vanek, "Time Spent in House Work."

23 On the reform of the American home at this time, see Wright, *Moralism and the Model Home*.

24 "Leaderette," *Women's Penny Paper*, 1 Dec. 1888, 5.

25 Panton, *Kitchen to Garret*, 161.

26 Ibid., 171–2.

27 Ibid., 160.

28 "Modern Housebuilding," 399.

29 Edgeworth was discussed in Harland, *Common Sense in the Nursery*.

30 Hardyment, *Dream Babies*, 35; Combe, *Physiological and Moral Management of Infancy*, 29. On the significance of Combe's work, see Hardyment, *Dream Babies*, 40.

31 Abbott, *Mother at Home*, 31.

32 On the role of women in evangelicalism, see Catherine Hall, "Early Formation of Victorian Domestic Ideology," 9–14, and Rendall, *Origins of Modern Feminism*, 73–107.

33 Hardyment, *Dream Babies*, 62. Jonathan Gathorne-Hardy traced the rise in employment of nannies by counting advertisements in the newspapers. See Gathorne-Hardy, *Rise and Fall of the British Nanny*, 66–9.

34 For examples, see Lasdun, *Victorians at Home*, 34–44.

35 Abbott, *Mother at Home*, 20–32.

36 Lasdun, *Victorians at Home*, 44.

37 Chappell, "A Parlour-Child," 261. Chappell was the author of *An Auntie's Notion about Children*.

38 Woolf, *Room of One's Own*.

39 Gathorne-Hardy, *Rise and Fall of the British Nanny*, 57. Edward Gelles claimed that apartments for the exclusive use of children were rare in the medieval period. See Gelles, *Nursery Furniture*, 28.

40 Girouard, *Life in the English Country House*, 286.

41 Franklin, *Gentleman's Country House* , 80–1.

42 *Country Life* 29 (1911): 601, as cited by Franklin in *Gentleman's Country House*, 81.

43 Hermann Muthesius, *English House*, 93.

44 Gathorne-Hardy, *Rise and Fall of the British Nanny*, 58.

45 See Banks, *Prosperity and Parenthood*; Brookes, "Women and Reproduction"; McLaren, *Birth Control in Nineteenth-Century England;* and Weeks, *Sex, Politics, and Society.*

46 Hardyment related the design of feeding bottles around 1868 to the "shift in baby-handling practice represented by perambulators and nursery wings" (*Dream Babies*, 51).

47 There is a vast literature on Victorian nurseries and their arrangement. Most books document nursery furniture as antiques. See Gelles, *Nursery Furniture;* King-Hall, *Story of the Nursery;* Mackay, *Nursery Antiques;* Miall and Miall, *Victorian Nursery Book;* Colin White, *World of the Nursery.*

48 Nurseries were clearly allocated in architectural plans of grander houses. See typical examples of plans in Girouard, *Life in the English Country House*, 286.

49 Warren, *How I Managed My Children*, 36, as cited in Hardyment, *Dream Babies*, 61.

50 Panton, *Kitchen to Garret*, 161.

51 Panton, *Suburban Residences*, 191–200.

52 Franklin, *Gentleman's Country House*, 81.

53 Lady Cook, "Moral Environment," 146–7.

54 Panton, *Kitchen to Garret*, 162.

55 Ibid., 164.

56 Ibid., 176.

57 Ibid., 177–9.

58 Ibid., 177.

59 Heal & Son sold special beds for children long before this; in the 1890s, however, their catalogues included distinct furniture for children and servants. In 1896 they published a separate catalogue of children's furniture. See Heal & Son, *Children's Cots, Cribs and Nursery Furniture* (1896), in Heal & Son Collection.

60 See, for example, Johnson, "Day and Night Nurseries," 181–3; and Blanchflower, "An Actual (and Ideal) Nursery for One Baby," 241.

61 Kerr, *Gentleman's House*, 159; J.J. Stevenson, *House Architecture*, 2:70.

62 Kerr, *Gentleman's House*, 160.

63 Ibid.

64 See Percival Gordon Smith, "Bed-rooms, Nurseries, and Bath-rooms," 89.

65 Squire, "Nursery," 843.

66 Blanchflower, "An Actual (and Ideal) Nursery for One Baby," 241.

67 The Carlyle home, formerly 5 Cheyne Row (now 24) is now a house-museum managed by the National Trust; for a description of the house when the Carlyles first rented it (1834), see Holme, *Carlyles at Home*, 2–3, 7–8.

68 Panton, *Kitchen to Garret*, 7.

69 Holme, *Carlyles at Home*, 44.

70 The Carlyles' private life became known when Jane Carlyle's diaries of 1855–56 were published after Thomas Carlyle's death in 1881; also, James Anthony Froude's biography of Carlyle, published in 1882, showed how "the great Carlyle, the sage and prophet, had been a terrible, a cruel, husband." For an account of their marriage, see Rose, *Parallel Lives*, 25–44, 243–59.

71 J.J. Stevenson, *House Architecture*, 70. For a typical house designed for a bachelor, see Audsley and Audsley, *Cottage*, 141–3.

72 This "feminization" of social life is explored at length in Davidoff, *Best Circles;* see also Neiswander, "Liberalism, Nationalism and the Evolution of Middle-Class Values," 40–1.

73 Control of the domestic garden was also linked to feminism in advice books for women. See Harris, "Cultivating Power."

74 Panton, *Way They Should Go*, 165, 198.

75 Panton, *Nooks and Corners*, 113.

76 "At the Health Exhibition," *Cabinet Maker and Art Furnisher*, 1 July 1884, 3. See fig. 18.

77 For a brief history of the metaphor of clothing in architectural thinking, see Forty, "Cars, Clothes and Carpets."

78 Haweis, *Art of Decoration*, 17, 10. For biographical information on Haweis, see Howe, *Arbiter of Taste*.

79 Clippings from 1860–69 in the Heal & Son Collection. In the 1870s, the store was described as having eight, ten, and sixteen separate rooms.

80 Katherine C. Grier has suggested that the use of model rooms in the United States began with kitchen models at the sanitary fairs of the 1860s. Before then, household goods were grouped by category "with no backdrop to suggest appropriate sites for their display." Model rooms assembled to sell household goods were an innovation of the Philadelphia Centennial Exhibition in 1876. See Grier, *Culture & Comfort*, 49.

81 Most of these model rooms were constructed in the Royal Pavilion, next to the Old London Street. For the most detailed analysis of the model rooms, see *Cabinet Maker & Art Furnisher*, 1 July, 1 Aug., and 1 Nov. 1884.

82 For a typical example, see *Queen* 76 (1884): 360.

83 Queen House or Queen's House was the former residence of the Pre-Raphaelite painter Dante Rossetti. Mrs Haweis said that a visit to the painter's house "opened [her] eyes to the importance of freedom of opinion in art." She and her husband, the Rev. H.R. Haweis, purchased the house in 1883. See "Interview: Mrs. Haweis," *Women's Penny Paper*, 15 Dec. 1888, 1. The house, built in 1717, was supposedly the one mentioned by Thackeray in *Henry Esmond*. See Howe, *Arbiter of Taste*, 15.

84 An account of the meeting was given in "Drawing-room Meeting at Mrs Haweis's," *Women's Herald*, 28 May 1892, 58.

85 Howe, *Arbiter of Taste*, 15–16. Neiswander has pointed out other feminist leanings in Mrs Haweis in the 1890s. She sent her daughter to the North London Collegiate School, "the most rigorous school for girls in the country"; she chose Elizabeth Garrett Anderson as her personal physician; she ran in the election for the Vestry of Chelsea, unsuccessfully, in 1895; and at the time of her death in 1898, she was writing a book on the history of the development of women. Mrs Ward was a well-known anti-suffragist, which may reflect changes in Mrs Haweis's political convictions. According to Neiswander, Haweis began as a "High Tory and fervent royalist" and then spent her final ten years as a passionate advocate of suffrage. See Neiswander, "Liberalism, Nationalism and the Evolution of Middle-Class Values," 55–61.

86 The rise in design "companies" in the late nineteenth century was the subject of Stefan Muthesius, "We Do Not Understand What Is Meant by a 'Company' Designing."

87 "Interview: Mrs. Pankhurst," *Woman's Herald*, 7 Feb. 1891, 241–2.

88 On the gendered character of interior decoration until the 1940s, see McNeil, "Designing Women."

89 On Millicent Garrett Fawcett's relation to politics, see Rubinstein, "Fawcett."

90 Neiswander, "Liberalism, Nationalism and the Evolution of Middle-Class Values," 51.

91 "Interview: Miss Agnes Garrett," *Women's Penny Paper*, 18 Jan. 1890, 146.

92 For a fascinating comparison of Haweis, Panton, and the Garretts, see Neiswander, "Liberalism, Nationalism and the Evolution of Middle-Class Values," 50–70.

93 Moncure Daniel Conway noted the Garretts' "admirable treatment of the new female colleges connected with the English universities" (*Travels in South Kensington*, 169). Standen has been owned and operated by the National Trust since 1972. See *Standen: West Sussex*.

94 This was at 4 Upper Berkeley Street in a building by T.H. Wyatt. See Girouard, *Sweetness and Light*, 54.

95 Mort, *Dangerous Sexualities*, 73. Mort has noted how doctors and feminists, who had earlier joined forces in sanitary reform, were split over the question of the Contagious Diseases Acts. This division may have fuelled Rhoda Garrett's interest in urban housing for women as a healthy alternative to the perceived danger of city living.

96 Neiswander, "Liberalism, Nationalism and the Evolution of Middle-Class Values," 52. The illustration is contained in the files of the Fawcett Library, London. This was particularly bold of Rhoda Garrett, since many feminists working for the suffrage cause, including Millicent Fawcett and John Stuart Mill, stood back from the repeal in fear that close association between the two causes might hurt the chance for enfranchisement. See Strachey, *Fawcett*, 52.

97 Strachey, *Fawcett*, 60.

98 Neiswander, "Liberalism, Nationalism and the Evolution of Middle-Class Values," 55.

99 "Notes on English Decorative Art in Paris," *British Architect and Northern Engineer*, 19 July 1878, 29.

100 Lady Margaret Hall, *Year-book of Women's Work* (1875), 84.

101 The sexual division of space into interior/female, exterior/male is found across cultures and long before the nineteenth century; the new responsibility of women as decorators, however, underlined this division. On the sexual division of space, see Lloyd, "Woman's Place, Man's Place."

102 Ruskin, *Sesame and Lilies*, 140–1. The reaction of Victorian feminists to these theories was voiced in "Women Never Invent Anything," *Englishwoman's Review*, 15 March 1876, 108–13.

103 On the antisuffragist campaign, see "Victorian Anti-Suffragism," in Pugh, *Women's Suffrage in Britain*, 5–13.

104 "The Ascent of Woman," *Young Woman* 7 (Oct. 1898–Sept. 1899): 183.

105 Fawcett, "Politics in the Home," 315–16.

106 "Ladies' Residential Chambers, Limited," *Englishwoman's Review*, 15 Feb. 1888, 84. The first was presumably the Ladies' Dwellings Company, responsible for the project on Lower Sloane Street.

107 "Ladies' Residential Chambers," *Englishwoman's Review*, 15 Jan. 1891, 57.

108 An architectural competition for "Erection, Arrangement, and Management of a block of Associated Dwellings adapted to the needs of single women" was sponsored by the journal *Work and Leisure* in 1887. See *Work and Leisure* 12 (Sept. 1887): 231, and Vicinus, *Independent Women*, 295. For a general history of these projects, see Pearson, *History of Cooperative Living*, 45–55.

109 "Ladies' Residential Chambers," *Englishwoman's Review*, 15 June 1889, 272.

110 "The Ladies' Dwellings Company, Limited," *Englishwoman's Review*, 15 March 1889, 140–1.

111 "Ladies' Residential Chambers," *Englishwoman's Review*, 15 Jan. 1891, 57–8.

112 Grainger, "Census Statistics as Indicative of the Employment of Women in London," 62–9. In 1891, Laura E. Morgan-Brown imagined a city larger than Vienna to accommodate the 900,000 women in England and Wales. See Morgan-Brown, "What the Census of 1891 Tells Us," 683, and Vicinus, *Independent Women*, 293–4. The plight of single women in late-nineteenth-century London was the subject of George Gissing's novel, *The Odd Women*.

113 Jones, "The Life of a Bachelor Girl in a Big City," 131.

114 H. Reinherz, "The Housing of the Educated Working Woman," 7. For an account of a spinster searching for an apartment, see "Seeking a Dwelling, by an Unglorified Spinster," *Women's Penny Paper*, 5 Oct. 1889, 8.

115 Zimmern, "Ladies' Dwellings," 98.

116 "The Ladies' Residential Chambers, Chenies Street," *Builder*, 9 Nov. 1889, 332.

117 Zimmern, "Ladies' Dwellings," 98.

118 Ibid., 99. In addition to these three projects, Zimmern mentioned an experimental apartment building for families, planned by Patrick Geddes in Cheyne Walk, and said that Lord Rowton was considering starting a "lodging-house" for women. See ibid., 96–104.

119 On Gilman's influence, see Allen, *Building Domestic Liberty*; Hayden, *Grand Domestic Revolution*, 183–277.

120 This description is based on Zimmern's remarks ("Ladies' Dwellings," 100–1). Parker's scheme was both criticized and praised by feminists (see

Jones, "The Life of a Bachelor Girl in a Big City," 132). His paper was published in 1889 as Gilbert Parker, "The Housing of Educated Working Women," in the *Report of the Transactions of the International Council of Women*.

121 The hospital was described in the *Builder*, 11 May 1889, 363. It was called the "new" hospital, since an earlier institution, the Hospital for Diseases of Women, had been founded in Red Lion Square in 1843. It was renamed the Hospital for Women in 1845. See Weinreb and Hibbert, eds., *The London Encyclopaedia*, 395–6.

122 *Builder*, 11 May 1889, 363.

123 The duration of the apprenticeship is unclear; the cousins initially trained with a glass painter named Cottier for eighteen months. Agnes Garrett stated that the training period with Brydon was three years in her interview in the *Women's Penny Paper* and in the *Year-book of Women's Work*, (1875), 85. Moncure Daniel Conway said that the Garretts were "formally articled" with Cottier for eighteen months (*Travels in South Kensington*, 169). Perhaps the total duration of apprenticeships with Cottier and Brydon amounted to three years. For biographical information on Brydon, see "Contemporary British Architects," *Building News*, 7 Feb. 1890, 221; Gibson, "The Late John McKean Brydon," 400–5; and his obituary in the *Builder*, 1 June 1901, 540–1.

124 Girouard, *Sweetness and Light*, 38.

125 Also, Stevenson's cousin was Martha Jane Loftie, wife of Walter J. Loftie, who published the Garretts' book in 1876.

126 Gray, *Edwardian Architecture*, 99.

127 Champneys also designed the first buildings of Bedford College when the college moved from Bedford to London in 1910. See ibid., 139.

128 On the architecture of Newnham College, see Girouard, "Victorian Sweetness and Light." For more information and contemporary accounts of the other buildings, see Cooke, "The Training of a Lady Doctor," 102–5; "Girls and Their Colleges," *Woman's Herald*, 19 Nov. 1892, 8–9; ibid., 21 Jan. 1893, 8–9, ibid., 2 March 1893, 18–19; ibid., 25 May 1893, 221; ibid., 15 June 1893, 259; PLP, "The Education of Women: A Visit to Somerville College," *Young Woman* 5 (Oct. 1896–Sept. 1897): 161–5; and Katharine St John Conway, "Life at Newnham," 99–103.

129 Weiner, *Architecture of Social Reform*, 65–80.

130 Ibid., 85.

131 Neiswander has noted how Queen Anne interiors were associated in novels of the time with challenging notions of class hierarchy. See Neiswander, "Liberalism, Nationalism and the Evolution of Middle-Class Values," 169.

132 The discussion of the acceptance of women to the RIBA was published in "The Admission of Lady Associates," *Journal of the Royal Institute of British Architects*, 11 March 1899, 278–81, and *Journal of the Royal Institute of British Architects*, 10 Dec. 1898, 77–8. See Lynne Walker, "Women and Architecture," 99.

133 "Mr. E.W. Godwin on Lady Architects," *British Architect*, 12 June 1874, 378. See also "Lady Architects," *Architect*, 13 June 1874, 335.

134 Panton, *Nooks and Corners*, 46.

135 Godwin designed furniture for several London department stores and may have been responsible for their model rooms; his correspondence and contracts in the Archive of Art and Design, London, document these commissions. He designed a conventional terrace house for himself in 1874 and described the design process in detail in an enlightening series of articles in the *Architect* in 1876.

136 Lynne Walker, "Women and Architecture," 104.

137 For an analysis of the "renaissance" of motherhood at the turn of the century, see Hardyment, *Dream Babies*, 98–115. This change in attitude was also marked by reactionary design changes – a new emphasis on wooden beds, the fireplace, a call for unity in decoration, and an obsession with the national past – as explained by Neiswander, "Liberalism, Nationalism and the Evolution of Middle-Class Values," 138–221.

CONCLUSION

1 The bungalow has been the subject of many scholarly publications, the broadest of which is King, *The Bungalow*. See also Robertson, "Male and Female Agendas."

2 This is the subject of a current paper. See Adams, "Home Economics Movement in America."

3 Cromley, *Alone Together*.

4 See Burnett, *Social History of Housing*; Clark, *American Family Home*; Handlin, *American Home*; Wright, *Moralism and the Model Home*.

5 *Sanitary Engineer*, 15 March 1883, 338. American domestic architecture was typically praised in the British press, both for its general level of comfort and its concern for health. For an example, see "American Architecture and Plumbing Seen through English Eyes," *Sanitary Engineer*, 18 Jan. 1883, 146.

6 Hoskins, *An Hour*, 12.

7 At McGill University, for example, director Ramsay Traquair was concerned that the mere presence of women in the drafting studio would require additional staff supervision at night. See Collins, "Notes on the Centenary," 13–14.

8 The change from a decidedly domestic and attached residence for nurses to a more institutional, detached building is the subject of my "Rooms of Their Own."

9 An example of this recent scholarship on women in public buildings is Van Slyck.

10 Quoted in Bartine, "Building of the Hospital Departments and Rooms," 285.

11 Historian Ludmilla Jordanova has noted how issues of gender have also intensified the *private* mode of medicine, emphasizing in particular the medical crusade to protect the public from images of disease, injuries, or malformations. See Jordanova, *Sexual Visions*, 140.

Bibliography

Abbott, Rev. John S.C. *The Mother at Home; or, The Principles of Maternal Duty.* London: Religious Tract Society, n.d.

Ackerknecht, Erwin H. "Anticontagionism between 1821 and 1867." *Bulletin of the History of Medicine* 22 (Sept.–Oct. 1948): 562–93.

Adams, Annmarie. "Charterville and the Landscape of Social Reform." In *Perspectives in Vernacular Architecture, IV,* ed. Thomas Carter and Bernard Herman, 138–45. Columbia, Mo.: University of Missouri Press 1991.

– *Corpus Sanum in Domo Sano: The Architecture of the Domestic Sanitation Movement, 1870–1914.* Montreal: Canadian Centre for Architecture 1991.

– "Rooms with a View: Domestic Architecture and Anglo-American Fiction." *Design Book Review* 20 (spring 1991): 61–2.

– "Waste Not, Want Not." *Winterthur Portfolio* 27 (spring 1992): 75–82.

– "Les representations des femmes dans la revue de l'Institut royal architectural du Canada, 1924–73." *Recherches féministes* 7, no. 2 (1994): 7–36.

– "The Healthy Victorian City: The Old London Street at the International Health Exhibition of 1884." In *Streets: Critical Perspectives on Public Space*, ed. Zeynep Çelik, Diane Favro, and Richard Ingersoll, 203–12. Berkeley: University of California Press 1994.

– "Rooms of Their Own: The Nurses' Residences at Montréal's Royal Victoria Hospital." *Material History Review* 40 (fall 1994): 29–41.

– "Building Barriers: Images of Women in the RAIC Journal, 1924–73." *Resources for Feminist Research* 23 (fall 1994): 11–23.

– "'The House and All That Goes On in It': Domestic Architecture and the Home Economics Movement in America." Paper presented at the annual meeting of the American Studies Association, Nashville, Tennessee, Oct. 1994.

Adams, Carol. *Ordinary Lives*. London: Virago 1980.

Adams, Maurice B. *Modern Cottage Architecture*. London: Batsford 1904.

Allbutt, Henry Arthur. *Wife's Handbook: How a Woman Should Order Herself during Pregnancy, in the Lying-in Room, and after Delivery*. London: Ramsey 1886.

Allen, Polly Wynn. *Building Domestic Liberty: Charlotte Perkins Gilman's Architectural Feminism*. Amherst: University of Massachusetts Press 1988.

Architect, 1869–93.

Architect and Contract Reporter, 1893–1918.

Ariès, Philippe. *Centuries of Childhood: A Social History of Family Life*. Trans. Robert Baldick. New York: Vintage 1962.

– "The Family and the City." *Daedalus* 106 (spring 1977): 227–35.

Art Journal, 1849–1912.

Aslin, Elizabeth. *E.W. Godwin: Furniture and Decoration*. London: Murray 1986.

At Home. London: MacIntosh 1874.

Attar, Dena. *Household Books Published in Britain 1800–1914*. London: Prospect 1987.

Attfield, Judy, and Pat Kirkham, eds. *A View from the Interior: Feminism, Women and Design*. London: Women's Press 1989.

Audsley, W., and G. Audsley. *Cottage, Lodge and Villa Architecture*. London: Mackenzie, n.d.

Baby: The Mothers' Magazine, 1887–1915.

Baker, Mrs. *The Companion to the Lying-in Room*. London: Cox 1857.

Ballantyne, J.W. "A Series of Thirteen Cases of Alleged Maternal Impressions." *Edinburgh Medical Journal*, May 1892, 1025–34.

Ballin, Ada S. "Health in Our Homes." *Baby: The Mothers' Magazine* 3 (Dec. 1889–Nov. 1890): 3.

– "Drainage." *Baby: The Mothers' Magazine* 3 (June 1890): 150–1.

– "Ventilation, Lighting, Warming, Furnishing." *Baby: The Mothers' Magazine* 3 (Nov. 1890): 269–71

Banks, J.A. *Prosperity and Parenthood: A Study of Family Planning among the Victorian Middle Classes*. London: Routledge 1954.

Banner, E. Gregson. *Wholesome Houses: A Handbook of Domestic Sanitation and Ventilation*. London: Stanford 1882.

Bardwell, William. *Healthy Homes and How to Make Them*. London: Dean and Son 1854.

Barker, Lady Mary Ann. *The Bedroom and the Boudoir*. London: Macmillan 1878.

Barker-Benfield, G.J. *The Horrors of the Half-Known Life: Male Attitudes toward Women and Sexuality in Nineteenth-Century America*. New York: Harper and Row 1976.

Barrow, Margaret. *Women 1870–1928: Guide to Printed and Archival Sources*. New York: Garland 1981.

Bartine, Oliver H. "The Building of the Hospital Departments and Rooms." *Transactions of the American Hospital Association* 18 (1916): 262–87.

Beckett, Jane, and Deborah Cherry, eds. *The Edwardian Era*. London: Phaidon 1987.

Beecher, Mrs Henry Ward. "Method and Regularity in the Home." *Woman's Herald*, 16 March 1893, 51.

Beeton, Isabella. *Beeton's Book of Household Management*. 1861. Reprint, London: Chancellor 1989.

Bégin, Monique. "'Inside-Out Men': Women in Medicine." 1991 Osler Lecture presented at the Faculty of Medicine, McGill University, Montreal, 6 Nov. 1991.

Benedict, Burton. *The Anthropology of World's Fairs*. Berkeley: Lowie 1983.

Benson, Susan Porter. *Counter Cultures: Saleswomen, Managers, and Customers in American Department Stores, 1890–1940*. Urbana: University of Illinois Press 1986.

Berch, Bettina. "Scientific Management in the Home: The Empress's New Clothes." *Journal of American Culture* 3 (fall 1980): 440–5.

Bigg, George Sherman. *The Wife's Health*. London: Adlard and Son 1889.

Black, George. *Young Wife's Advice Book: A Guide for Mothers on Health and Self-Management*. 6th ed. London: Ward, Lock 1888.

Blackmar, Elizabeth. *Manhattan for Rent, 1785–1850*. Ithaca: Cornell University Press 1989.

Blake, Edward T. *Sewage Poisoning: Its Causes and Cure*. London: Spon 1880.

Blanchflower, Mary. "An Actual (and Ideal) Nursery for One Baby." *Baby: The Mothers' Magazine* 12 (Dec. 1898–Nov. 1899): 241.

Blau, Eve. "Patterns of Fact: Photography and the Transformation of the Early Industrial City." In *Architecture and Its Image: Four Centuries of Architectural Representation*, ed. Eve Blau and Edward Kaufman, 36–57. Montreal: Canadian Centre for Architecture 1989.

Bledstein, Burton J. *The Culture of Professionalism: The Middle Class and the Development of Higher Education in America*. New York: Norton 1976.

Blodgett, Harriet. *Centuries of Female Days: Englishwomen's Private Diaries*. London: Sutton 1989.

Bohun, Florence. "Back to the Home." *Englishwoman's Review*, 15 July 1910, 182–6.

Bose, Christine E., Philip L. Bereano, and Mary Malloy. "Household

Technology and the Social Construction of Housework." *Technology and Culture* 25, no. 1 (1984): 53–82.

Bourdillon, Hilary. *Women as Healers: A History of Women and Medicine.* Cambridge: Cambridge University Press 1988.

Boyle System of Ventilation, The. London: Boyle 1900.

Boys, Jos. "Is There a Feminist Analysis of Architecture?" *Built Environment* 10, no. 1 (1984): 25–34.

Brack, Mark. "The Architecture of Health: The Role of Hygiene in the Architecture and Planning of Nineteeth-Century London." Department of Architecture, University of California at Berkeley, 3 May 1988. Photocopy.

Branca, Patricia. *Silent Sisterhood: Middle-Class Women in the Victorian Home.* London: Croom Helm 1975.

Briggs, Asa. *Victorian People: A Reassessment of Persons and Themes, 1851–67.* Chicago: University of Chicago Press 1972.

– "Public Opinion and Public Health in the Age of Chadwick." In *The Collected Essays of Asa Briggs*, 2:129–52. Urbana: University of Illinois Press 1985.

– *Victorian Cities.* Harmondsworth: Penguin 1985.

– *Victorian Things.* London: Batsford 1988.

Brightfield, Myron F. "The Medical Profession in Early Victorian England, as Depicted in the Novels of the Period (1840–1870)." *Bulletin of the History of Medicine* 35, no. 3 (1961): 238–56.

British Architect, 1874–1919.

Brookes, Barbara. "Women and Reproduction c.1860–1919." In *Labour and Love*, ed. Jane Lewis, 149–71. Oxford: Basil Blackwell 1986.

Brooks, S.H. *Rudimentary Treatise on the Erection of Dwelling Houses.* London: Weale 1860.

Brown, James Baldwin. *The Home in Its Relation to Man and Society.* London: Clarke 1883.

Brown, M. Harriette. *To Those About to Marry.* Paisley: Alexander Gardner [1905].

Browne, Phyllis. "House-cleaning." In *Our Homes, and How to Make them Healthy*, ed. Shirley Forster Murphy, 869–94. London: Cassell 1883.

– "The Profession of Housewifery." *Young Woman* 8 (Oct. 1899–Sept. 1900): 223–5.

Bruegmann, Robert. "Central Heating and Forced Ventilation: Origins and Effects on Architectural Design." *Journal of the Society of Architectural Historians* 37 (Oct. 1978): 143–60.

Buchan, William. *Domestic Medicine.* New York: Lindsay 1812.

Buchan, W.P. "Recent Improvements in House Drainage." *Sanitary Record*, 15 Oct. 1888.

Buckley, Cheryl. "Made in Patriarchy: Toward a Feminist Analysis of Women and Design." *Design Issues* 3 (fall 1986): 3–24.

Buckton, Catherine M. *Our Dwellings, Healthy and Unhealthy.* London: Longmans 1885.

Builder, 1842–.

Building News, 1857–1926.

Bull, Thomas. *The Maternal Management of Children, in Health and Disease.* London: Longman 1840.

– *Hints to Mothers for the Management of Health during the Period of Pregnancy, and in the Lying-in Room.* 4th ed. London: Longman, Brown, Green, and Longmans 1844.

Bunting, Evelyn, et al. *A School for Mothers.* London: Horace Marshall and Son 1907.

Burdett, Henry C., and F. de Chaumont, eds. *Report of the Fourth Congress of the Sanitary Institute of Great Britain.* London: Sanitary Institute 1880.

Burnett, John. *A Social History of Housing, 1815–1985.* 2nd ed. London: Methuen 1986.

Burton, Anthony. "Looking Forward from Ariès? Pictorial and Material Evidence for the History of Childhood and Family Life." *Continuity and Change* 4 (1989): 203–29.

Bynum, W.F., Stephen Lock, and Roy Porter, eds. *Medical Journals and Medical Knowledge.* London: Routledge 1992.

Cabinet Maker and Art Furnisher, 1882–84.

Calder, Jenni. *The Victorian Home.* London: Batsford 1977.

Callen, Anthea. *Angel in the Studio: Women in the Arts and Crafts Movement, 1870–1914.* London: Astragal 1979.

Carter, Jenny, and Therese Duriez. *With Child: Birth through the Ages.* Edinburgh: Mainstream 1986.

Cartwright, Frederick F. *A Social History of Medicine.* London: Longman 1977.

Cassedy, James H. "Hygeia: A Mid-Victorian Dream of a City of Health." *Journal of the History of Medicine and Allied Sciences* 17 (1962): 217–28.

– "The Flamboyant Colonel Waring: An Anticontagionist Holds the American Stage in the Age of Pasteur and Koch." *Bulletin of the History of Medicine* 36 (1962): 163–76.

Cassell's Household Guide. 4 vols. London: Cassell, Pelter, and Galpin 1869–71.

Chadwick, Edwin. *Report to Her Majesty's Principal Secretary of State for the Home Department, from the Poor Law Commissioners, on an Inquiry into the Sanitary Condition of the Labouring Population of Great Britain.* London: Clowes 1842.

Chappell, Jennie. "A Parlour-Child." *Baby: The Mothers' Magazine* 10 (Dec. 1896–Nov. 1897): 261.

Chavasse, Pye Henry. *Advice to a Mother*. 14th ed. London: Churchill 1886.

– *Advice to a Wife*. 12th ed. London: Churchill 1887.

Clark, Clifford Edward, Jr. "Domestic Architecture as an Index to Social History: The Romantic Revival and the Cult of Domesticity in America, 1840–1890." *Journal of Interdisciplinary History* 7 (summer 1976): 33–56.

– *The American Family Home, 1800–1960*. Chapel Hill: University of North Carolina Press 1986.

– "The Vision of the Dining Room: Plan Book Dreams and Middle-Class Realities." In *Dining in America, 1850–1900*, ed. Kathryn Grover, 142–72. Amherst: University of Massachusetts Press 1987.

Coke, Mrs Talbot. *The Gentlewoman at Home*. London: Henry [1890].

Collection of Feeding Bottles. Wells: Cow and Gate Ltd., n.d.

Collins, Peter. "Notes on the Centenary of the Faculty of Engineering of McGill University: Its Origin and Growth." N.p., n.d.

Colomina, Beatriz, ed. *Sexuality and Space*. Princeton: Princeton Architectural Press 1992.

Combe, Andrew. *Treatise on the Physiological and Moral Management of Infancy*. Edinburgh: Maclachlan 1840.

Concerning Carpets and Art Decoration of Floors. London: Waterlow and Sons 1884.

Connor, J.T.H. "Listerism Unmasked: Antisepsis and Asepsis in Victorian Anglo-Canada." *Journal of the History of Medicine and Allied Sciences* 49 (April 1994): 207–39.

Conquest, John Ticker. *Letters to a Mother on the Management of Herself and Her Children in Health and Disease*. London: Longman 1848.

Contemporary Review, 1866–.

Conway, Katharine St John. "Life at Newnham." *Young Woman* 3 (Oct. 1894–Sept. 1895): 99–103.

Conway, Moncure Daniel. *Travels in South Kensington*. London 1882. Reprint, New York: Garland 1977.

Cook, Lady. "Moral Environment." *Baby: The Mothers' Magazine* 11 (Dec. 1897–Nov. 1898): 146–7.

Cook, Millicent Whiteside. *Tables and Chairs: A Practical Guide to Economical Furnishing*. London: Routlege [1876].

Cooke, Grace. "The Training of a Lady Doctor: Life and Work at the School of Medicine for Women." *Young Woman* 7 (Oct. 1898–Sept. 1899): 102–5.

Corfield, W.H. *Dwelling Houses: Their Sanitary Construction and Arrangements*. London: Lewis 1894.

– *Disease and Defective House Sanitation*. London: Lewis 1896.

Cosgrove, J.J. *History of Sanitation*. Pittsburgh: Standard 1909.

Cowan, Ruth Schwartz. *More Work for Mother: The Ironies of Household Technology from the Open Hearth to the Microwave*. New York: Basic 1983.

Creese, Walter. "Fowler and the Domestic Octagon." *Art Bulletin* 28 (1946): 89–102.

Cromley, Elizabeth Collins. "Sleeping Around: A History of American Beds and Bedrooms." *Journal of Design History* 3, no. 1 (1990): 1–17.

– *Alone Together: A History of New York's Early Apartments*. Ithaca: Cornell University Press 1990.

Crouch, Joseph, and Edmund Butler. *The Apartments of the House: Their Arrangement, Furnishing and Decoration*. London: Unicorn 1900.

Daunton, M.J. *House and Home in the Victorian City: Working Class Housing, 1850–1914*. London: Edward Arnold 1983.

Davidoff, Leonore. *The Best Circles: Society Etiquette and the Season*. London: Cresset 1973.

– "Mastered for Life: Servant and Wife in Victorian and Edwardian England." *Journal of Social History* 7 (summer 1974): 406–28.

Davidoff, Leonore, and Catherine Hall. "The Architecture of Public and Private Life: English Middle-Class Society in a Provincial Town, 1780–1850." In *The Pursuit of Urban History*, ed. Derek Fraser and Anthony Sutcliffe, 326–45. London: Edward Arnold 1983.

– *Family Fortunes: Men and Women of the English Middle Class, 1780–1850*. London: Hutchison 1987.

Davidoff, Leonore, Jean L'Esperance, and Howard Newby. "Landscape with Figures: Home and Community in English Society." In *Rights and Wrongs of Women*, ed. Juliet Mitchell and Ann Oakley, 139–75. London: Penguin 1976.

Davidson, Caroline. *A Woman's Work Is Never Done: A History of Housework in the British Isles 1650–1950*. London: Chatto and Windus 1982.

Davies, Celia. "Making Sense of the Census in Britain and the USA: The Changing Occupational Classification and the Position of Nurses." *Sociological Review* 28 (1980): 581–609.

Davin, Anna. "Imperialism and Motherhood." *History Workshop Journal* 5 (spring 1978): 9–65.

Davison, Graeme. "The City as a Natural System: Theories of Urban Society in Early Nineteenth-Century Britain." In *The Pursuit of Urban History*, ed. Derek Fraser and Anthony Sutcliffe, 349–70. London: Edward Arnold 1983.

Day, Lewis F. "The Woman's Part in Domestic Decoration." *Magazine of Art*, 1881, 457–63.

Decoration, 1880–90.

DeLacy, Margaret. "Puerperal Fever in Eighteenth-Century Britain." *Bulletin of the History of Medicine* 63 (1989): 521–56.

Delamont, Sara, and Lorna Duffin, eds. *The Nineteenth-Century Woman: Her Cultural and Physical World*. London: Croom Helm 1978.

Delaporte, François. *Disease and Civilization: The Cholera in Paris, 1832*. Cambridge: MIT Press 1986.

Dethier, Kathryn. "The Spirit of Progressive Reform: The *Ladies' Home Journal* House Plans, 1900–1902." *Journal of Design History* 6, no. 4 (1993): 247–61.

Dixon, Roger, and Stefan Muthesius. *Victorian Architecture*. New York: Oxford University Press 1978.

Dodd, Helen. *The Healthful Farmhouse by a Farmer's Wife*. Boston: Whitcomb and Barrows 1906.

Dodds, S.W. *Health in the Household; or, Hygienic Cookery*. New York 1891.

Donnison, Jean. *Midwives and Medical Men: A History of Inter-Professional Rivalries and Women's Rights*. London: Heinemann 1977.

Downing, Andrew Jackson. *The Architecture of Country Houses*. 1850. Reprint, New York: Dover 1969.

Drysdale, J. *Health and Comfort in House Building*. 2nd ed. London: Spon 1876.

Drysdale, J., and J.W. Hayward. *Health and Comfort in House Building*. London: Spon 1872.

Duffy, John. *The Sanitarians: A History of American Public Health*. Urbana: University of Illinois Press 1990.

Durham Patent System of Screw-joint Iron House Drainage, The. New York: de Vinne 1889.

Dwork, Deborah. "Victorian Child Care: Lay Medical Manuals." *Maternal and Child Health*, May 1983, 207–14.

Dyhouse, Carol. *Girls Growing Up in Late Victorian and Edwardian England*. London: Routledge and Kegan Paul 1981.

– *Feminism and the Family in England 1880–1939*. Oxford: Basil Blackwell 1989.

Dyos, H.J. *Victorian Suburb: A Study of the Growth of Camberwell*. Leicester: Leicester University Press 1961.

Dyos, H.J., and Michael Wolff, eds. *The Victorian City: Images and Realities*. 2 vols. London: Routledge and Kegan Paul 1973.

Eassie, William. *Healthy Houses: A Handbook to History, Defects and Remedies of Drainage*. London: Simpkins, Marshall 1872.

– *Sanitary Arrangements for Dwellings*. London: Smith, Elder 1874.

Eastlake, Charles L. *Hints on Household Taste*. 1878. Reprint, New York: Dover 1969.

Edinburgh Medical Journal, 1855–1954.

Edis, Robert W. *The Decoration and Furniture of Town Houses*. London: C. Kegan Paul 1881.

– "Internal Decoration." In *Our Homes, and How to Make Them Healthy*, ed. Shirley Forster Murphy, 309–64. London: Cassell 1883.

Ehrenreich, Barbara. *Witches, Midwives and Nurses: A History of Women Healers*. Old Westbury: Feminist Press 1973.

Ehrenreich, Barbara, and Deirdre English. *For Her Own Good: 150 Years of Experts' Advice to Women*. London: Pluto 1979.

Elder-Duncan, John Hudson. *The House Beautiful and Useful*. London: Cassell 1907.

Elliot, James. *The City in Maps: Urban Mapping to 1900*. London: British Library 1987.

Ellis, Edward. *Manual of What Every Mother Should Know*. London: Churchill 1881.

Ellis, Sarah. *The Wives of England*. London: Fisher 1843.

Englishwoman's Domestic Magazine, 1852–79.

English Woman's Journal, 1858–63.

Englishwoman's Review, 1866–1910.

Englishwoman's Review and Drawing Room Journal of Social Progress, Literature and Art, 1857–59.

Englishwoman's Year Book, 1875, 1881–1916.

Erlemann, Christine. "What Is Feminist Architecture?" In *Feminist Aesthetics*, ed. Gisela Ecker, trans. Harriet Anderson, 125–34. Boston: Beacon 1986.

Etiquette of Love, Courtship and Marriage. Halifax: Milner and Sowerby 1859.

Fawcett, Mrs. "Politics in the Home." *Woman's Herald*, 6 July 1893, 315–16.

Finch, Casey. "'Hooked and Buttoned Together': Victorian Underwear and Representations of the Female Body." *Victorian Studies* 34 (spring 1991): 337–63.

Finer, S.E. *The Life and Times of Sir Edwin Chadwick*. London: Methuen 1952.

Forty, Adrian. "The Modern Hospital in England and France: The Social and Medical Uses of Architecture." In *Buildings and Society: Essays on the Social Development of the Built Environment*, ed. Anthony D. King, 61–93. London: Routlege and Kegan Paul 1980.

– *Objects of Desire: Design and Society since 1750*. New York: Pantheon 1986.

– "Of Cars, Clothes and Carpets: Design Metaphors in Architectural Thought." *Journal of Design History* 2, no. 1 (1989): 1–14.

Fowler, O.S. *A Home For All*. New York: Fowlers and Wells 1854.

Fox, Selina F. *Mother and Baby: Outlines for a Young Mother on the Care of Herself and Her Baby*. London: Churchill 1912.

Foyle, Arthur M. "Henry Roberts, 1802–1876, a Pioneer of Housing for the Labouring Classes." *Builder*, 2 Jan. 1953, 5–8.

Franklin, Jill. *The Gentleman's Country House and Its Plan, 1835–1914*. London: Routledge and Kegan Paul 1981.

Fraser, Derek, and Anthony Sutcliffe, eds. *The Pursuit of Urban History*. London: Edward Arnold 1983.

Freedman, Estelle. "Separatism as Strategy: Female Institution Building and American Feminism, 1870–1930." *Feminist Studies* 5 (1979): 512–29.

Galton, Douglas. *Observations on the Construction of Healthy Dwellings*. Oxford: Clarendon 1880.

– "Warming and Ventilation." In *Our Homes, and How to Make Them Healthy*, ed. Shirley Forster Murphy, 484–614. London: Cassell 1883.

– "The International Health Exhibition." *Art Journal*, n.s., 4 (1884): 153–6, 161–4, 293–6.

– *Healthy Hospitals*. Oxford: Clarendon 1893.

Gardiner, Florence Mary. *Furnishings and Fittings for Every Home*. London: Record 1894.

Gardner, E.C. *The House That Jill Built, after Jack's Had Proved a Failure*. New York: Fords, Howard, and Hulbert 1882.

Garrett, Rhoda, and Agnes Garrett. *Suggestions for House Decoration*. London: Macmillan 1876.

Gaskell, Elizabeth Cleghorn. *My Diary: The Early Years of My Daughter Marianne*. London: Shorter 1923.

Gaskell, S. Martin. *Model Housing: From the Great Exhibition to the Festival of Britain*. London: Mansell 1987.

Gathorne-Hardy, Jonathan. *The Rise and Fall of the British Nanny*. London: Weidenfeld and Nicolson 1985.

Gauldie, Enid. *Cruel Habitations: A History of Working-Class Housing, 1780–1918*. London: Allen and Unwin 1974.

Gelles, Edward. *Nursery Furniture*. London: Constable 1982.

Gibson, James Sivewright. "The Late John McKean Brydon." *Journal of the Royal Institute of British Architects*, 22 June 1901, 400–5.

Gillow's: A Record of a Furnishing Firm During 2 Centuries. London: Harrison 1901.

Gilman, Charlotte Perkins. *The Yellow Wallpaper and Other Writings*. New York: Bantam 1989.

Gilman, Sander L. "Black Bodies, White Bodies: Toward an Iconography of Female Sexuality in Late Nineteenth-Century Art, Medicine, and Literature." *Critical Inquiry* 12 (fall 1985): 204–42.

Girouard, Mark. "Victorian Sweetness and Light: Newnham College, Cambridge." *Country Life*, 16 Dec. 1971, 1704–6.

– *Sweetness and Light: The Queen Anne Movement 1860–1900*. London: Yale University Press 1977.

– *Life in the English Country House: A Social and Architectural History*. London: Yale University Press 1978.

Gissing, George. *The Odd Women*. London: Nelson, n.d.

Gladstone, Mrs Catherine. *Healthy Nurseries and Bedrooms, including the Lying-in Room*. London: Clowes 1884.

Gleason, Rachel B. "Household Cares: Cannot We Reduce Them?" *Woman's Signal*, 2 June 1898, 342.

Godwin, E.W. *Dress in Its Relation to Health and Climate*. London: Clowes 1884.

Gorham, Deborah. *The Victorian Girl and the Feminine Ideal*. Bloomington: Indiana University Press 1982.

Goubert, Jean-Pierre. *The Conquest of Water: The Advent of Health in the Industrial Age*. Trans. Andrew Wilson. Princeton: Princeton University Press 1989.

Grainger, Allerdale. "Census Statistics as Indicative of the Employment of Women in London." *Englishwoman's Yearbook*, 1881, 62–9.

Granshaw, Lindsay. "'Upon This Principle I Have Based a Practice': The Development and Reception of Antisepsis in Britain, 1867–90." In *Medical Innovations in Historical Perspective*, ed. John V. Pickstone, 17–46. New York: St Martin's Press 1992.

Gray, A. Stuart. *Edwardian Architecture: A Biographical Dictionary*. London: Duckworth 1985.

Green, A.F. "The Problem of London's Drainage." *Geography* 41 (1956): 147–54.

Green, Harvey. *The Light of the Home: An Intimate View of the Lives of Women in Victorian America*. New York: Pantheon 1983.

Grier, Katherine C. *Culture and Comfort: People, Parlors, and Upholstery, 1850–1930*. Rochester: Strong Museum 1988.

Guide to the Sanitary and Insanitary Houses. London: International Health Exhibition 1884.

Gulick, Dr Luther. "The Home Maker: What She Ought to Know." *Young Woman* 8 (Oct. 1899–Sept. 1900): 64.

Haley, Bruce. *The Healthy Body and Victorian Culture*. Cambridge: Harvard University Press 1978.

Hall, Catherine. "The Early Formation of Victorian Domestic Ideology." In *Fit Work for Women*, ed. Sandra Burman, 15–32. New York: St Martin's Press 1979.

Hall, Lesley. *Hygeia's Handmaids: Women, Health and Healing*. London: Wellcome Institute for the History of Medicine 1988.

Hamlin, Christopher. "Providence and Putrefaction: Victorian Sanitarians and the Natural Theology of Health and Disease." *Victorian Studies* 28 (spring 1985): 381–411.

Handlin, David. "Efficiency and the American Home." *Architectural Association Quarterly* 5 (winter 1973): 50–4.

– *The American Home: Architecture and Society, 1815–1915*. Boston: Little 1979.

Hardyment, Christina. *Dream Babies: Child Care from Locke to Spock*. London: Cape 1983.

Harland, Marion. *Common Sense in the Nursery*. Glasgow: Morrison 1886.

Harper, Roger. *Victorian Building Regulations*. London: Mansell 1985.

Harris, Dianne. "Cultivating Power: The Language of Feminism in Women's Garden Literature, 1870–1920." *Landscape Journal* 13 (fall 1994): 113–23.

Hart, Ernest. "The International Health Exhibition: Its Influence and Possible Sequels." *Journal of the Society of Arts*, 28 Nov. 1884, 35–58.

Hartman, Mary, and Lois W. Banner, eds. *Clio's Consciousness Raised*. New York: Harper 1974.

Haweis, Mrs H.R. *The Art of Decoration*. London: Chatto and Windus 1881.

Hayden, Dolores. *The Grand Domestic Revolution: A History of Feminist Designs for American Homes, Neighborhoods and Cities*. Cambridge: MIT Press 1981.

Heal and Son Collection. Archive of Art and Design. London.

Health Exhibition Literature, The. 19 vols. London: Clowes 1884.

Hellyer, S. Stevens. *The Plumber and Sanitary Houses*. London: Batsford 1893.

Hersey, George. "Godey's Choice." *Journal of the Society of Architectural Historians* 18 (Oct. 1959): 104–11.

Himmelfarb, Gertrude. *Marriage and Morals among the Victorians*. New York: Knopf 1986.

Hinchcliffe, Tanis. *North Oxford*. New Haven: Yale University Press 1992.

Hoffert, Sylvia D. *Private Matters: American Attitudes toward Childbearing and Infant Nurture in the Urban North, 1800–1860*. Urbana: University of Illinois Press 1989.

Holdsworth, Angela. *Out of the Doll's House: The Story of Women in the Twentieth Century*. London: BBC 1988.

Holme, Thea. *The Carlyles at Home*. London: Oxford University Press 1965.

Holmes, Oliver Wendell. *Medical Essays*. New York: Houghton, Mifflin 1883.

Homoeopathic Medical Directory of Great Britain and Ireland, and Annual Abstract of British Homoeopathic Serial Literature, The. London: Turner 1868.

Horsfall, Mrs. *The House and Its Surroundings*. London: Hardwicke and Bogue 1878.

Hosking, William. *Healthy Homes: A Guide to the Proper Regulation of Buildings, Streets, Drains, and Sewers*. London: Murray 1849.

Hoskins, George Gordon. *An Hour with a Sewer Rat*. London: Simpkins, Marshall 1879.

Houghton, Walter. *The Victorian Frame of Mind, 1830–1870*. New Haven: Yale University Press 1957.

Howe, Bea. *Arbiter of Taste*. London: Harvill 1967.

Howells, William Dean. *A Hazard of New Fortunes*. 1890. Reprint, Oxford: Oxford University Press 1965.

Illustrated Household Journal and Englishwoman's Domestic Magazine, 1880–81.

Illustrated London News, 1842–.

International Health Exhibition Official Guide, The. London: Clowes 1884.

International Medical and Sanitary Exhibition Official Catalogue. London: Parkes Museum of Hygiene 1881.

Jarcho, S. "Yellow Fever, Cholera, and the Beginning of Medical Cartography." *Journal of the History of Medicine and Allied Sciences* 25 (1970): 131–42.

Jeffrey, Kirk. "The Family as Utopian Retreat from the City: The Nineteenth-Century Contribution." *Soundings* 55 (1972): 21–41.

Jephson, Henry. *The Sanitary Evolution of London*. London: T. Fisher Unwin 1907.

Johnson, Mrs H.A. "Day and Night Nurseries." *Baby: The Mothers' Magazine* 13 (Dec. 1899–Nov. 1900): 181–3.

Jones, Dora M. "The Life of a Bachelor Girl in a Big City." *Young Woman* 8 (Oct. 1899–Sept. 1900): 131–3.

Jordanova, Ludmilla. *Sexual Visions: Images of Gender in Science and Medicine between the Eighteenth and Twentieth Centuries*. Madison: University of Wisconsin Press 1989.

Journal, 1893.

Journal of the Royal Institute of British Architects, 1893–.

Journal of the Society of Arts, 1852–1907.

Kerber, Linda K. "Separate Spheres, Female Worlds, Woman's Place: The Rhetoric of Women's History." *Journal of American History* 75 (June 1988): 9–39.

Kerr, Robert. *The Gentleman's House; or, How to Plan English Residences*. London: Murray 1864.

King, Anthony D. *The Bungalow: The Production of a Global Culture*. London: Routledge and Kegan Paul 1984.

King-Hall, Magdale. *The Story of the Nursery*. London: Routledge and Kegan Paul 1958.

Kunzle, David. "Dress Reform as Antifeminism: A Response to Helene E. Roberts's 'The Exquisite Slave: The Role of Clothes in the Making of the Victorian Woman.'" *Signs* 2, no. 3 (1977): 570–9.

Lady's Realm, 1896–1915.

Lancet, 1823–.

Lanchester, Henry J. *How to Make a House Healthy and Comfortable*. London: Simpkins, Marshall 1873.

Larimore, F.C. "Hygiene of the Sick-room." *Sanitarian* 20 (March 1888): 220–3.

Larson, Magali Sarfatti. *The Rise of Professionalism: A Sociological Analysis.* Berkeley: University of California Press 1977.

Lasdun, Susan. *Victorians at Home.* New York: Viking 1981.

Leared, Arthur. "Infant Mortality and Its Causes." *English Woman's Journal,* 1 Nov. 1862, 173–83.

Leverton, Mrs Edith Waldemar. *Small Houses and How to Furnish Them.* London: Pearson 1903.

Lewes, George Henry. *The Physiology of Common Life.* Edinburgh and London: Blackwood 1859.

Lewis, Jane. *Women in England 1870–1950: Sexual Divisions and Social Change.* Sussex: Wheatsheaf 1984.

– ed. *Labour and Love: Women's Experience of Home and Family, 1850–1940.* Oxford: Basil Blackwell 1986.

Lewis, Judith Schneid. *In the Family Way: Childbearing in the British Aristocracy, 1760–1860.* New Brunswick: Rutgers University Press 1986.

Lewis, R.A. *Edwin Chadwick and the Public Health Movement, 1832–54.* London: Longmans, Green 1952.

Lipstadt, Helene. "Housing the Bourgeoisie: Cesar Daly and the Ideal Home." *Oppositions* 8 (spring 1977): 33–47.

Lloyd, Bonnie. "Woman's Place, Man's Place." *Landscape* 20 (Oct. 1975): 10–13.

Lochhead, Marion. *The Victorian Household.* London: Murray 1964.

Loftie, Martha Jane. *The Dining-Room.* London: Macmillan 1878.

– *Comfort in the Home.* London: Leadenhall 1895.

Loftie, William J. *A Plea for Art in the House.* London: Macmillan 1876.

Long, Helen C. *The Edwardian House: The Middle-Class Home in Britain, 1880–1914.* Manchester: Manchester University Press 1993.

Longmate, Norman. *King Cholera: The Biography of a Disease.* London: H. Hamilton 1966.

Lukacs, John. "The Bourgeois Interior." *American Scholar* 39, no. 4 (1970): 616–30.

Lupton, Ellen, and J. Abbott Miller. *The Bathroom, the Kitchen, and the Aesthetics of Waste: A Process of Elimination.* Princeton: Princeton University Press 1992.

McClary, Andrew. "Germs Are Everywhere: The Germ Threat as Seen in Magazine Articles 1890–1920." *Journal of American Culture* 3 (1980): 33–46.

McDannell, Colleen. *The Christian Home in Victorian America.* Bloomington: Indiana University Press 1986.

McDowell, Linda. "City and Home: Urban Housing and the Sexual Division of Space." In *Sexual Divisions: Patterns and Processes,* ed. Mary Evans and Clare Ungerson, 142–63. London: Tavistock 1983.

Mackay, James. *Nursery Antiques.* London: Ward Lock 1976.

McLaren, Angus. *Birth Control in Nineteenth-Century England.* London: Croom Helm 1978.

– *Reproductive Rituals: The Perception of Fertility in England from the Sixteenth Century to the Nineteenth Century.* London: Methuen 1984.

McMurry, Sally. "Women in the American Vernacular Landscape." *Material Culture* 20 (spring 1988): 33–49.

– *Families and Farmhouses in Nineteenth-Century America: Vernacular Design and Social Change.* New York: Oxford University Press 1988.

McNeil, Peter. "Designing Women: Gender, Sexuality and the Interior Decorator, c.1890–1940." *Art History* 17 (Dec. 1994): 631–57.

Magazine of Art, 1878–1904.

Maguire, William R. *Domestic Sanitary Drainage and Plumbing.* 3rd ed. London: Kegan Paul, Trench, Trubner 1901.

Mallet, Mrs. "National Association for Housewifery." *Women's Penny Paper,* 28 Sept. 1889, 7.

Mangan, J.A., and James Walvin, eds. *Manliness and Morality: Middle-Class Masculinity in Britain and America, 1800–1948.* Manchester: Manchester University Press 1987.

Martin, Emily. *The Woman in the Body: A Cultural Analysis of Reproduction.* Boston: Beacon 1987.

Martineau, Harriet. *Household Education.* London: Smith, Elder 1867.

Matrix. *Making Space: Women and the Man-made Environment.* London: Pluto 1984.

Mechling, Jay. "Advice to Historians on Advice to Mothers." *Journal of Social History* 9 (fall 1975): 44–63.

Merchant, Carolyn. "Gender and Environmental History." *Journal of American History* 76 (March 1990): 1117–21.

Miall, Antony, and Peter Miall. *The Victorian Nursery Book.* London: Dent 1980.

Mitchell, Juliet, and Ann Oakley, eds. *The Rights and Wrongs of Women.* London: Penguin 1976.

Montague, Ken. "The Aesthetics of Hygiene: Aesthetic Dress, Modernity, and the Body as Sign." *Journal of Design History* 7, no. 2 (1994): 91–112.

Montgomery, Rachel. "Careers for Women." In *The Lady's Realm,* 200–1. 1904–05. Reprint, London: Arrow 1972.

Montgomery, W.F. *An Exposition of the Signs and Symptoms of Pregnancy.* London: Sherwood, Gilbert, and Piper 1837.

Morantz, Regina Markell. "Nineteenth-Century Health Reform and Women: A Program of Self-Help." In *Medicine without Doctors: Home Health Care in American History,* ed. Guenter B. Risse, Ronald L. Numbers, and Judith Walzer Leavitt, 73–93. New York: Science History Publications 1977.

– "Making Women Modern: Middle Class Women and Health Reform in 19th Century America." *Journal of Social History* 10 (1977): 490–507.

Morantz-Sanchez, Regina. "The Female Student Has Arrived: The Rise of the Women's Medical Movement." In *'Send Us a Lady Physician': Women Doctors in America, 1835–1920*, ed. Ruth J. Abram, 59–69. New York: Norton 1985.

Morgan-Brown, Laura E. "What the Census of 1891 Tells Us." *Woman's Herald*, 15 Aug. 1891, 683.

Morris, Malcolm. "Arsenic in Wall-papers and Paints." In *Our Homes, and How to Make Them Healthy*, ed. Shirley Forster Murphy, 365–72. London: Cassell 1883.

Mort, Frank. *Dangerous Sexualities: Medico-Moral Politics in England since 1830*. London: Routledge and Kegan Paul 1987.

Mother's Home-book, The. London: Ward, Lock, n.d.

MSA and MRAS. *The Grammar of House Planning*. Edinburgh: Fullarton 1864.

Murphy, Shirley Forster, ed. *Our Homes, and How to Make Them Healthy*. London: Cassell 1883.

Muthesius, Hermann. *The English House*. 1904–05. Reprint, New York: Rizzoli 1979.

Muthesius, Stefan. *The English Terraced House*. New Haven: Yale University Press 1982.

– "'We Do Not Understand What Is Meant by a "Company" Designing': Design versus Commerce in Late Nineteenth-Century English Furnishing." *Journal of Design History* 5, no. 2 (1992): 113–19.

Neale, Shirley. "An Architect Presents Arms." *Country Life*, 14 Nov. 1985, 1570–2.

– "Robert William Edis, 1839–1927." *Victorian Society Annual*, 1985–86, 12–20.

Neiswander, Judith Ann. "Liberalism, Nationalism and the Evolution of Middle-Class Values: The Literature on Interior Decoration in England, 1875–1914." PH D diss., University of London 1988.

New England Quarterly Journal of Medicine and Surgery, 1842–43.

Nicholls, Phillip A. *Homoeopathy and the Medical Profession*. London: Croom Helm 1988.

Nicholson, Shirley. *A Victorian Household*. London: Barrie and Jenkins 1988.

Oakley, Ann. *Sex, Gender and Society*. London: Maurice Temple Smith 1972.

– *The Sociology of Housework*. New York: Pantheon 1974.

– *Woman's Work: The Housewife, Past and Present*. New York: Vintage 1974.

– "Wisewoman and Medicine Man: Changes in the Management of Childbirth." In *Rights and Wrongs of Women*, ed. Juliet Mitchell and Ann Oakley, 1–58. London: Penguin 1976.

– *The Captured Womb: A History of the Medical Care of Pregnant Women*. Oxford: Basil Blackwell 1984.

Ogle, Maureen. "All the Modern Conveniences: American Household Plumbing, 1840–1870." PH D diss., Iowa State University 1992.

O'Hara, Georgina. *The World of the Baby*. London: Michael Joseph 1989.

Olsen, Donald J. "Victorian London: Specialization, Segregation and Privacy." *Victorian Studies* 17 (spring 1974): 265–78.

– *Town Planning in London: The Eighteenth and Nineteenth Centuries*. 2nd ed. New Haven: Yale University Press 1982.

– *The City as a Work of Art: London, Paris, Vienna*. New Haven: Yale University Press 1986.

O'Neill, Hannah Cox, and Edith A. Barnett. *New Life: Its Genesis and Culture*. London: Swan Sonnenschein 1890.

On the Evils Resulting from Rising Too Early after Childbirth. London: Ladies' Sanitary Association, n.d.

Orrinsmith, Lucy. *The Drawing Room: Its Decoration and Furniture*. London: Macmillan 1876.

Panoramic Views of the International Health Exhibition. London: Andres, Lehmaier 1884.

Panton, Jane Ellen. *From Kitchen to Garret: Hints for Young Householders*. London: Ward and Downey 1888.

– *Nooks and Corners*. London: Ward and Downey 1889.

– *Suburban Residences and How to Circumvent Them*. London: Ward and Downey 1896.

– *The Way They Should Go: Hints to Young Parents*. London: Ward and Downey 1896.

– *Leaves from a Life*. London: Eveleigh Nash 1908.

Parent's Review, 1890–.

Parker, Gilbert. "The Housing of Educated Working Women." In *Report of the Transactions of the International Council of Women*, 258–73. London: T. Fisher Unwin 1889.

Parkes Museum of Hygiene International Medical and Sanitary Exhibition Official Catalogue. London: Parkes Museum 1881.

Parsons, Gail Pat. "The British Medical Profession and Contagion Theory: Puerperal Fever as a Case Study." *Medical History* 22 (April 1978): 138–59.

Pearson, Lynn F. *The Architectural and Social History of Cooperative Living*. London: Macmillan 1988.

Peel, Dorothy Constance. *The New Home*. London: Constable 1898.

Pennington, T.H. "Listerism, Its Decline and Its Persistence: The Introduction of Aseptic Surgical Techniques in Three British Teaching Hospitals, 1890–99." *Medical History* 39, no. 1 (1995): 35–60.

Peterson, M. Jeanne. *Family, Love, and Work in the Lives of Victorian Gentlewomen*. Bloomington: Indiana University Press 1989.

Playfair, W.S. "Defective Sanitation as a Cause of Puerperal Disease." *Lancet*, 5 Feb. 1887, 251–4.

Plunkett, Mrs H.M. *Women, Plumbers, and Doctors; or, Household Sanitation*. New York: D. Appleton 1885.

Poore, George Vivian. *The Dwelling House*. London: Longmans, Green 1887.

– *London (Ancient and Modern): From the Sanitary and Medical Point of View*. London: Cassell 1889.

Poovey, Mary. *Uneven Developments: The Ideological Work of Gender in Mid-Victorian England*. Chicago: University of Chicago Press 1988.

Prior, Lindsay. "The Architecture of the Hospital: A Study of Spatial Organization and Medical Knowledge." *British Journal of Sociology* 39, no. 1 (1988): 86–113.

– "The Local Space of Medical Discourse: Disease, Illness and Hospital Architecture." In *The Social Construction of Illness: Illness and Medical Knowledge in Past and Present*, ed. Jens Lachmund and Gunnar Stollberg, 67–84. Stuttgart: Steiner 1992.

Pugh, Martin. *Women's Suffrage in Britain 1867–1928*. London: Historical Association 1980.

Punch, 1841–.

Queen, 1861–.

Quiney, Anthony. *House and Home: A History of the Small English House*. London: BBC 1986.

Reinherz, H. "The Housing of the Educated Working Woman." *Englishwoman's Review*, 15 Jan. 1900, 7–11.

Rendall, Jane. *The Origins of Modern Feminism: Women in Britain, France and the United States, 1780–1860*. London: Macmillan 1985.

Report of the Transactions of the International Council of Women. London: T. Fisher Unwin 1889.

Reynolds, Osborne. *Sewer Gas, and How to Keep It Out of Houses*. London: Macmillan 1872.

Richardson, Benjamin Ward. *Hygeia*. London: Macmillan 1876.

– "Woman as a Sanitary Reformer." In *Report of the Fourth Congress of the Sanitary Institute of Great Britain*, ed. Henry C. Burdett and F. de Chaumont. London: Sanitary Institute 1880.

– "Health in the Home." In *Our Homes, and How to Make Them Healthy*, ed. Shirley Forster Murphy, 1–32. London: Cassell 1883.

– *National Health*. London: Longmans, Green 1890.

– "Light in the Sick-room." *Sanitarian* 24 (April 1890): 313–14.

Richardson, Dorothy M. *Pilgrimage.* 1916. Reprint, New York: Knopf 1967.

Roberts, Helene E. "The Exquisite Slave: The Role of Clothes in the Making of the Victorian Woman." *Signs* 2, no. 3 (1977): 554–69.

Robertson, Cheryl. "Male and Female Agendas for Domestic Reform: The Middle Class Bungalow in Gendered Perspective." *Winterthur Portfolio* 26 (summer–fall 1991): 123–41.

Rolt, L.T.C. *Victorian Engineering.* London: Penguin 1970.

Rose, Phyllis. *Parallel Lives: Five Victorian Marriages.* New York: Vintage 1983.

Rosen, George. *A History of Public Health.* New York: MD Publications 1958.

– "Disease, Debility, and Death." In *Victorian City*, ed. H.J. Dyos and Michael Wolff, 2:625–67. London: Routledge and Kegan Paul 1973.

Rosenberg, Charles E. "Florence Nightingale on Contagion: The Hospital as Moral Universe." In *Healing and History: Essays for George Rosen*, ed. Charles E. Rosenberg, 116–36. New York: Science History Publications 1979.

– *Explaining Epidemics and Other Studies in the History of Medicine.* Cambridge: Cambridge University Press 1992.

Roth, Leland. "Getting the Houses to the People: Edward Bok, the *Ladies' Home Journal*, and the Ideal House." In *Perspectives in Vernacular Architecture, IV*, ed. Thomas Carter and Bernard L. Herman, 187–207. Columbia: University of Missouri Press 1991.

Rubinstein, David. "Millicent Garrett Fawcett and the Meaning of Women's Emancipation, 1886–99." *Victorian Studies* 34 (spring 1991): 365–80.

Ruskin, John. *Sesame and Lilies.* Chicago: Donohue [1865].

Ryan, Mary P. "The Explosion of Family History." *Reviews in American History* 10 (Dec. 1982): 181–95.

– *The Empire of the Mother: American Writing about Domesticity 1830–1860.* New York: Harrington 1985.

– *Women in Public: Between Banners and Ballots, 1825–1880.* Baltimore: Johns Hopkins University Press 1990.

Saint, Andrew. *Richard Norman Shaw.* New Haven: Yale University Press 1976.

– *The Image of the Architect.* New Haven: Yale University Press 1983.

Sala, George Augustus. "The Health Exhibition: A Look Around." *Illustrated London News*, 2 Aug. 1884, 90–5.

Sandweiss, Eric. "Around the World in a Day: International Participation in the World's Columbian Exposition." *Illinois Historical Journal* 84 (spring 1991): 8–9.

Sanitarian, 1873–1904.

Sanitary Engineer, 1881–89.

Sanitary Record, 1874–1916.

Scott, Joan Wallach. *Gender and the Politics of History.* New York: Columbia University Press 1988.

Semmelweis, Ignaz. *The Etiology, Concept, and Prophylaxis of Childbed Fever.* Trans. K. Codell Carter. Madison: University of Wisconsin Press 1983.

Shammas, Carole. "The Domestic Environment in Early Modern England and America." *Journal of Social History* 14 (fall 1980): 3–19.

Sheppard, F.H.W. *London 1808–1870: The Infernal Wen.* Berkeley and Los Angeles: University of California Press 1971.

– ed. *Survey of London.* Vol. 38. London: Athlone 1975.

Shonfield, Zuzanna. "The Expectant Victorian." *Costume* 6 (1972): 36–42.

Shorter, Edward. *A History of Women's Bodies.* New York: Basic 1982.

Shortt, Samuel E.D. "Physicials, Science and Status: Issues in the Professionalization of Anglo-American Medicine in the Nineteenth Century." *Medical History* 27, no. 1 (1983): 51–68.

Shuttleworth, Sally. "Female Circulation: Medical Discourse and Popular Advertising in the Mid-Victorian Era." In *Body/Politics: Women and the Discourses of Science,* ed. Mary Jacobus, Evelyn Fox Keller, and Sally Shuttleworth, 47–68. London: Routledge 1990.

Simpson, James Young. *Selected Obstetrical and Gynaecological Works of Sir James Y. Simpson: Containing the Substance of His Lectures on Midwifery.* 3 vols. Ed. J. Watt Black. Edinburgh: A. and C. Black 1871–72.

Smith, Francis B. *The People's Health, 1830–1916.* New York: Holmes and Meier 1979.

Smith, Percival Gordon. "Bed-rooms, Nurseries, and Bath-rooms." In *Our Homes, and How to Make Them Healthy,* ed. Shirley Forster Murphy, 86–91. London: Cassell 1883.

Smith, T. Roger. "A Public Health Exhibition." *Architect,* 5 Jan. 1884.

Smith-Rosenberg, Caroll. "Puberty to Menopause: The Cycle of Femininity in Nineteenth-Century America." In *Clio's Consciousness Raised,* ed. Mary Hartman and Lois W. Banner, 23–37. New York: Harper 1974.

– "The Female World of Love and Ritual: Relations between Women in Nineteenth-Century America." *Signs* 1 (1975): 1–29.

Solis-Cohen, Myer. *Woman in Girlhood, Wifehood, Motherhood.* London: T. Werner Laurie 1908.

Squire, William. "The Nursery." In *Our Homes, and How to Make Them Healthy,* ed. Shirley Forster Murphy, 841–68. London: Cassell 1883.

Stacpoole, Florence. "Maternity Rules for Mothers' Meetings." *Women's Penny Paper,* 6 July 1889, 4.

– "Maternity Readings." *Women's Penny Paper,* 13 July 1889, 8.

– *Advice to Women on the Care of the Health before, during, and after Confinement.* London: Cassell 1892.

Standen: West Sussex. London: National Trust 1989.

Stevenson, Christine. "Who Shall Make the Plan? European Architects and Medical Professionals on the Hospital Site, 1750–1850." Paper read at a meeting of the Society of Architectural Historians, Boston, 30 March 1990.

Stevenson, J.J. *House Architecture.* 2 vols. London: Macmillan 1880.

Stevenson, Lloyd G. "Science Down the Drain: On the Hostility of Certain Sanitarians to Animal Experimentation, Bacteriology and Immunology." *Bulletin of the History of Medicine* 29, no. 3 (1955): 1–26.

Stokes, A.W. "Arsenic in the Home." *Sanitary Record*, 15 Nov. 1888, 213–14.

Strachey, Ray. *Millicent Garrett Fawcett.* London: Murray 1931.

Taylor, Jeremy. *Hospital and Asylum Architecture in England 1840–1914.* London: Mansell 1991.

Teale, T. Pridgin. *Dangers to Health: A Pictorial Guide to Sanitary Defects.* London: Churchill 1878.

Temkin, Oswei. *The Double Face of Janus and Other Essays in the History of Medicine.* Baltimore: Johns Hopkins University Press 1977.

Thompson, F.M.L. *The Rise of Respectable Society: A History of Victorian Britain, 1830–1900.* Cambridge: Harvard University Press 1988.

Thompson, J.D., and G. Goldin. *The Hospital: A Social and Architectural History.* New Haven: Yale University Press 1975.

Thomson, Gilbert. "The Inspection of Plumber-work." *Sanitary Record*, 15 Feb. 1890, 377.

Tomes, Nancy. "The Private Side of Public Health: Sanitary Science, Domestic Hygiene, and the Germ Theory, 1870–1900." *Bulletin of the History of Medicine* 64 (winter 1990): 509–39.

Tristram, Philippa. *Living Space in Fact and Fiction.* London: Routledge, Chapman and Hall 1990.

Tuckey, C. Lloyd, "Maternal Impressions, and Their Influence on the Offspring." *Baby: The Mothers' Magazine* 5 (Dec. 1891–Nov. 1892): 287–8.

Upton, Dell. "Pattern Books and Professionalism: Aspects of the Transformation of Domestic Architecture in America, 1800–1860." *Winterthur Portfolio* 19, nos. 2–3 (1984): 107–50.

Valverde, Mariana. *The Age of Light, Soap, and Water: Moral Reform in English Canada, 1885–1925.* Toronto: McClelland and Stewart 1991.

Vanek, Joann. "Time Spent in House Work." *Scientific American* 231, no. 5 (1974): 116–20.

Van Slyck, Abigail Ayres. *Gender and Space in American Public Libraries, 1880–1920.* Report. Tucson: Southwest Institute for Research on Women 1992.

Vicinus, Martha. *Independent Women: Work and Community for Single Women, 1850–1920.* Chicago: University of Chicago Press 1985.

– ed. *A Widening Sphere: Changing Roles of Victorian Women.* Bloomington: Indiana University Press 1977.

– *Suffer and Be Still: Women in the Victorian Age.* Bloomington: Indiana University Press 1980.

Walker, Jane H. *A Handbook for Mothers.* London: Longmans, Green 1893.

Walker, Lynne. "Women and Architecture." In *A View From the Interior*, ed. Judy Attfield and Pat Kirkham, 90–105. London: Women's Press 1989.

– ed. *Women Architects: Their Work.* London: Sorella Press 1984.

Wallace, Mrs Willoughby. *Woman's Kingdom.* London: Archibald, Constable 1905.

Walvin, James. *Victorian Values.* London: Cardinal 1987.

Warren, Eliza. *How I Managed My Children from Infancy to Marriage.* London: Houlston and Wright 1865.

Weeks, Jeffrey. *Sex, Politics, and Society: The Regulation of Sexuality since 1800.* London: Longman 1981.

Weiner, Deborah E.B. *The Architecture of Social Reform in Late-Victorian London.* Manchester: Manchester University Press 1994.

Weinreb, Ben, and Christopher Hibbert, eds. *The London Encyclopaedia.* London: Macmillan 1983.

Wekerle, Gerda R. "Women in the Urban Environment." *Signs* 5, no. 3, suppt (1980): s188–214.

Welter, Barbara. "The Cult of True Womanhood: 1820–1860." *American Quarterly* 18 (summer 1966): 151–74.

Westland, Albert. *The Wife and Mother: A Medical Guide to the Care of Her Health and the Management of Her Children.* London: Griffin 1892.

Wheeler, Marianna. *Before the Baby Comes.* New York and London: Harper 1914.

White, Colin. *The World of the Nursery.* London: Herbert 1984.

White, Cynthia. *Women's Magazines 1693–1968: A Sociological Study.* London: Michael Joseph 1970.

Wilkie, Jacqueline. "Submerged Sensuality: Technology and Perceptions of Bathing." *Journal of Social History* 19 (1986): 649–64.

Wilmott, Peter, and Michael Young. *Family and Class in a London Suburb.* London: Routledge and Kegan Paul 1960.

Wohl, Anthony S. *Endangered Lives: Public Health in Victorian Britain.* Cambridge: Harvard University Press 1983.

– ed. *The Victorian Family: Structure and Stresses.* London: Croom Helm 1978.

Woman's Herald, 1891–93.

Woman's Signal, 1894–99.

Women's Penny Paper, 1888–90.

Wood, Ann Douglas. "'The Fashionable Disease': Women's Complaints and Their Treatment in Nineteenth-Century America." In *Clio's Consciousness*

Raised, ed. Mary Hartman and Lois W. Banner, 1–22. New York: Harper 1974.

Wood, Catherine J. "The Sick-room and Its Appliances." *Baby: The Mothers' Magazine* 1 (Dec. 1887–Nov. 1888): 179.

Wood-Allen, Mary. *The Marvels of Our Bodily Dwelling*. Ann Arbor: Wood-Allen Publishing 1899.

Woolf, Virginia. *A Room of One's Own*. London: Hogarth Press 1929.

Work and Leisure, 1875–93.

Wright, Gwendolyn. *Moralism and the Model Home: Domestic Architecture and Cultural Conflict in Chicago, 1873–1913*. Chicago: University of Chicago Press 1980.

– "Domestic Architecture and the Cultures of Domesticity." *Design Quarterly* 138 (spring 1987): 13–19.

Year-book of Women's Work, 1875.

Young Woman, 1892–1915.

Zimmern, Alice. "Ladies' Dwellings." *Contemporary Review* 77 (Jan. 1900): 96–104.

Zone 1–2 (1987), special issues on "The City."

Index